Abraham Lurie, PhD, is Director, Department of Social Work Services, Long Island-Hillside Medical Center, Glen Oaks, New York.

Gary Rosenberg, PhD, is Associate Professor of Community Medicine (Social Work), The Mount Sinai School of Medicine of the City University of New York; Director, Department of Social Work Services, The Mount Sinai Hospital; and Vice President of Human Resources, The Mount Sinai Medical Center, New York, New York.

Social Work Administration in Health Care

Social Work Administration in Health Care

Edited by
Abraham Lurie
Gary Rosenberg

The Haworth Press
New York

The Haworth Press, Inc., 28 East 22 Street, New York, NY 10010

Library of Congress Cataloging in Publication Data
Main entry under title:

Social work administration in health care.

Includes bibliographies and index.
1. Medical social work—United States—Administration. I. Lurie, Abraham. II. Rosenberg, Gary. [DNLM: 1. Hospital departments—Organ. 2. Social work department, Hospital. W 322 S6733]
HV687.5.U5S62   1984   362.1′0425′068   84-799
ISBN 0-917724-42-9
ISBN 0-86656-314-8 (pbk.)

CONTENTS

Contributors

Neil A. Cohen, PhD, is Associate Professor, Department of Sociology and Social Work, California State University at Los Angeles.

Claudia J. Coulton, PhD, is Associate Professor, School of Applied Social Sciences, Case Western Reserve University.

Gary L. Ellis is Superintendent of the Danville State Hospital, Danville, Pennsylvania. He was formerly Executive Director of the H. K. Cooper Clinic, Lancaster, Pennsylvania.

Hans S. Falck, PhD, is Regenstein Professor of Social Sciences, Menninger Foundation, Topeka, Kansas.

Eugenie Walsh Flaherty, PhD, is Senior Research Associate, Philadelphia Health Management Corporation, Philadelphia, Pennsylvania.

Thomas J. Kiresuk, PhD, is Chief Clinical Psychologist, Hennepin County Mental Health Service and Director, Program Evaluation Resource Center.

Sander H. Lund is Associate Director of the Program Evaluation Resource Center, Minneapolis, Minnesota.

Frances G. Martin, MS, is a doctoral candidate, Graduate School of Education, Psychology and Education Department, University of Pennsylvania.

Raymond Sanchez Mayers, PhD, is Assistant Professor, Graduate School of Social Work, University of Texas at Arlington.

James J. McNamara, DSW, is Director, Department of Social Work, University of Utah Medical Center, and Associate Professor, School of Social Work, University of Utah.

Martin Nacman, DSW, is Director, Social Work Division, The University of Rochester, School of Medicine and Dentistry, Strong Memorial Hospital.

Seishi Oka, DDS, PhD, is Executive Director of the H. K. Cooper Clinic, Lancaster, Pennsylvania.

Helen Rehr, DSW, is Edith J. Baerwald Professor of Community Medicine (Social Work) and Director, Division of Social Work, Department of Community Medicine, Mount Sinai School of Medicine, City University of New York.

Kurt Reichert, PhD, is Professor and Coordinator of the Health Concentration, School of Social Work, San Diego State University.

Gary B. Rhodes, MSW, is Associate Professor, Kent School of Social Work, University of Louisville.

Lawrence L. Schkade, PhD, is Professor and Chairman, Systems Analysis Department, College of Business Administration, University of Texas at Arlington.

Richard J. Schoech, PhD, is Assistant Professor, Graduate School of Social Work, University of Texas at Arlington.

Robert M. Spano, ACSW, is Director, Social Work Department, University of Minnesota Hospitals, and Professor, University of Minnesota School of Social Work.

Philip Starr, ACSW, is Chief of Social Research at the H. K. Cooper Clinic, Lancaster, Pennsylvania.

John J. Stretch, PhD, is Professor and Assistant Dean, School of Social Services, St. Louis University.

Patricia J. Volland, LCSW, MBA, is Senior Director for Patient Services, The Johns Hopkins Hospital.

Andrew Weissman, DSW, is Associate Professor of Community Medicine, Mount Sinai School of Medicine, City University of New York.

Harold H. Weissman, DSW, is Associate Professor, Hunter College School of Social Work, New York, New York.

Paul A. Wilson, PhD, is Associate Professor, School of Social Work, University of Illinois, Urbana.

John A. Yankey, PhD, is Professor, School of Applied Social Sciences, Case Western Reserve University.

Foreword

The role of management in the health care setting is receiving, and will continue to receive, increased attention as efforts to control the cost of medical care are accelerated by governmental agencies, business groups, insurers and consumers. The explosive growth of proprietary hospital chains, their successes in the marketplace and the increased value of their stocks are credited to a management approach which has tended to suggest that the health care industry should function as "a business" rather than as a part of this country's social fabric.

In the face of such a thrust, the role of social work managers in the health care setting takes on added importance. (Someone must maintain the basic sense of the organizational mission which we would assume to be the delivery of high quality, humane patient care and not, solely, the generation of profits for stockholders.) To do so effectively, however, social work managers themselves must be accepted as competent managers and must prove their ability to meet "bottom line" responsibilities lest their credibility with the decision makers is diminished or destroyed. Social work's proven competence in "process" and its proven commitment to the principles of organizational strength resulting from employee participation in the management of the affairs of the organization should further cement its place in the hierarchical structure of the increasingly complex health care organization.

For these reasons, *Social Work Administration in Health Care* by Lurie and Rosenberg is a welcome addition to the literature and is must reading for all those who aspire to meaningful administrative positions in the health care industry. This book should not be looked upon merely as a primer for those aspiring to become directors of social work departments in hospitals or nursing homes; rather, it should be viewed as a source for helping in the education of social workers who aspire to influential managerial positions in health care which, while they certainly do not exclude departments of social work, may also include such areas as human resource administration or total institutional administration.

Harold Light, President
Long Island College Hospital
Brooklyn, New York

Preface

The word *administrator* derives from the root "ministrare"—to serve, to tender to another, to aid, to minister to. This connotation provides a needed corrective to the not uncommon perspective which distorts the concept of administration into a concern with a series of burdensome tasks, regulations and procedures willfully superimposed to sap the vitality and creativity of the clinician. Clinicians often see administrators as bureaucrats, paper pushers, drop outs from the "real" clinical world, i.e. those who can't "do", become teachers, researchers, and administrators.

Yet, the heart of administration, as its roots imply, lies in the doing of things needful and helpful, in the processes of serving others, of enabling them to do their work. Applied to social work this means the administrator serves the practitioner by providing the resources, structures, and ambience which make possible the practice and art of helping patients and clients. The most skilled and dedicated providers of human services cannot deliver them without administrative underpinnings creatively and capably wrought to support their implementation and institutionalization.

In health care settings, the administrator and the line social worker share an equal commitment to providing needed services to patients and families. Neither has the monopoly on the care mission. But their work is different. The administrator serves by successfully mobilizing and managing the human and material resources prerequisite to implementing the functions of that mission, whether it be service alone, or whether it includes education and research. Capable performance of this work requires the acquisition of many areas of knowledge and the development of many skills not always on tap for the professional social worker. This book is a good resource in this regard as it contains reviews of the major administrative systems comprising the functions and processes of management. Within its broad range, it nonetheless gives specific attention to the major tasks of administration of social work in health care so that it should be a useful and helpful reference to practicing and evolving administrators as well as educators and students.

It will come as no surprise to the readers of this book that the practical and seemingly prosaic concerns of budget, space, information systems, financial management, staffing patterns, and evaluations require at least as highly developed levels of interpersonal and interprofessional skills as do matters of safeguarding patient and family access to social work, of ensuring quality of service, education and research, of establishing program priorities, and of developing accountability mechanisms.

E.M. Forster's admonition "above all—connect" is apt here. Dynamic administration of health care social work comes from the administrator's ability to connect to the myriad systems of complex organizations. To learn the language of these systems, the social worker with basic knowledge and skills need to add an armamentarium of management skills and tools. Many of these derive from the business and corporate world and so are suspect to some. But there are professional issues in all facets of any operation dedicated to helping people and these provide the connective and catalyst for merging practical and professional components into a dynamic gestalt of administration viewed as service.

Sylvia S. Clarke, MSW
Editor
Social Work in Health Care

Social Work Administration in Health Care

Introduction

Social work managers in health care make an important contribution in managing direct service activities, in translating direct service activities to other managers in the institution, in situations which link the organization to the community and to the broader issues of social policy and legislation. The manager is often embroiled in conflicting situations. As a member of the health care management team, with a commitment to client-focused care in a very complex environment, action can cause stress between what is right for the organization and what is right for the client system.

Martin Rein[1] has referred to this as the difference between the hot knowledge of the practitioner and the cold knowledge of the administrator. He suggests that the emotional reactions and worries of the practitioner in touch with the people who are hurting and in need are different than the demands on the administrator for sorting out and dealing with this hot knowledge and turning it into a rational basis for decision and action or interpretation and analysis. Stein[2] suggests that the administrator has both the opportunity and responsibility to be tuned into the experience of the professionals in direct contact with people served and to draw necessary inferences and conclusions. While the administrator's job is viewed most frequently in terms of the internal management to the organization, the administrator's external role as the key communicator and frequently a leading figure in planning and policy deliberations needs a special focus. The social work manager in health care is the direct linkage between the direct line practitioners and the planners and policy makers, both in the institution and in government organizations. The administrator constitutes a vital link among these groups as well as being a provider of expert experience.

The purpose of this book is to provide a set of useful ideas about management of social work in health care settings. There are many fine books which describe the theories of management, social work administration, the ethics of social work administration and the principles of organizational development and personnel practices.[3] We believe that it is unnecessary to duplicate what has already been done. There is, how-

[1]Martin Rein, "Practice Worries in the Helping Professions," *Society*, Vol. 19, No. 6, September/October 1982.

[2]Herman Stein, unpublished paper delivered at the Mount Sinai Medical Center Department of Social Work Services, May 18, 1983.

[3]See, for example, Amitai Etzioni, ed., *A Sociological Reader on Complex Organizations*, 2d

ever, in the literature a group of articles which demonstrate the practical know-how of social work managers, each of which is deeply rooted in the theory, practice and values of the social work profession. Each of the articles selected is by a recognized leader in health care management or in the social work profession and we believe provides state-of-the-art knowledge to the new manager and the student of management whose main focus is the health care system.

An attempt was made to select articles which would be relevant to large complex health settings with larger departments and to the smaller one- or two-person departments and those in between. With this in mind we divided the book into chapters reflecting our point of view about the need to ground social work in the missions and functions of social work in the health care setting, the need to be accountable and therefore the need to develop management information systems ranging from hand collected data to more complex computer assisted systems. The logic of such systems must be looked at and the articles we have selected will help the social work manager and student do just that. For any responsible profession continuing education plays a crucial part in the development and growth of professional skills. It is our belief that it is the manager's responsibility to make sure this happens and therefore articles on innovations in continuing education have been included.

One management skill necessary for successful performance as a health care manager is that of financial management and we have included articles that discuss financial management of hospital social work departments. A major management dilemma today is staffing patterns. We offer articles on staffing patterns and articles that discuss organizational goals and performance appraisal in relation to staffing. A manager who stays close to his staff and close to the practice field can serve as an innovator. We have included in our book examples of the social work manager as innovator in health care.

Our last chapter is entitled "Managing the Community Linkage System." The social work manager serves as a key facilitator of the social work focus inside the organization, the transition of the patient from entry to exit and the planning and identification of health care resources in the community. It is from the community linkage system that future practice innovations will probably emanate. The social work manager serves as a key link in practice, management, policy and program.

---

ed. (New York: Holt, Rinehart & Winston, 1969); Simon Slavin, ed., *Social Administration: The Management of the Social Services* (New York: Haworth Press and the Council on Social Work Education, 1978); Felice Davidson Perlmutter and Simon Slavin, eds., *Leadership in Social Administration* (Philadelphia: Temple University Press, 1980); Rosemary C. Sarri and Yeheskel Hasenfeld, eds., *The Management of Human Services* (New York: Columbia University Press, 1978); and Herman D. Stein, ed., *Organization and the Human Services: Cross-Disciplinary Reflections* (Philadelphia: Temple University Press, 1981).

There are many articles that could have been included and were not. The authors take full responsibility for their judgments of inclusion and believe that the readings provided herein are excellent examples of management theory and management practice, and in many respects serve as a key casebook for social work management in health care settings. It is our belief along with Stein that social work management will be most effective when management stays close to the practice base of social work, translates this practice base to hospital administrators with broader responsibilities, translates the knowledge base into an effective community linkage system and serves as expert witness to gaps in service and hardships faced by people entering the service system and those deprived of services. The social work manager can also contribute to policy, program and in general to the patient care system. It is our belief that social workers will be called upon more frequently to fill our general hospital management positions and will face the dilemmas of leaving the profession to assume these positions or bringing in the profession along with their new position.

The readings included in this book should serve as a stimulating, exciting descriptive analysis of what social workers can achieve in health care settings and can serve as a challenge for the future managers of social work to carry forth the rich tradition of those professionals who are courageous enough to innovate and describe their work.

Gary Rosenberg, PhD

PART I

The Missions and Functions
of Social Work in Health Care

From a modest and often barely tolerated existence, the social worker in health care has become one of the more widely accepted team members in the delivering and administration of comprehensive health care services.

The social worker in a modern health care institution is active in primary, secondary, and tertiary care programs, participating in planning, prevention, and predicting health care trends. Four areas in which the social worker or social work skills play a significant role in health care in addition to offering direct services to patients and families are as a (1) consultant, (2) educator, (3) researcher, and (4) as a staff member whose knowledge and experience is sought to provide the psychosocial dimension which is an integral part of health care.

The articles in this section represent concepts which can help to clarify the main objectives of the social work services in the health care field, and lead to the unending search for innovative ideas.

The central theme among the three articles selected is the concept "social" which is dealt with in depth in Hans Falck's article. As he points out in his article, there is a need to define social work in health settings because this determines the focus of the work. He puts it succinctly when he states that work is not automatically social work because social workers do it. And, therefore, a rationale is required to identify and make distinct the area of competence which social workers require to deal with specific problems that are a result primarily of the social effects of illness and not the illness itself.

The problems inherent in the tasks which social workers undertake to help hospitalized patients are discussed. A caution in attempting this is to point out that social workers within their own competence must conceptualize their interventions as help with the social situation, and this is not the same as treating the illness per se. The sharp definition of social work in the medical setting delineates the work of the social worker dramatically. To carry this forward into the future is somewhat hazardous, but the next article deals with some of the trends that are currently apparent and could and will lead to work areas in which social workers will find themselves.

Many of the trends apparent when the article by Lurie was written have manifested themselves even more dramatically at the present time. The importance of quality and quantity controls, cost containment, and function definition bear out some of the cautions of which Hans Falck reminded us in his article. Lurie continues this caution and carries it forward into suggesting strongly that indeed social workers will have to be much clearer about their ability to intervene with more limited and sharply defined problems in working with hospitalized patients.

The final article in this section by Spano and Lund suggests a scheme in which a hospital social service department can develop goals based on a program philosophy and function. It is suggested that a system of peer review mechanism can be developed which will help a social work department expose its practice to mandated reviews by helping to define its functions and monitor its activities from a cost perspective. Parallel to the main theme, which is to clarify and maintain the social perspective in social work interventive practice, is the constant reminder that these interventive strategies should aid social workers to sustain goals and objectives in a multidisciplinary system such as a hospital. A social work department has to be sustained and judged not only from a quality standpoint, but from the point of view of effectiveness.

Abraham Lurie, PhD

Chapter 1

Social Work
in Health Settings

Hans S. Falck, PhD

ABSTRACT. The distinctiveness of social work in health settings is that people served are clients rather than patients; that the focus of work is on the social effects of illness, not illness; that problem formulation and intervention rests on clear understanding of social cause, social manifestation, and social intervention as group phenomena.

This paper is primarily, yet not exclusively, addressed to health care social workers. Although it is true that such workers' practice is influenced and guided by the setting in which they work—hospital, clinic, community mental health center, and others—the vicissitudes of such work strongly suggest that they need a clear link also to their profession, its methods, theories, assumptions, and values. Beyond the clear advantages morale-wise lies a great need. That need is to spell out how such work is social work, not only attitudinally but also theoretically and, by extension, practically. The work is not automatically social work because social workers do it. More than that is needed.

It stands to reason as common sense that in a health care setting one needs to learn all one can about the illnesses that afflict the patients. No graduate school can teach more than a small portion of that; most of it is acquired in practice, from colleagues and especially from patients. But what cannot be taught by non-social work colleagues is the social work aspect of helping clients who are there because they are patients, too. That part must rely on social workers who can conceptualize the social work role, who spell out the logic and the reasoning of social work, as well as the goals and ideologies of the profession. Each worker can then make his/her own adaptations befitting the work, his ideas and preferences, and, above all, the needs of his clients.

The thesis of this paper is that medical social work will play its most effective role to the extent that medical social workers display and confirm their identity by what they know and by what they can do. In the absence of either or both, university credentials as well as professional credentials (ACSW or licenses) work to the detriment of workers and the profession; and most of all to patients; and lastly, in relation to other professions.

What this paper will not do is to berate social workers. This is not the proper occasion to compare social workers with physicians or other occupational groups. All professions display a whole range of qualities and there is no evidence to the author's knowledge that any one of them distinguishes itself from all others in its achievements and its failures.

THE PROBLEM

Medical social workers are expected and are committed to render social services to hospitalized patients. Much of what is being said here also applies to social workers in mental health settings. The term "medical" is convenient but could to some extent be expanded to cover workers in psychiatric settings, inpatient as well as community mental health. Secondly, medical social workers almost always work as part of treatment groups in which they play but one role. They are expected and are committed to perform as such and usually at a level of unspecified quality.

In the first case, the patient treatment level, the usual assumption is that the social worker, as others, is an assistant to the physician who is in charge of the patient. The patient is "his" patient, and, as is true of other ownership processes, he exercises control over who works with the patient, toward what ends, if indeed he does so at all. A great many social workers either accept this situation as it is because they agree with it, or they submit more or less unwillingly and resignedly, or they rebel and leave. Few rebel and stay. Many develop an interpersonal modus vivendi that satisfies them, the physicians, and other members of the treatment group.

A cursory review of social work journals suggests, however, the changes that are taking place in social work. One of these is the increase in research work, another is the increasing sophistication of social workers in terms of their knowledge, still another their increasing political sophistication which makes them much less willing than heretofore to take orders from non-social workers, and fourthly, the opportunity to join the widespread disillusionment with physicians, the quality of medical practice, the increasing costs, and the general reduction of confidence in the medical establishment. Unquestioned reliance on things and persons medical is on the decline, and the opportunity for more equal participation by social workers in medical work is on the increase. Yet, for fear of overstating the brightness of the new sun, it is still true that hierarchy and authority play extraordinary roles in the allocation of personnel and services to patients.

Yet all of this is not enough. The insufficiency in our own argument lies in the fact that social workers continue to function by the leave of others, rather than autonomously, and would thus continue to react rather than act. To be sure, there is an important qualitative difference between being "let" to work with the patient and not being so "let." The hierarchy may be benign or venal, but it is still *hierarchy without collegiality*. That, then, is another way of stating the problem before us. Hierarchy alone results in restricted and constricted practice. Its central feature is the inability to serve the patient in ways deemed qualitatively desirable (if not necessary!) by those best qualified to make judgments about it. In medicine that is the physician; in social service it is the social worker. Yet, when the major emphasis in the administration of treatment is on hierarchical considerations, the tendencies are very pronounced to let power rather than expertise rule, and at that power uninformed (if not antagonistic on ideological or other grounds) to that over which it is exercised. The choice before us is not between administrative or clinical power as such; instead it is that *hierarchy when standing by itself is insufficient to achieve the desired result, namely, services of quality*. All professions teach their students that central to responsible practice is the exercise of autonomous judgment. Autonomous judgment in the professions consists of data collection, informed decision making regarding the meaning of the data, plus decisions about interventions. The word "autonomous" can be taken to mean independent, but it need not be. It can also be taken to imply and mean that workers exercise their functions by the light of their own profession while at the same time exercising their responsibility, that is, with due consideration of the needs, the rights, and the knowledge and skills of others. Autonomy can be conceptualized in the context of others' functions and rights, as well as one's own. That, then, is also how I would define collegiality. It rests on the commitment to let the patient have his multiple needs met. It recognizes that colleagues with different interests, skills, as well as attitudes are able to offer help with the enormous complexities of being both alive and sick. That places great responsibilities on all members of the treatment group. A corollary to the thesis with which the paper began is that physicians (as others) will play their most effective role to the extent that they display and confirm their identity by what they know and by what they can do. The mutual recognition of the universal validity of that statement is both the basis for true teamwork and for autonomous practice. *One does not confirm one's competence by attempting to practice what one does not know or by exercising noncollegial control over functions not one's own.*

THE NATURE OF SOCIAL WORK IN MEDICAL SETTINGS

Rather than list all the functions social workers perform in medical settings, it will be more useful (if not more instructive) to talk about the logic of social work. The assumption is that one can identify the underlying logical structure of many activities considered part of social work, and that one can also suggest generalizations that could be studied further to see whether or not they stand the test of experience. The identification of logical structure enables us to find integrative principles, which in turn make it possible to view the work holistically rather than episodically, or in terms of single events. The systematic application of principles or generalizations also has the virtue of defining what makes for a profession.

Not all structures are logical. For example, it seems illogical to define groups in the language of personality. To cite one example, groups are sometimes said to "feel," or they are said to "resist." Groups are at times described as possessing an unconscious. All these are terms not made to explain collectivities. One author suggests that social workers mediate between clients and society (Schwartz, 1961, 1976). He never explains what he means by the implication of "mediate," that is, to be located "between." How is one to take that when we are not really told? Could one not just as well—and probably more logically—argue that by virtue of people's interdependence all are members of society; and that social problems arise precisely *because* we are all members and yet not treated fairly, or evenly, or justly? Or, for that matter, how can one expect to help professionally if the prerequisite be that one stands not as *part of* but outside (if indeed that were imaginably possible) of the society we wish to change? These considerations are not mere word quibbles; they go to the heart of how we think, by what logic, and from where come our claims to goal, competence, function, and method. When we make single cause statements about groups, we fail to understand the complexities of human networks. *When social workers in medical settings conceptualize their clients as patients they imply that they treat illness; but that also prevents them from doing what they ought to be doing, namely, to maximize their functioning abilities in their social situation.* That social situation may be concomitant with illness but it is not the same, so that in one sense people are patients and in the other (social work) they are clients who are ill. The latter, then, is a consequence of the illness (for example, unemployment, loss of pay, compromised self-esteem), but it is not illness treated by social workers.

I said in another context (Falck, 1977) that social workers who can diagnose in a social work way declare their competence by taking responsibility for reasoned judgment, and by devising intervention plans. I believe that this is the heart of the issue for medical social work as for all other social work. The statement is intended to point to the heart of the issue of disciplinary (and therefore interdisciplinary) practice. Thus viewed, interdisciplinary practice is also seen as a variant of disciplinary practice. If one does not know his discipline, he has nothing to be interdisciplinary about!

DISCIPLINARY SOCIAL WORK

I should like to begin this section with the listing of what I believe to be the essential aspects of social work logic, and therefore social work practice:

1. The problems to which social workers address themselves are social in nature and encompass a high degree of probability that they can be alleviated by changes in social arrangements. *Social* means that their causes have to do with behavior involving more than one person, both present and future. *Arrangement* means action(s) by several persons in relation to each other.
2. The method of problem alleviation and resolution is social, that is, persons acting in relation to each other such that the outcomes are more desirable than the conditions giving rise to the requirement for help. Participants in that process are client(s) and social worker. It should be noted that in a situation that is social there are frequently clients, namely, in group work, in family work, in institutions, *who help each other* and therefore also themselves.
3. The social worker brings the resources available to him, and it is part of his function to make these available to his clients through the way both clients and workers employ them. The following is a list of such resources:
   a. Knowledge of human life and development in general terms, that is, what is common to most people.
   b. Knowledge about the particular client(s) in the specific situation (problem) under discussion.
   c. Specific skills (and techniques) assumed applicable to this situation, and based on past experiences with others.
   d. The worker's ability to control the quality of his performance by self-observation in action, related to ongoing awareness of what is happening to the client(s) in the process of being helped.
   e. The ability of both client(s) and social worker to evaluate the results of their mutual work.

All these dimensions are descriptive of social work practice. They explain why social workers are necessary in health settings.

I think it is necessary now to say more about the use of the term "social." It is obvious that the work has become so all-inclusive that it is difficult to render it specific meaning. That becomes clear when one considers that it is used for everything from what happens in any given family or other group to vast problems such as unemployment and poverty, to say nothing of mental illness. From the vantage point of its most general use, everyone and anyone who addresses social concerns would be doing social work. It would include schoolteachers and policemen, welfare workers and top-level government officials. The need exists, therefore, to delimit the use of the term—at lease for social work purposes—where it stands somewhat apart from its most general meaning in order to communicate with some degree of precision. This can be accomplished in two ways. The first of these is by problem conceptualization and the second by problem resolution. But even then we will not be totally satisfied, and we will be unconvincing that only social workers deal with social problems and through social work methods. We shall be unable to claim uniqueness (or monopoly) of function even in the doubtful case that this were desirable.

1. A problem is conceptualized as social when by cause or effect more than one person would experience gain or loss by its nature, its consequences, or its resolution.
2. The work is considered social work when methods of problem resolution (or alleviation) are utilized that emphasize *the behaviors of people toward each other* as means toward the achievement of desired results. This includes the reciprocal behavior of workers and clients, as well as clients among themselves.

The fact that most social workers view social problems as social is not to be taken too lightly, although self-evident to social workers themselves. We do live in a society, after all, that holds the ideal of individualism in very high esteem, as well as in one beset by profound doubts about the collective responsibility for the poor, for children, for minorities. Individual achievement is as important to social workers as to other Americans, and a mature view of communalism is largely absent in American society to this very day. Torn by dissent, philosophically and politically, it should hardly be surprising to read that even in the "people" professions there is little understanding of the relation of person and community, that is, the meaning of *social* (Falck, 1969, 1971, 1973, 1976).[1] Of particular importance in this connection, and particularly to psychiatric

---

[1] The author's main points have to do with viewing individuation as a result of and a contributor to groupness, referred to as the individuality-groupness (I-G) effect, rather than continuing to distinguish between individual and group.

and medical social workers, is the strong inclination to think and talk of patients as having "the social environment" as if it were something outside of them, as an additional consideration regarding a personally held illness. That may be true in the medical tradition. I submit that it has no place in a social work view. From a social work standpoint illness is not a medical event; it is a social event. The members of the patient's social context are as affected by the person's illness as they are by all else he/she does. They are affected, they are responsible, their lives are influenced by it, they in turn influence the course and often the nature of illness: The situation is social, the event is social, the intervention is social. All of this defines and spells out our social work values, which deny American individualism, in its isolating forms; and they acclaim the interdependence of man, not only as ideal but as scientifically demonstrable fact. My reading of the social work ethic says that social work believes in the sacredness of *the person in the social context,* rather than in individualism apart from it, or at most marginally related to it. That is how and why illness is a social event, perhaps not even really illness as social work would see it, but social dysfunction along with or in addition to illness. It is also the place where our values and our knowledge merge, yet are clearly identifiable. From a social work standpoint, I submit, the needful unit is always a group (the meaning of social), although it is also true that the medical and psychiatric worker may talk with one person at a time. But what they talk about, what they focus on, what is of the essential concern is the person as part of others. That is a social view as I see it, and I recommend it in this context in order to delineate what social—irreducibly—ought to be about. The term "irreducibly," to emphasize my point further, means that man as part of the social context is not a part that one puts in and takes out, as it were, but that he is to be seen as individuated within the social situation, not separated from it and individualized.

It would be beyond the scope of a single paper to elucidate at length the linkages between social man and psychological man, or the relation of sociological and psychodynamic thought. Various attempts have been made in that effort (Falck, 1976; Parsons, 1958; Pollak, 1956). I shall confine myself here to a brief consideration of psychodynamically oriented work in a social framework.

Every helping (or therapeutic) interaction is social, simply because it presupposes two or more people, active in some relationship to each other. What makes it *social* or *psychological* (it is always both anyway) is the problem conceptualization which emphasizes the one more than the other. When the emphasis is primarily psychological the work is conceptualized as reflecting how by use of the client's personality he/she experiences himself/herself, and presumably, how modification in personality dimensions would lead to different and presumably more satisfying behavior. Social work is problem solution, both in the conceptualization of it as social and, therefore, in its method. It emphasizes not what the personality produces, but the options (choices) clients have that are realistically available in order to cope (behave) more effectively. *The test in both personality- and behavior-oriented work is more desirable behaving.* It is not in whether one or the other is better or deeper. It lies in what is needed by the patient and what works. Deeper is not always better, and coping more efficiently may engage so much energy and spell so many difficulties for the client that it would often be far better to try a more psychiatrically centered approach. There need be no conflict, therefore, between social workers, psychologists, and psychiatrists when the issue is viewed from the standpoint of resource availability. The problems arise primarily over power, domination, and envy. They are pushed under the rug when role blurring takes the place of making multiple methods and resources available.

The discussion, then, leads back to a logical extension of the concept *social* as here given. That in turn suggests that the medical concept *patient* (in distinction to Parsons' sick role formulation) ought to be revised to client. Client has the advantage of being consistent with the rest of social work, resolves the confusion over whether nonmedical people "treat" patients, clarifies that social workers help clients cope socially by invoking the client's family and/or other social structures, and thereby *dampen the individualistic bias that underlies everything from medicine to education, social work, religion, and business.*

Medical and psychiatric social work should come to terms with the fact, as I see it, that the central logic of its work is social, that is, group related. This does not suggest that "one-to-one" work is not as legitimate as it ever was, but that the point of view workers bring to it is determined by the individuality-groupness dimension which irreducibly describes man to social workers.

I think that the educational implications of this intellectual attitude need to be spelled out, but not in this piece. May it be sufficient to point out that they lie primarily in the area of how man is viewed psychologically and sociologically, and by derivation how this affects the formulation of intervention theory.

CONCLUSIONS

The concept *social* has its own logic in both problem conceptualization and in intervention management. It is the central intellectual building block for social work practice. It does not need to stand in conflict with other approaches, either in problem conceptualization or in methodology of helping. Social work and social workers are defined as persons committed intellectually, attitudinally, and methodologically to the understanding and practice of social intervention.

If the tone of this article is "editorial," this is my intention. There are issues where the facts should lead one to suggest, also, how they ought to be changed.

REFERENCES

Falck, H. S. Thinking styles and individualism. *Bulletin of the Menninger Clinic,* 1969, *33*(3).

Falck, H. S. Individualism and the psychiatric hospital system. *Bulletin of the Menninger Clinic,* 1971, *35*(1).

Falck, H. S. Magic in the perception of the self-made man. *Menninger Perspective,* 1973, *4*(6).

Falck, H. S. Individualism and communalism: Two or one? *Social Thought,* Summer 1976.

Falck, H. S. Interdisciplinary education and its implications for social work practice. *Journal of Education for Social Work,* 1977, *13*(2).

Parsons, T. Social structure and the development of personality: Freud's contribution to the integration of psychology and sociology. *Psychiatry,* 1958, *21*(4).

Pollak, O. *Integrating sociological and psychoanalytic concepts.* New York: Russell Sage Foundation, 1956.

Schwartz, W. The social worker in the group. *Social Welfare Forum 1961.* New York: Columbia University Press, 1961.

Schwartz, W. Between client and system: The mediating function. In R. W. Roberts & H. Northen (Eds.), *Theories of social work with groups.* New York: Columbia University Press, 1976.

Chapter 2

Social Work in Health Care in the Next Ten Years

Abraham Lurie, PhD

ABSTRACT. The social worker in health settings in the future will have more medical knowledge that affects his practice, be a more active psychosocial counselor, and be prepared to work in group practice that includes a number of disciplines. The social work department of the future will be organized in a more decentralized fashion, and will develop stronger links to other clinical and administrative departments within the medical center, to departments of social work of other medical centers, and particularly with community groups outside of the hospital. The department will need to assign manpower expertise in such areas as knowledge of changing social and welfare systems, legislation affecting programs, as well as in research, computerization, data gathering, and retrieval.

HAZARDS OF PREDICTIONS

The making of predictions in these hazardous times is an exercise fraught with difficulties. The pace of change has quickened, knowledge is increasing by leaps and bounds, and relationships among decision-making groups are in flux. Although fundamental relationships have not changed significantly, enough is in the process of constant change that predictions made with some assurance often turn out in retrospect to be objects of ridicule and amazement. Social work manpower shortages predicted by experts for the mid-seventies proved to be an unfortunate illusion. However, predictions that an economic recession in the seventies would follow the affluent sixties were accurate. Few would have expected, though, that health and welfare services would be so severely contracted. Nacman and Shulman wrote in 1971 "that it is difficult to predict the future of social work in the health field."[1] Perhaps it is with more courage than wisdom that I accepted the burden of attempting to forecast practice in the health field in the next ten years. I do this believing that forecasting practice is a step in influencing its future through the suggestion of innovation and change.

THE PAST

To suggest the future of social work a brief classification of historical epochs in social work in health care is needed. If we review social work in health care settings by its historical epochs, it can be said to have had its beginnings during the period 1905 to 1920. This includes the establishment of social work in psychiatric hospitals. The particular reasons for the growth of social work in different settings were different, but the essential basis for this thrust was the same.

The 1920s were the years in which public health programs grew rapidly. The orthopsychiatric movement in the health field reflected this. Preventative programs in the educational system brought together social workers, public health nurses, psychiatrists, and others who worked closely in the child guidance movement.

The 1930s saw the great development of social work as a result of federal programs. Social work departments began in some larger hospitals, particularly those serving lower economic and disadvantaged groups.

The period 1940 through 1950 can be classified as the psychiatric social work period in which the psychoanalytic approach was reflected in emphasis on depth psychology in training and practice with many social workers trying to become psychotherapists.

The fifties were the period of stability with steady expansion in the health field. Social action was the hallmark of the sixties, sparked by President Johnson's Great Society Program, the War Against Poverty, and most importantly the struggle for civil liberties. The emphasis was on involvement and the need to eliminate causes for social and psychological dysfunction.

The present period, 1970 through 1980, may be characterized as the period of professionalism. The social work profession is turning inward, away from social action. It is a time of self-criticism and evaluation, of trying to gather data, develop sounder theoretical approaches, increase technical skills, and greater development toward specialization. There is a greater self-seeking on the part of the profession, greater pursuit of legal regulation to get public sanction for function and funding from new sources. Increased funding can provide social services to more segments of the population and affords the profession more independent status.

SHIFT TO AMBULATORY CARE

Expansion of social work functions will take place in such key areas as the emergency room, ambulatory care, and admissions and discharge planning. Bedside social work services will continue to be provided but more by physicians, nurses, and physician associates. Social workers often represent through concrete services "advocacy and humaneness" that counterbalances the impersonal and mechanistic nature of the inpatient hospital culture. However, with emphasis in current medical and nursing education on psychosocial causation it is likely that these and other disciplines will assume more caring relationships with patients. In emergency rooms, in admissions and discharge planning—areas of great and dramatic need and quick use of community resources—social workers will be more valued and their use will expand.

Ambulatory or outpatient services will grow. The drive to curtail bed utilization will be strengthened by increase in technology, knowledge, and costs. The major delivery of health care including psychiatric services will be on an ambulatory basis. Satellite dialysis clinics, geriatric clinics, and general health care facilities will be located in the neighborhoods where people live or work.

Home care programs will be expanded. The need for hospitalization will diminish, and services formerly provided through inpatient hospitalization will shift to ambulatory care. Support systems to enable patients to cope with physical and social problems in their homes or in alternative hospital programs will entail a greater use of social workers. Such workers will have training in mobilizing community resources and serving as mediators and consultants as well as in direct practice.

Posthospitalization care and home care programs will require developing forms of social support systems such as nursing, housekeeping, and rehabilitation care. Social workers will be used in these programs because of their skill in working with groups and individuals as well as their knowledge of other social and welfare systems.

EMPHASIS ON COMMUNITY WORK

Phillips has described the modern hospital "as a health center in every sense of the word."[2] She points out that the hospital must be concerned not only with curing and caring but also, by definition, with prevention. Prevention includes education, and this demands involvement with social agencies and with a host of new community group constellations. Most disciplines working exclusively within the hospital have not developed the expertise to forge linkages to such groups. Since social workers have been aware of this need and have made knowledge and expertise in network building an important element of their armamentaria, this aspect of social work in health settings will expand. The dynamics of the changing health structure make it imperative that we devote some manpower resources to this work even though budgetary restrictions may limit the rate of progress.

The importance of community work for health care will be accelerated by health legislation that has already been enacted providing for community participation in development of health programs. As community groups become more sophisticated to the loci of power that reside in hospitals and health agencies, their participation in decision making will become more significant. Social workers, by virtue of their training and practice, will be used for liaison and mediation in the development of programs consistent with local community needs and high professional expectations and demands.

DIRECT PRACTICE

Despite what many have predicted about future roles I believe social workers will continue to spend the major portion of their effort and time in the next ten years in direct practice working with individuals and groups of clients. I do not foresee significant change in basic orientation or capability to help people beyond the theoretical and conceptual formulations presently in use. Unless radical new theories are validated or another Freud or Piaget bursts on the scene I doubt that there will be a substitution of current practice theory in the immediate future.

Social work treatment models will be shaped and influenced by a variety of forces.

Influence of Regulation

Increased governmental control over financing will strongly influence program development and the structure of the health services, and, hence, will impact directly on treatment models. For example, the closer supervision of the expenditure of Medicaid and Medicare funds, mandated shortening of hospital stays, and increased auditing of professional and administrative practices will affect the delivery of health services. There will be more rather than less regulation. The regulations may come from different levels of government with closer local and consumer auditing. The rationale is obvious. Of the gross national product, approximately 8.4 percent goes to health care, a level deemed excessive by government financial advisers. Social work departments will need to shape their service delivery models and articulation of responsibility to this climate of public mandate and understanding.

Social Control

Another factor that will affect social work practice in health settings is the inherently dangerous recognition that social service structures can be used as agents of social control. As social problems in all areas of human activity become apparent, the significance of social work as the provider of services that minimize or alleviate social disorganization and dysfunction is recognized. The tactical advantage is evident. In health care settings social workers will be used increasingly to mediate and to serve as consultants to those requiring help in resolving multidisciplinary problems within the health care system. In dealing with community groups and mobilizing community resources external to the medical center their skills will be useful. The inherent dangers are that the profession will be viewed as allied with the establishment or that its function will actually be corrupted to become institutionally self-serving and alien to the disadvantaged in the community who desperately need our work.

Advocacy

The moral imperative to be an advocate or, as Dean Hyman Weiner of the New York University Graduate School of Social Work indicated, "be the loyal opposition" has existed from the time that social work began. The imperative to help the poor has been diluted by the thrust toward professionalism and more material gains for practitioners. While we are now emulating other more prestigious and lucrative professions such as medicine and law, the moral imperative remains as strong as ever. Our role as advocates must be strengthened even if it produces professional discomfort and hardship. This will be very difficult for social workers to do because most are employed by health agencies whose special vested interests impose constraints on all staff including social workers. Tenure rights that would guarantee freedom to disseminate personal/professional ideology are a possible solution, and some staff in hospital settings have already achieved this. Social workers will need to find ways in which advocacy can become an integrated part of their armamentarium.

Advocacy also carries the expectation that social workers will participate more actively in political and social groups and fraternal organizations, such as the local library board or directorial positions in agencies, school boards, and local planning groups. From such positions health care social workers can more readily advocate for the handicapped, lower socioeconomic groups, and others in need. Only continued emphasis from schools of social work and the profession itself will motivate social workers to take on with greater enthusiasm the discouraging and unpopular role of advocating for those who need it most.

Collaboration

The medical profession, coming from a position of supreme authority in the early 1900s, has begun to share decision making and responsibility for some areas of practice. No other professionals have given up as much as physicians, although it should be added that they have had more power to share than most other professionals and they continue to retain a great deal of authority. As multidisciplinary practice is extended we expect that there will be greater success in training all disciplines in productive collaboration. To some extent education has failed to socialize prospective members of the health professions.[3] Social work departments will also need a sustained effort in continuing education and staff development in this area.

Centralization

University and teaching hospitals will become more important as focal points in administration, treatment, research, and training functions, the hub of networks of services that will develop prototypes for other health agencies to follow. The principles of social Darwinism will be operative, and the stronger, more flexible and innovative institutions will survive while weaker hospitals will consolidate, merge, or develop affiliations with the university hospital systems. Weaker hospitals will probably be less significant in the total service delivery pattern. Governmental influence and control tends to foster centralization. Vertical complexes in the health field will develop as a result of budgetary controls much like the vertical combines in industry. In the health industry, preventive facilities and ambulatory, inpatient, and follow-up services together with health-related facilities will be combined under the umbrella of the major medical institutions.

Health care facilities will also be forced to avoid duplication of services. Social work departments will cooperate more effectively with each other and with community agencies. Some medical center home care programs will be more highly developed than others and because of special equipment and staffing will be more effective. Social work services can be regionalized, and interchange of staff and using each other as consultants will become more prevalent. The bigness may have the advantage of forcing institutions to be more cooperative in terms of sharing not only facilities but staff as well.[4] Social workers should be pioneers in this effort.

Quality and Quantity Controls

Social work in the next ten years will still be looking for its own theoretical framework. Treatment approaches will continue to be innovative but will need to be backed with much firmer evaluative data. We will be unable to continue approaches based on anecdotal or personalized experiences. All approaches will be scrutinized for effectiveness. Measurement will need to be by criteria developed out of rational and scientific experimentation.

By 1980 anecdotal recording will be minimal. The chart will need to reflect all activities of the worker and will be so organized that it will document all social work intervention. Statistical information obtained by social workers will be computerized. By 1980 computers will be cheap enough so that most medical centers and health facilities will be able to afford their own. This will be valuable in developing data important for case finding, developing high-risk data, and for discharge planning. Departments will have available to them either consultants or their own specialists who will develop systems of information based on data put into the medical charts as well as retrievable data for social work planning and intervention. There will be a greater emphasis on crisis intervention, short-term treatment, and lessened use of analytically oriented therapy. The use of the more active therapies, such as behavior modification, reality and assertive therapies, game therapies, and consciousness raising, will increase. Social workers will be expected to be more active and verbal in the therapeutic context and will make expanded use of family and group therapies in health settings.

Social Dysfunction and Role

There will be more emphasis on role functioning in social work practice. As values and attitudes change, such institutions as the family, school, and church will change their approach to their constituencies. Knowledge about this interplay will need to be introduced into the curricula of the schools of social work, and social workers will develop different approaches to modifying the helping process in the resolution of social dysfunction caused by illness.

Technology

Technological advances will continue in health care. This kind of knowledge will be mandatory for social workers entering health settings in the future. The moral, ethical, and practice issues involved in helping patients and families resolve difficulties caused by such procedures as organ transplants will have a profound effect on social work techniques and function.

Function Definition

Social workers in health settings will need to reorient their approach to individuals in terms of life and space context. More specific limits will need to be placed on those problem areas that social workers can deal with, and those that are beyond the scope of social work will need to be referred elsewhere. The use of limits based on hard knowledge will be applied.

Morris and Anderson have proposed that psychosocial understanding is only a prelude to complete professional function.[5] They suggest that personal care services be considered an extension of concrete services. In health settings personal care services would include, for example, homemaker services, home health services, day care for children, and services in day care for the mentally ill. Personal care services could be more easily supported as social interventions because they would be consonant with the goals of the health and welfare system as defined nationally. Mogulof has suggested that services that affect the productivity of individuals would be more apt to receive the attention and support of our society.[6] Within the health care system social workers who help persons dependent as a result of an illness to return to gainful employment would merit governmental support. Mogulof defines these types of services as "interventions or service systems which would aid in maximizing in health setting the patient's use of medical treatment and also in discharge planning."[7] Psychological counseling is not likely to receive continued governmental support because it is not directly related to moving persons in and out of hospitals or maximizing their utilization of expensive medical care treatment.

Using the partialization principle, social workers will be clearer about their ability to intervene with more limited and sharply defined problems.

Networks

The hospital will be forced to become a multiservice agency dealing with issues tangential but related to health problems. The medical center will need to consider whether it should be involved with such a wide variety of problems. If so, what resources will be needed to do the job? Are there other welfare sources that must be used by a hospital or be integrated into health care delivery systems to make possible the fulfillment of a more comprehensive mandate? Questions can be raised as to how a social work department will fit into this system and into these expanded functions. Should the social work service be external or internal to the system? If the department is to exist externally, as some have concluded, a new approach to the problem of organization of social work services for patients in the health care system needs to be developed. Teague has concluded that the present pattern of organization and orientation to services is outmoded and radical reform is urgently needed. He has proposed a model that consists of a new external agency structure that is separate from the hospital and other health care facilities in a defined service area.[8] I believe the social work department can be an integral part of the medical care system dealing with the problems arising from the newer functions. But there will be reliance on external social work systems also.

Social work departments may require different resources to be generated and developed. These may take a form that now exists in an embryonic state within some departments or they may take completely new forms. If the hospital is to become the hub of a large network of health agencies, then community organization workers will become a more important section of a social work service than heretofore. Social worker specialists of another sort may be required, or perhaps other disciplines will be attached to a social work department. Perhaps public health nurses should be attached to social work departments to participate in preventive educational programs that will be developed. Or it may well be that social workers in health settings will require different training. Social workers should know more about the practical applications of medical knowledge in a preventive or emergency situation. It is conceivable that just as public health nurses use stethoscopes, social workers in preventive areas in the community should become familiar with certain medical instruments, to use the stethoscope and do thermometer readings as well, and to develop approaches that will be helpful in aiding the physician and other medical specialists in preventive programs.

Confidentiality

The right to treatment and the right to privacy and confidentiality will become increasingly important. This will affect social work in health settings in a variety of ways. One of the major concerns now is how to involve community agencies in the treatment of individuals.

Because hospitalization will be shorter there will be more dependence on maintaining services through use of community health and social agencies. How will the principle of privacy and confidentiality affect the giving and sharing of information with agencies? How do these principles affect research?

Overlapping Functions: Specialist and Generalist

There will be a greater meshing of professions with continued overlapping of functions. There are many disciplines now involved in the health field because of the vast areas of new knowledge that have been developed as well as the increasing knowledge available in the old areas. As disciplines continue to overlap, new professions can emerge. It would be foolhardy to deny that specialization is the order of the day. In the next ten years social workers will tend to become more expert in narrower fields of knowledge. This can be most unfortunate, and we have seen the results of this highly specialized trend in medicine. An alternative is to develop group practice as is occurring with greater frequency and success in medicine. Teams of social workers consisting of different levels from the social work assistant through postmaster's training will be used. Another alternative is to use a generic social worker to perform as the basic manpower unit in all settings and as in medicine to supplement the effort of the generalist with the specialist through consultation or in direct practice when called upon. This requires greater autonomy for social work practitioners, a less rigid form of supervision, and greater security on the part of social work management. These are not easily met conditions.

Role of the Supervisor

The supervisor, as a middle manager within a large social work department or as the director in a small department, will be an educator as well as a manager. The primary function will be to upgrade the skills of the worker, moving him continuously toward autonomous practice, through consultation, direct service, offering new and alternative plans for treatment, and availability as a resource person to all practitioners. Preparation for this administrative and educational role will demand continuing education beyond that offered on the master's level.[9]

CONCLUSION

Donald F. Phillips raises the issue that "solutions to today's health delivery problems may become problems for tomorrow's hospitals."[10] He discusses the integration of a regional network of health care services, the participation of the hospital in comprehensive health care, and its dependency upon interaction with other health care institutions. A limitation on the total amount of resources available for institutional health, much more extensive accountability, and much more active demand for consumer involvement are all to be expected. We can anticipate that social work as an integral part of the comprehensive health care system will be involved in these problems.

As we look forward to the 1980s we review some of the great problems that we faced ten years ago. We have managed to resolve some of them. Others seem more harsh and difficult than they were then. There is some basis for confidence based on the growth of social work in the health care field. More than one out of every three professional social workers are working in health agencies. Almost 60 percent of all the hospitals in the United States have staff identified as social workers or as consultants. The validity of the social work approach in the health field has made this possible. If social workers did not produce a service that is wanted and needed by patients and their families, there could not have been this rapid growth. So long as we retain our commitment to the human aspect of the cure system I believe we will have the knowledge, flexibility, and strength to fulfill and enhance our tradition of caring and advocacy in changing and stressful times ahead.

REFERENCES

1. Martin Nacman and Lawrence Shulman, "Social Work: Its Future in the Health Field," mimeographed, 1971.

2. Beatrice Phillips, "Development and Deployment of Social Work Staff in the Health Setting" (Paper delivered at the Annual Meeting of the Society of Hospital Social Work Directors, Denver, September 1973).

3. Bess Dana, H. David Banta, and Kirk W. Deuschle, "An Agenda for the Future of Interprofessionalism," in *Medicine and Social Work,* ed. Helen Rehr (New York: Prodist, 1974), pp. 77–88.

4. Allen L. Applebaum, "New York City Hospitals: The Financial Crunch," *Hospitals, Journal of the American Hospital Association* 50 (January 16, 1976):59–62.

5. Robert Morris and Delwin Anderson, "Personal Care Services: An Identity for Social Work," *Social Service Review* 49, no. 2 (June 1975):157–61.

6. Melvin Mogulof, "Future Funding of Social Services," *Social Work,* September 1974, pp. 607–14.

7. Ibid.

8. Doran Teague, "Social Service Enterprises: A New Health Care Model," *Social Work* 16, no. 3 (July 1971):66–74.

9. Abraham Lurie and Gary Rosenberg, "The Current Role of the Hospital Social Work Director," *Hospitals, Journal of the American Hospital Association* (Reference article, June 1973).

10. Donald F. Phillips, "American Hospitals: A Look Ahead," *Hospitals, Journal of the American Hospital Association* 50 (January 1, 1976).

Chapter 3

Management By Objectives in a Hospital Social Service Unit

Robert M. Spano, ACSW
Sander H. Lund

ABSTRACT. A Management By Objectives (MBO) system has been installed in the Social Service Department of the University of Minnesota Hospitals. MBO involves administering organizations through establishment and follow-up of goals. In order to accommodate a human service milieu two additions have been made to the usual MBO format: (a) a statement of program philosophy, and (b) a statement of essential program functions. Staff reaction to the system has been mixed, while hospital administration has been uniformly favorable. In the future the MBO system will be integrated with a management information system, and "significant others" will be surveyed to get more outside input into the formulation of objectives. MBO meets organizational needs for effective planning, management of resources and control, while at the same time maximizing staff input into the overall operation.

There is a rich tradition in the social sciences that distinguishes formal organizations from other human service groups by the dedication on the part of organization members to attain collectively accepted goals. Building on this literature, Peter Drucker,[1] a prominent management consultant, has promulgated an administrative technique called "Management By Objectives" (MBO) wherein organizations are directed through formulation and evaluation of express program objectives. Management By Objectives has been adopted successfully by many business organizations but has received relatively little attention in the human services.[2] The purpose of this paper is to help fill this gap by describing the installation of an MBO system in a hospital social service department. The mechanics of the system will be presented, the advantages will be highlighted, and it will be shown how the usual MBO format was modified to fit a human service milieu.

SETTING

The setting for this venture was the Social Service Department of the University of Minnesota Hospitals. Founded in 1909, the department employs 22 full-time MSWs, 2 BA staff, and 1 case aide, and provides a full range of services to the hospital's patients and their families. In 1974, 10,000 clients were served by the department.

MANAGEMENT BY OBJECTIVES

As the name implies, Management by Objectives involves direction of an organization through the periodic establishment and review of formal objectives. Objectives are typically derived from and serve to expand a statement of the organization's mission and are in turn elaborated by subordinate goals, which represent the specific outcomes that must occur in a given time period if the objectives and larger mission are to be achieved. Goals and objectives are formulated with input from staff at all levels of the hierarchy. Evaluation, in Management by Objectives, consists of comparing the actual outcome with the original goal and using this information to judge organizational effectiveness and formulate new goals.

At the University of Minnesota Hospitals Social Service Department a modified version of Management by Objectives was used to derive a four-tiered organizational goal structure (Figure 1). As can be seen, there are two changes in the usual MBO format: (a) derivation of a mission statement from a formal department philosophy and (b) inclusion of "department functions" between the mission statement and objectives. The philosophy is an attempt to incorporate the department's value system into its formal operation. The functions serve as a mechanism to insure that attention is paid to all appropriate professional standards.

Philosophy

At the apex of the goal structure is the Social Service Department's philosophy. Derived from literature reviews, community meetings, hospital policies, and staff discussion, it is a statement of the department's overall dedication and serves as background for examination and revision of the goal structure. The philosophy attempts to give continuity and subjective meaning to the department's operation by providing a sense of its fundamental, but not previously articulated, value system. The importance of this can be that unlike private operations, which tend to be accountable only to themselves, public service providers have a multiplicity of "significant others," and as a result the values served by an agency are subject to many points of view. A formal philosophy can mitigate poten-

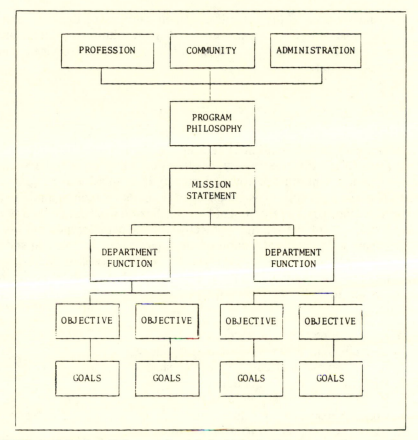

FIGURE 1. University of Minnesota Hospitals Social Service Department goal structure format.

tial turmoil by insuring that a program's values are subject to public scrutiny and by providing a channel for integrating legitimate external input into a program's operation.

Mission Statement

The philosophy serves as a platform for development of the department's mission statement, which is a brief description of its fundamental reason for existence. The following mission statement was formulated by the director of the department based upon the philosophy and upon his understanding of the role of professional social work in the provision of medical services:

MISSION: It is the mission of the Social Service Department to enhance the delivery of comprehensive health services by providing social services to the patients and their families of the University of Minnesota Hospitals and to assist in resolution of social and emotional problems related to illness, medical services and rehabilitation.

Functions

Subordinate to the mission statement are the department functions. Each function is a discrete activity, or cluster of activities, that the Social Service Department must perform adequately if its mission is to be realized. The list of functions is based upon a series of recommendations from the Social Service Department Director Search Committee, and provides rubrics to link the setting of objectives to the department's mission. Unless there is a major redirection of the department, the mission statement and functions will rarely be revised. The objectives, however, are evaluated and reformulated on an annual basis. The current department functions are to:

1. Provide direct patient services.
2. Maintain liaison with community agencies.
3. Foster professional development of staff.
4. Participate in hospital programs.
5. Provide educational programs.
6. Conduct research projects.
7. Administer and coordinate programs.

Objectives and Goals

Each objective is a separate event, or group of related events, that must occur in a specified time period if a function is to be adequately served. An objective consists of: (a) the title of the objective; (b) the staff responsible for activities in regard to the title; (c) a statement of current activities in regard to the title; (d) a statement of the outcome expected in regard to the title; and (e) the date at which the expected outcome is to occur (Figure 2). In cases where attainment of an objective involves a series of related outcomes, each such outcome is presented as a separate goal under that objective. Objectives and goals were formulated by department staff, under review of the director. There was at least one staff committee for each function, and in many cases temporary subcommittees were established as well.

DEPARTMENT FUNCTION: PARTICIPATION IN EDUCATION PROGRAMS

Function Objectives	Responsible Staff	Current Level of Functioning	Expected Level of Functioning	Completion Date	Outcome Level
FORMULATE TEACHING ROLE IN APPROPRIATE UNIVERSITY AND HOSPITAL COURSES.	Formal Teaching Role Committee	Minimal use of staff as consultant teachers; usually on informal basis with no departmental recognition.	Recognition and sanction of work done now. Establish committee to evaluate further department involvement in teaching.	June, 1974	Recommendations made as to recognition and sanction of present work. Committee appointed; evaluation of further teaching will be continued.
PARTICIPATE IN TRAINING OF STUDENTS IN ALLIED HEALTH CARE DISCIPLINES.	Formal Teaching Role Committee	Minimal: occurs primarily in departments of Neurology and Psychiatry.	Documentation and evaluation of role in Neurology and Psychiatry.	January, 1975	Volume and direction of teaching in this area has been documented.
CONSULTATION TO OTHER HEALTH CARE DISCIPLINES.	Formal Teaching Role Committee	Provided informally and on request; has low department priority.	Improve and expand consultation.	January, 1975	It has been suggested that a coordinator for educational consultation be appointed; procedures have been set up to process requests for consultation.
STUDY THE POSSIBILITY OF FACILITATIVE ASSISTANCE TO RELATIVES OF PATIENTS IN ICU'S & WAITING ROOMS.	Two Students	Need for assistance has been brought to attention of department for investigation.	Determine potential involvement of department, either on its own or in conjunction with other departments.	April, 1974	Study complete and presented to department and administration.

FIGURE 2. Administrative portion of the Social Service Department's 1974 goal structure.

INSTALLATION OF THE SYSTEM

During the fall of 1972, the senior authority was selected by the Social Service Department Director Search Committee to take charge of the University of Minnesota Hospitals Social Service Department. Concurrent with this appointment, the department was receiving administrative encouragement to expand its community and hospital activities, and there were signs that staff desired a more direct involvement in the development of departmental policy. Consequently, a request by hospital administration for a statement of the new director's goals served as a stimulus to supplant the previous administrative system, which focused power on the office of the director, with Management by Objectives. It was hoped that this move would both tighten the linkage with higher administration and provide a rational structure for the management of new programs, while at the same time serving as a mechanism for significantly increasing staff influence in the department's overall operation.

Following the request for his goals, the director met with staff, explained his desire to implement an MBO system, and called for committees to be formed in each function area to establish departmental objectives and goals. Seventeen out of 24 staff volunteered, and within 1 month a goal structure containing 42 objectives and goals was constructed. The director reviewed the goal structure, met with committee chairpersons to discuss his reactions and negotiate revisions, and forwarded the final document to hospital administration. Accompanying the final version was a cover letter that stated the director's belief that the goal structure represented both a work plan for the department and a contract with hospital administration.

One year later, each staff committee reported on the attainment of the objectives and goals in its function area, and the junior author was retained to review these reports and help compose the annual report. The results were positive: During the 1st year, 31 of the 33 objectives and goals scheduled for attainment had actually been achieved. The completed annual report was sent to hospital administration, and staff committees were reconvened to initiate the second iteration of the MBO goal-setting process.

Reaction to the System

The MBO system was a striking departure from the previous administrative style, and drew attention from a variety of sources. The reaction of the Social Service Department staff was mixed. Some staff eagerly seized the opportunity to make their priorities heard in the operation of the program. Other staff saw the system as bureaucratic paperwork, and treated it as a nuisance to be avoided. A few appeared to view it as a threat, and resisted the implicit accountability that accompanies formulation and evaluation of program goals. After the 1st year of operation, 10 staff members had left the department and had been replaced by individuals whose values were congenial with the new system. In addition, goal setting was established as an integral part of each staff person's annual performance review.

The reaction of the University of Minnesota Hospitals' administration was uniformly favorable. Shortly after submission of the first annual report, the director was requested to present the full system at a meeting of the hospitals' department chiefs, and subsequently the University of Minnesota Hospitals implemented Management By Objectives in all administrative units. The authors like to believe that this event was influenced by the successful experience of the Social Service Department. The system has also been presented at the Minnesota Chapter of the Society of Hospital Social Service Directors, at an international exchange program for social workers, at the national meeting of Hospital Social Service Directors, and at a workshop on Management by Objectives sponsored by the American Hospital Association. In addition, the system was described in the *Program Evaluation Resource Center Newsletter,* and copies of the first report have been requested by over 300 national and international human service programs. At least two University of Minnesota management courses have also used the report as an educational aid.

Future Developments

The values and objectives of a public human service organization are often a matter of conflict and negotiation. The next stage in the development of the Social Service Department's MBO system will involve periodically surveying groups and individuals with a continuing interest in the department's development. Sources of input will include clients, legislators, community agencies, hospital administrators, and professional social work organizations. A panel of individuals representing each group will be contacted annually to get both input on future priorities and feedback on the degree to which past priorities have been satisfied. The results of the surveys will be incorporated into the department's overall goal structure.

The second future development will be integration of the MBO format with the department's Management Information System. Developed by the director and an independent evaluation consultant, the system is an automated staff accountability mechanism wherein all personnel report their professional activities in specific function categories.[3] The function categories used in the system are based upon standards developed by the Southern Regional Educational Board and may be modified so they are consistent with the department functions presented previously. Particularly when linked to decentralized budgeting, this creates the potential to determine the expense required to support objectives in each function area and allows the director to make programmatic decisions based on cost-effectiveness information.

DISCUSSION

Like most formal organizations, human service programs typically have two distinct, and occasionally conflicting, needs: (a) rational and orderly allocation of limited resources, and (b) creation of an atmosphere that allows maximum use of diverse staff talents. Students of Fredrick Taylor's[4] "Scientific Management" school argue that the basic requirement of organization is "structure," and contend that effectiveness can best be assured through construction of a formal supervisory hierarchy with sanctions allocated according to the degree that staff meet specific and detailed role expectations. However, disciples of Chester Barnard[5] and Elton Mayo's[6] "Human Relations" approach to management believe that "participation" is essential to organization, and counter that open communication, decentralized decision making, and personalized task expectations are the key to optimal functioning.

The authors believe that organizational needs for "structure" and "participation" are not mutually exclusive. The Management By Objectives system presented here is an attempt to develop the three "structural" administrative functions mentioned by Allen Schick (i.e., planning, management, control),[7] while at the same time using human relations theorist Douglas MacGregor's[8] Theory Y assumption of management to allow maximum staff impact on the course of the Social Service Department's development.

The first structural requirement of organization mentioned by Schick, "planning," involves anticipating future needs, deciding on the resources necessary to meet these needs, and formulating policy to govern allocation of the resources. In the Planning, Programming, and Budgeting system (PPB) advocated by Schick, planning represents an attempt to project the activities of an organization ahead through time by formulating organizational objectives. The core of this process, of course, is identical with Management By Objectives. The very act of establishing objectives compels consideration of future contingencies, and the existence of an organizational goal structure provides a natural framework for examining the relationship of an organization's activities to its basic dedication.

"Management" according to Schick is the means through which resources are organized in the attainment of program objectives. In the same way that "planning" corresponds to the MBO process of forming objectives, "management" represents the setting of operational goals to attain them. This is the step in which each rather global objective is transformed into the clear, realistic, and concrete event(s) that will signal its attainment. An integrated goal structure of organizational goals facilitates the management function by providing a vehicle for distribution of resources and monitoring of staff task responsibilities. Such a structure also provides a coherent description of the organization's operating structure, which facilitates identification of weaknesses and redundancies.

"Control" according to Schick is the function insuring that specific activities are performed in an efficacious and efficient manner. Regarding Management By Objectives, "control" relates to evaluation and feedback, and involves assessing goal attainment and using such information to monitor organizational development. MBO enhances the control function in two ways. First, of course, it provides a means of evaluating performance. Predetermined goals, stated clearly and concretely, are effectiveness standards that avoid the potential biases of unstructured post hoc judgment. Second, Management By Objectives provides a catalyst for improving organizational communication. An open statement of organization reduces conflicts due to idiosyncratic interpretation of the organization's mission.

Subscribing to MacGregor's Theory Y assumption of management, which holds that under appropriate circumstances human beings will actively seek increased responsibility, the authors believe that inflexibility and excessive centralization of power can deny formal organizations the full creative potential of their personnel. Under the present Management By Objectives system this problem is mitigated through the direct staff establishment of goals, an arrangement that provides a mechanism for controlled opening of a hierarchy. Placing responsibility for goal setting on staff, rather than merely enforcing strict task instructions, increases flexibility and nurtures personal growth at the same time that it creates a structure for formal staff accountability. Staff are simultaneously provided with an opportunity to take a personalized approach to their work and accorded public responsibility for both the level of their expectations and the quality of their output. In the long run, this increases the energy and inspiration leveled against any particular problem, and tends to increase morale and efficiency as well, since staff tend to be most committed to goals of their own formulation. At the same time, MBO opens a useful channel of reciprocal communication between staff and administration, providing for open debate on issues directly related to improved organizational functioning. This dialogue helps clarify organizational priorities and places them "up front" where they may be examined by staff, consumers, and community.

CONCLUSION

During the past 2 years, the Social Service Department has accomplished goals that have guided staff in directions similar to those shaping the health care delivery system at large. Government has mandated certain responsibilities to health professionals through the passage of recent amendments to the Social Security Act. These include the establishment of local Professional Standards Review Organizations (PSRO) and, within them, the utilization review programs, medical audit programs, and quality assurance programs. Health professionals will be required to expose their practice to peer review mechanisms and to function within the standards, norms, and criteria developed in the geographic area by each PSRO.

Nonphysician health care practitioners will become involved in the PSRO review process at all levels. The implications for the social work profession and social work practitioners in health care delivery are becoming clear. The profession will be required not only to define its functions and monitor its activities from a cost perspective but also to evaluate the effectiveness of its intervention strategies from a quality standpoint as well.

The Social Service Department at the University of Minnesota has begun this process by stating its philosophy, articulating its mission, defining its functions, and establishing a procedure for setting yearly objectives and goals. In addition, the department is monitoring staff effort with an information and reporting system. What remains is to define the kinds of client problems the department will address and to implement an evaluation system to determine effectiveness in these areas.

REFERENCES

1. Drucker, Peter. *Managing for Results*. New York: Harper & Row, 1964.

2. Brady, Rodney. "MBO Goes to Work in the Public Sector." *Harvard Business Review*, March–April 1973.

3. Baxter, James. "An Automated Professional Staff Accounting System." Unpublished manual, University of Minnesota Hospitals Social Service Department, 1974.

4. Taylor, Fredrick. *Scientific Management*. New York: Harper & Row, 1947.

5. Barnard, Chester. *The Function of the Executive*. Cambridge, Mass.: Harvard University Press, 1938.

6. Mayo, Elton. *The Social Problems of an Industrial Civilization*. Cambridge, Mass.: Harvard University Press, 1945.

7. Schick, Allen. "The Road to PPB: The Stages of Budget Reform." *Public Administration Review* 26 (1966):243–58.

8. MacGregor, Douglas. *The Human Side of Enterprise*. New York: McGraw-Hill, 1960.

PART II

Management Information
for Planning, Operating and Controlling
the Social Work Contribution

The social work manager is responsible for a group of accountabilities to the client system, the organization which employs third party payers, the profession as a whole and for the quality of practice and the utilization of resources. Management information systems are the important foundation for implementing these accountabilities. Additionally management information systems serve as a base for research. The conceptual base of management information is far more important than whether a system is hand-tallied or computerized. A partnership between professional staff and management is necessary for any management information system to be functional.

Volland authors a social work accountability system which is an excellent example of one hospital's struggle to enact its accountabilities and to use data in a research-oriented way for practice, collaboration and accountability. Harold Weissman's article is a more general discussion which emphasizes the collaboration of researchers, staff and clients in managing information systems. Spano and Kiresuk describe another model of accountability which forms the base of a management information system, a research system and a performance evaluation system. Schoech describes a far more technologically advanced system which is specifically designed for computer applications. In sum, the articles provide the social work manager and student of management with a set of examples and ideas which provide state-of-the-art knowledge on management information systems.

Gary Rosenberg, PhD

Chapter 4

Social Work Information and Accountability Systems in a Hospital Setting

Patricia J. Volland, LCSW, MBA

ABSTRACT. Information and accountability systems for departments of social work are a major concern for the profession, particularly within the health care sector. This paper describes the development of such a system within a large university hospital, the forces that led to its development, and the multiple expectations for its usefulness in planning and implementing social work services most effectively, within the lowest cost. It includes potential for building research projects and is utilized as a communication mechanism for recording. Collaboration within the profession is essential for implementing objective standards to be utilized in reviewing delivery of professional social work services.

"To move forward in the coming decade, social work must make substantial progress in at least three tasks: (1) to find better ways to account for what it does, (2) to determine the effectiveness of its programs, and (3) to develop more potent means of effecting change in social problems."[1] To do what Dr. William Reid suggests, and to do it responsibly, the profession must continue to develop and perfect information and accountability systems that collect, store, and analyze a wide range of information to answer questions of program effectiveness, costs, and operating systems. It is to the credit of the profession that social work is asking these questions of itself in planning for a future where nothing will be taken for granted. All services in the health care sector are coming under critical scrutiny in an attempt to provide the highest level of care at the lowest possible cost. Health care providers are being asked to define and account for their services through cost-effective processes. Both third-party payers, including government agencies, and consumers are focusing on the escalating cost of health care and understanding the quality of the care provided.[2] Where social work is part of a health care delivery system, the profession is participating in this process.

This paper describes the design and implementation of an information and accountability system within a university hospital. It reviews the purposes of the system and relates these to the needs of the profession in general, and social work in health care in particular.

ACCOUNTABILITY AND SOCIAL WORK INFORMATION SYSTEMS

There are forces at local and federal levels that sharpen the need for definitions of quality and quantity of work by the profession. In the state of Maryland, the Maryland Health Services Cost Review Commission has been established.[3] This commission has responsibility for investigating, reviewing, and establishing rates of reimbursement for hospital services. In establishing a rate review methodology, this commission has accepted the Revenue Center as a means for defining service. Each revenue center makes bills and establishes relative value units. Departments of social work are not considered revenue centers. Rather, social work services are charged off through the per diem established within the revenue center where the service is provided. A relative value unit has been established for each professional service; for social work this unit of measure is total number of cases. This unit of measure does not accurately define quality or quantity of services provided or their benefit to patients. In response to this, directors of social work departments, through the Maryland Chapter of the American Society for Hospital Social Work Directors, have taken responsibility for defining and ranking types of social work services.[4] One approach to relative value is time spent in delivering each service with level of professional skill necessary to provide these services.

On the federal level, passage of Professional Standards Review Organization (PSRO) regulations mandates the requirement for both concurrent and retrospective review.[2] The objectives of this legislation suggest that reduction of health care costs is compatible with increased effectiveness of service. Establishment of criteria for a standard for services for each health care professional addresses the possibility of reduced cost and increased effectiveness. One approach for the establishment of such criteria for social work is through defining service categories with minimum criteria necessary to delivery these services effectively,[4] a process that is part of an information system.

In addition to addressing accountability, a good information system has potential as the basis for research and evaluation of services. Attempts within the profession of social work to research adequately the content and effectiveness of services have tended to be anecdotal and limited to case examples at best.[5] Predictions for future studies suggest that future focus will be on effectiveness of certain techniques, established in advance, rather than total review of process retrospectively.[1] Emphasis is on defining and testing observable changes or "hard" data. One approach to developing these data is to categorize psychosocial problems that are frequently utilized to define cause and effect relationship to illness and health. These psychosocial problems, frequently used to define need for social work interventions in health care, could form the basis for a taxonomy of "hard" data.

Changes in The Johns Hopkins Hospital focused on decentralized management and implementation of "Management By Objectives" concepts. The Department of Social Work experienced a change in leadership. This resulted in overall goals being sharpened, as the new leadership was charged with defining program objectives and establishing effectiveness criteria while understanding the costs to a given revenue center. A cost system was needed to establish this clearly. These developments reflect the situation faced by many departments of social work.

ESTABLISHMENT OF SYSTEM OBJECTIVES

Having considered all of these factors, what then should the objectives of an information and accountability system in a large university hospital setting be? This author determined that a multifaceted system with the following objectives would be functional for the Department of Social Work at The Johns Hopkins Hospital:

1. To establish and define social work services.
2. To communicate these services to all other health care professionals.
3. To measure the outcome of these services.
4. To develop an information system that lays a basis for developing and executing research projects on health care problems pertinent to social work interventions.

The first approach was a review of developments in other hospital social work departments. In Maryland, one such program with potential for adaptation was developed at the Sinai Hospital of Baltimore.[6] The same consultant to that program was employed by our department to review our needs and to assist in the design of a workable system. The system that has been developed at The Johns Hopkins Hospital reflects and has similarities to the design developed at the Sinai Hospital of Baltimore.

The system at The Johns Hopkins Hospital has been developed within the framework of problem identification, goal-directed services provided to alleviate the defined problem, and measurement of service outcome. In setting such a framework, services are defined into categories; each category has a set of criteria that will be utilized in the peer review process.[2,7] Further definition of services results from collection of demographic information on each patient. For example, review of patients who receive discharge planning services clearly establishes patients at risk for this service. Patients needing social work services can be defined and enter the social work system more effectively. This also leads to implementation of concurrent review[2] as has already been demonstrated at The Johns Hopkins Hospital where patients "at risk" are automatically referred to the Department of Social Work by the Quality Assurance Office. Effective implementation of concurrent review is accomplished, and outcome of such service delivery benefits the patient (effective discharge planning) and the hospital (improved utilization of beds).

Objective definition of services leads to a better understanding of social work services. Further, by comparing time spent and level of professional expertise necessary to provide said service, a relative value for each service category will be established. Service categories will then become the unit of measure for defining the cost of social work service, thus providing a more accurate cost base and a more effective means of comparing social work departments within like hospitals. The potential of charging for social work services, based on actual services provided, should have greater appeal for third-party payers in considering separate reimbursement for social work.

Collection of data, both qualitative and quantitative, can lead to demonstration of cost-effectiveness. For example, when the commission or hospital administration questions the high cost of social work services in an outpatient clinic where service to patients in groups is focused on reducing somatic complaints while dealing with psychosocial problems of depression and social isolation, this service can be demonstrated as being less costly than utilization of physician time with patients individually. The above discussion of objective data collection also has value in working with hospital administration. Psychosocial problems that interfere with or complicate health and medical care are defined for a particular patient population. Such systematic problem identification combined with defined service categories and measurement of outcome of such services defines for hospital administration the type of program being implemented and the contribution it makes to the hospital's objective to provide quality care. Effectiveness of program planning is demonstrated by comparing services with outcomes such as length of stay in the hospital. The potential for reducing length of stay in the hospital through early entry into the social work system can be demonstrated while providing comprehensive service to the patient. Through preliminary review, the Department of Social Work has demonstrated already that time is lost in planning when the patient's refusal to cooperate is disregarded.[8] Further, both service definition and outcome measures are better understood through the reporting of obstacles to service. Internal and external obstacles such as late referral or lack of resources are known. This information can be utilized to define ways of saving health costs. Communication through objective methodologies and utilizing the concept of problem-oriented record keeping enhances understanding of social work services while leading to clarification of role responsibilities for patient care. Problems and service intent are clearly stated to enhance team responsibilities for patient care.

Finally, there is great potential for such a system to lay a basis for developing and executing research projects. Demographic patient information, problem taxonomy, service goals and outcomes, and obstacles to service delivery can be compared and studied separately in evaluative as well as descriptive research projects.

DESCRIPTION OF THE SYSTEM

The Recording and Reporting System itself contains a standardized problem list and four recording forms. The problem list has two levels:

1. *Initial problems* represent the point of entry into the social work system from the overall health care system. Classifications include: (a) difficulties with medical regime; (b) acceptance/adjustment to conditions; (c) inadequate/harmful care; (d) personal adjustment/behavior problem; (e) environmental difficulties; and (f) terminal illness.

2. *Follow-up or resultant problems* are defined following a social work assessment. The problems here may coexist with health-related problems, or they may be the cause or result of these health-related problems. Classifications include the following: (a) individual function related to illness; (b) family conflicts; (c) living conditions; (d) interpersonal relationship difficulties; (e) economic conditions; (f) other specific conditions; and (g) individual psychiatric disorders—behavioral symptomatology, thought and feeling disorders, and lifelong maladaptive behavioral patterns. Each is further broken down into specific problem areas to aid in focusing for social work services. Each problem is numbered for computerization.

Recording Forms

Patient case record. This form is completed by the social worker at the time of referral for assessment. It contains demographic information regarding the patient and his family, a medical diagnosis, as well as a description of the referring agent and the referring problem. This form never appears in the Medical Record, as all information contained on it should already be there. One copy of this form goes to data processing; the social worker keeps the other for his own records.

Service plan. Following initial assessment where the social worker decides to open a case, this form is completed and a copy is placed in the Medical Record within 48 hours. The Service Plan Form contains specific problems identified for social work services. Service goals are defined, and activities to be performed are described. These are coded for computer analysis.

Service completion form. At the completion of a service episode this form is completed. A copy is placed in the Medical Record. Problems worked, service goals and activities, and outcome achieved for each are recorded descriptively and coded. Obstacles that may have interfered with the social work services are described and coded. The worker then has the option of closing the case or redefining problems and new services to be provided.

Service plan change. When, in the process of providing service, the worker determines a need to redefine problems and/or services, the Service Plan Change Form is completed. A copy is placed in the Medical Record. This represents either a shift in problem focus or in goal focus. The Service Plan Change is similar to the Service Plan. It is primarily an indicator of the shift.

With the decision to computerize this system, it becomes possible to store information indefinitely and to expand the number of variables to be compared. In devising and implementing this system, it was determined that a system was needed that served both recording and reporting purposes. Each suggested design was analyzed for its potential usefulness in collecting the necessary information and then was tested on limited staff. Attention was focused on creating a problem list that contained mutually exclusive items. The current problem list is close to this goal. A sample system was devised and implemented on a trial basis in April of 1975 and was utilized through August of 1975. Feedback was gathered from each of the staff members with suggestions for improving the system. The formal system was implemented in September 1975.

IMPLEMENTATION AND POTENTIAL VALUE

No formal system of recording existed previously. Therefore, worker response to this system was very ambivalent: There was excitement in developing and participating in a new system; however, the ultimate expectation that each worker would be required to utilize it created concern. Time considerations in learning to use and maintain such a system are still being discussed. Social workers tend to view this process of record keeping as unnecessary paperwork. Time spent away from direct contact with patient and/or family is frequently seen as time wasted. Administrative staff spent much time attempting to resolve such concerns.

The value of this system in planning and implementing comprehensive treatment services was stressed as was the responsibility for maintenance of profession accountability within the hospital. Since the administration of The Johns Hopkins Hospital views any attempt at objective definition and planning of services within realistic cost as positive, necessary funds to develop and build this system were readily available. The Medical Records Department was reluctant to approve still another form for the Medical Record. However, this was a minor obstacle, and the focus on problem-oriented records further reduced resistance as Medical Records would like the hospital to adopt this format.

Building a foundation for future research projects posed a minor problem in that it was necessary to develop a system that combined a mutually exclusive problem list and collected relevant patient demographic information. Outcome measures, while somewhat objective, will need continued review.

The value of this system can be stated in terms of how it benefits and relates to: (a) outside regulatory agencies such as the Maryland Health Services Cost Review Commission; (b) hospital administration; (c) the director and supervisory personnel of the social work department; (d) the social work profession, particularly as it has impact on PSRO regulations and research potential; and (e) patients and families.

As previously stated, the Department of Social Work's relationship to the Maryland Health Services Cost Review Commission is in establishing service categories as the unit of measure and of costing social work services more effectively. Future budgets will be built on this cost system, not on total number of cases or total number of staff. At any given time the director of the Department of Social Work is prepared to say, by revenue center, exactly what social work services are provided, to what population, with what problems, at what cost (time and money), with what outcome.

Management information, for the director and supervisory staff, is gathered and disseminated in a useful form. The social work administrator utilizes this information to understand and evaluate the quality of work of each staff member. Services can be understood both as they alleviate problems for patients and their families and as they alleviate problems within the institution. Comparison of services for a given problem will aid in understanding which services for which problem are most effective within the shortest time and the least cost to the patient and the institution. The teaching of medical students and other health care professionals about patient and family psychosocial needs is more clearly focused. Subjective assessment of quality of work is reduced as is assessment of clinical social work skills. Activities can be reviewed regularly, and innumerable variable comparisons can be retrieved.

When cost reduction programs are begun, the social work administrator is prepared to define what these potential reductions will mean. Conversely, when fiscal year budgets are submitted the administrator is prepared to demonstrate need and value (outcome) for additional services. Thus by defining costs for each service the administrator can compare this with the potential cost to the institution when a service is not provided. Future program planning becomes a process of defining services necessary within a given patient population. These objective data presented to the chief of a medical division allow him to establish a value for these services, plan for quality patient care, and analyze where dollars will be most effectively spent.

For the social work professional the system's problem, service, and outcome criteria are readily adaptable for PSRO requirements. It represents a conceptual framework through which social workers in a health care setting can function effectively. This framework is not new. With the focus on objectifying problems and goal expectations it allows the social worker to anticipate service effectiveness and validate this by outcome measures. The social worker must contract with a patient and/or his family for specific service focused on clearly defined problems, which reinforces the social work principle of self-determination.

Such a system tends, as well, to reduce jargon and to clarify role responsibilities for social work within the health care team. Services provided for the psychosocial needs of patients, from a variety of health care professionals, can be compared in terms of process as well as outcome effectiveness. The profession has labored diligently to establish a role as evaluator and treater of psychosocial factors that affect health and medical care. The medical profession has struggled to understand the effect of these factors on illness and health. Objectifying problems in a systematic taxonomy can establish a basis through which we view psychosocial factors as they affect or cause illness.

A standardized problem list is a beginning step for building a system taxonomy as a scientific framework through which social work research can focus in the future on specific etiologies of medical problems. Collection of demographic information regarding population served establishes potential for reviewing and comparing populations within a given health care system. Comparisons between the population receiving social work service and the population that is not can prove invaluable for understanding the effectiveness and the future of social work programs in health care planning.

Definitions of social work services with outcome measures established are the basis of evaluation of effectiveness. The service categories are defined objectively, and standardized outcomes have been established. Evaluative research projects can be conducted easily where population allows, emphasizing objective factors to be considered.

This article has described the forces that moved a department of social work toward an experimental information and recording system and has emphasized the potential in such a system. This effort is being paralleled in many other departments of social work within health care settings. It is essential that those experiences be shared with the social work community in health settings with the goal of a single system combining the most productive components of each system.

REFERENCES

1. Reid, William. "Developments in the Use of Organized Data." *Social Work* 5 (1974):585–93.

2. Department of Health, Education, and Welfare, *PSRO Program Manual*. Washington, D.C.: United States Government Printing Office, 1974.

3. State of Maryland, Health Services Cost Review Commission. "Position Paper on Selected Problems and Issues." Baltimore, Maryland, May 1975.

4. American Society for Hospital Social Work Directors, Maryland Chapter, Ad Hoc Committee on Peer Review. *Final Report* in process. Documentation available in minutes of chapter meetings from September 1975 through present. Unpublished.

5. Fischer, Joel. "Is Casework Effective: A Review." *Social Work* 18 (1973):5–20.

6. Fassett, Jacqueline D. Paper presented at the 1974 Annual Meeting of the Society for Hospital Social Work Directors, Atlanta, Georgia. Unpublished.

7. National Association of Social Workers. *PSRO Basic Information for Social Workers Action Guide*. Washington, D.C.: NASW, 1975.

8. The Johns Hopkins Hospital, Department of Social Work. "Nine Month Report from Continuity of Care Office." Baltimore, Maryland, September 1975. Unpublished.

Chapter 5

Clients, Staff, and Researchers: Their Role in Management Information Systems

Harold H. Weissman, DSW

ABSTRACT. A management information system being developed by researchers at the Henry Street Settlement in New York City has stimulated management and staff to begin to explicate program objectives, to develop indices of success, and to carry out exploratory studies of program effectiveness. In these studies, systematic feedback of client perceptions of service had significant impact on workers' behavior and attitudes. Decisions to be made dictated the information to be collected. Interest in and understanding of evaluative research were stimulated.

In the fifties and sixties the question was asked, "Why is there not more program evaluation in social agencies?" and now in the seventies, similarly, the question is asked, "Why is there not better management in social agencies?" These are not unrelated questions. One of the requisites of better management is a workable system of program evaluation that can provide ongoing guidance to program managers. That this system is needed is seldom denied, yet the means for its achievement remains elusive. This paper will describe the beginning steps taken at the Henry Street Settlement to integrate service staff and clients into a viable evaluation and management information system. It also takes the point of view that this integration is necessary if such management systems are to become operational.

PERSPECTIVES ON AGENCY RESEARCH

Historically, social welfare agencies have operated on the assumption that the programs they were offering were by their nature good, and that

This project was initiated through a pilot-project grant from the Esther A. and Joseph Klingenstein Fund and was continued with support from the Robert Sterling Clark Foundation and the Henry Luce Foundation.

to question their efficacy would somehow be to challenge their value. By the mid-fifties this view had given way under the impact of social science on social welfare. The need for proof of effectiveness was increasingly accepted.

In the sixties the War on Poverty brought forth a good deal of evaluative research related to social programs. While the quality and substantive value of the program evaluation varied, a great deal was learned about the problems and difficulties of carrying out research in social agencies.[1]

The essence of the classical research design is the control group. Yet in the actual operation of social programs it is very difficult to establish control groups. First, there is the problem of denying service to certain elements of the population who may very well need it. Second, there is the practical problem of randomization so that in fact those who receive service and those who do not are similar. Third, there are problems in maintaining confidentiality and control over the subjects so that those in the experimental group do not influence those in the control group and vice versa. Last, there is a natural desire of program staff to alter their programs when they realize changes need to be made, no matter what the canons of research may call for.

While none of these problems are necessarily insurmountable they are compounded by the inability of researchers and practitioners to understand each other.[2] Very often administrators complain that the results of research are abstract and are not related to practical problems. Too often the research results reveal that practitioners and researchers were not in agreement as to the purposes of the research. Frequently the goals of the program that were identified for the researcher were not really the actual goals the agency had in mind.

Etzioni notes that organizations usually have both public and private goals.[3] Administrators and researchers have often ignored this difference prior to initiating a research project. For their part, researchers have taken such statements as delinquency prevention, inculcation of social values, and family stability as the operating goals of programs. More likely, these were broad outcome goals or missions linked to a chain of objectives such as foster placement, counseling of natural parents, and reuniting the family. Administrators accustomed to using broad goals or missions for fund raising and securing public legitimacy were outraged at researchers who called these ends into question by their findings.

In such situations researchers did not insist vigorously enough that practitioners and administrators specify their impact model, the links between program components and subobjectives to ultimate objectives.[4] Thus, their outcome evaluation told only whether an agency was in fact achieving its public goals, not *how* it achieved them or, if it failed to do so, where in the chain of subobjectives and procedures the breakdowns occurred.

Likewise, researchers were often hired to look at specific programs. They tended to underplay the effect of the organizational aegis of programs. Thus, unintentionally researchers have tended to present a model that implicitly has the view that an organization such as a social agency is merely the sum of its programs. The way to evaluate the effectiveness of a child care agency, for example, is to evaluate the effectiveness of its component programs. Such a model assumes that specific goals can be evaluated and modified in isolation from other goals being sought by an agency.[5]

Yet, in addition to the achievement of goals and subgoals, organizations are concerned with the effective coordination of the subunits, the acquisition and maintenance of needed resources, and the adaptation of the organization to its environment. Some of an organization's means must be devoted to such functions as custodial activity, maintenance of morale of the staff, and securing the public commitment and support necessary for agency survival.

From the viewpoint of the above, maintenance activities are functional and actually increase organizational effectiveness. Thus, rather than evaluating an organization in terms of its degree of success in reaching specific objectives, an organizational model is required that establishes the degree to which an organization realizes its goals under a given set of conditions. It is this latter given set of conditions that has often been ignored by researchers and administrators in setting up agency evaluations. It becomes obvious that these conditions cannot be ignored, if a true picture of the agency and its program is to be given.

In an interesting dyad of articles, Chommie and Hudson make the point that the context of research must be given as much weight as the canons of research.[6] What has been discovered in relation to a variety of fields of practice from child welfare to drug addiction—that differential treatment is required for different types of clients—has been discovered for research. There is no one ideal design or methodology of research that will fit every situation.

Chommie and Hudson note that "the information needs of policymakers and funding agencies may require an outcome-focused strategy that attempts to verify through measurement the relationship between the program and its specified outcomes or effects. On the other hand, information concerning program success or failure often arrives too late to serve the needs of program administrators, clients and staff."[7]

Thus, if research is to be an aid in promoting better management, certain policies and procedures must be clearly articulated:

1. Administrators, staff, and researchers must agree on the purposes

and potential consequences of the research prior to its being initiated.

2. Research should not begin until indices of success and goal attainment are adequately described. There is nothing more devastating to program staff than an evaluation showing that clients are neither better off nor worse off for having been involved in the program. No doubt there are many cases where these results are accurate, but, as will be amplified later, there are clear reasons to believe that simplified indices of success can distort the value of programs, both negatively as well as positively.

3. An overemphasis on the desire to establish scientific proof when the requisites, both intellectual and organizational, are not present must be avoided. The mere fact that one cannot establish cause and effect outside of the classical experimental design does not mean that it is valueless to gather information systematically in order that program judgments may be based on the best available information.

4. It is absolutely vital that the impact model implicit in any social program be completely explicated, that is, how in fact the program is to achieve its desired ends. For example, if a counseling program and a work training program are designed to help an adolescent prepare for return to his natural parents, how does this occur? What are the exact connections between changes of attitude, behavior, and program? Does counseling provide the sense of self-esteem that makes it possible for an adolescent to complete a training course that will provide him with the sense of competence and self-mastery that will ultimately make it possible for him to secure a job and then stick with it? If this does not occur, where, in this chain, is the breakdown? Perhaps the skills training course is inadequate, or the teacher is inadequate, or the counseling is not useful. Is the program goal unrealized because the counseling does not result in a sense of self-esteem, or is it because the labor market does not have jobs available for adolescents?

It is crucial to know where in the sequence of activities the breakdown occurs, if there is to be any improvement in the program. It is safe to say that in most programs the impact model has not been sufficiently explicated.

RECONNAISSANCE RESEARCH

Given the above, the conclusion can be drawn that a good deal of intellectual homework must be done before social agencies can adequately evaluate their programs. The first task of a research consultant is to help agencies do this homework. This task may be termed reconnaissance research. Rossi uses the phrase ''reconnaissance'' to refer to soft evaluation techniques such as correlational designs.[8] He does not spell out the other types of soft designs. Reconnaissance research in this paper refers specifically to soft designs *implemented and carried out by program staff*. In essence, they represent a "tooling up" phase, not only in the research process but also in the information-gathering process. Such a tooling up would involve staff in defining goals and indices of success, clarifying impact models, and developing a design for gathering and interpreting data.[9]

Given the complexity of these tasks, it may legitimately be asked, "Do service staff have the interest and capacity to deal with them?" In a demonstration evaluation project in a counseling and group services program, the assumption was made that they would if certain policies were followed. First, the evaluation must provide operating staff directly with information not only about how well or how poorly they are doing their job but much more significantly with information that will offer guidance on how they can improve their work. If staff are merely held accountable for results but are not given the kind of information that will help them improve, there is a strain toward falsification.[10]

In order to mitigate the reactions of staff over whether "they are being evaluated," the issue of program evaluation must initially be separated from the issue of staff evaluation. When the focus is on program evaluation, staff are freer to develop their own procedures and program evaluation tools apart from the implied threat to job security and promotion.

Thus, the first step in the demonstration project was to engage staff in gathering information about the current state of their program. This involved developing a questionnaire to tap clients' responses to service. In this task staff were mainly concerned with the efficacy of the means they were using to achieve program ends: "Should I make demands on clients?" "Should I make home visits?" "Are regular appointments a hindrance to developing trust?" Nevertheless, questions about outcome or results of service were also included.

In the staff meetings, where client responses to the questionnaires were discussed, it became apparent that clients were concerned not only about results but also about procedures: "I could always call my worker on the phone." "He really cared about me because he came to our house." "He talked to the teacher himself."

Such responses were hardly unexpected. What was unexpected was the reaction of the staff: "I'm really going to get out of my office more." "I never realized how important little amenities are."

What was even more striking was the changed perception and increased understanding of research: "I'm glad we didn't start simply by evaluating the results." "We have to be a lot clearer about what we want to achieve." The actual experience of administering a questionnaire to clients resulted in a greater staff commitment to measuring results than could have been achieved through the most intelligent and rational explanations of research consultants.

While reconnaissance research is quite soft in relation to standards of proof, systematic reporting of client reactions to service may be quite hard in relation to program change. It seems highly likely that even when results are measured, the key issue will be how to get the staff to alter their procedures. The experience in a variety of settings has been that facts alone seldom change procedures; rather, facts tend to undergo alteration to fit old procedures. In this project, client perceptions of program results as well as program procedures were an excellent prod for procedural changes.

In the group services program a similar pattern developed among both staff and clients. While the goals of the program from the adolescent participants' point of view included fun, friendship, employment, and cultural experiences, they were equally concerned with means: "It's how it's said as well as what is said." "I don't want anyone to tell me to shape up." "If you make rules, enforce them."

Those participant responses had a similar effect on the group services staff. In addition, it is highly likely that participants' responses offer the best clue about the stages or processes involved in achieving any particular effect. As noted earlier, a major impediment to conducting research on social programs is the unavailability of impact models, the links between objectives, subobjectives, and tasks. Client responses should be of considerable help in developing these models.

They will also be of considerable help in establishing indices of success. Nevertheless, the indices of success must be related to the overall functions of an agency. The agency as a whole must decide whom it wishes to serve and the relative emphasis to be given to its various functions.[11] For example, a foster care agency, if left on its own, would probably set its function as remedial, given the training of its staff in therapeutic modalities. Yet the agency may desire to allocate some of its resources to preventing the necessity of placement. The specification of the extent to which the indices of success for a foster care agency are remedial or preventive is, therefore, a responsibility of agency management.

To this end, in the project described above, the research consultant met with the program directors and executives of the agency. The discussions were focused on their views of what the organization should be aiming to achieve as well as what information they required to improve the functioning of their various departments. Similar to line staff, the responses of top management focused mainly on procedural issues—how to motivate staff, how to secure funds, and the like.

If there is any conclusion that can be drawn, it is that program evaluation that merely reports results would probably create considerable frustration. Program evaluation must not only tell managers what is right or wrong but, in the case of the latter, must provide the information needed to help them improve. Otherwise, one will merely be creating a new shopping list of unavailable information.

A MANAGEMENT INFORMATION SYSTEM DESIGN

On the basis of the year's project experience, top management has developed a series of operating policies for continued work: (a) evaluative research cannot be divorced from the ongoing administration of programs; (b) evaluative research requires considerable prior thought and conceptualization on the part of an agency as to its goals, impact model, and indicators of success; (c) evaluative research can best be stimulated and developed out of systematic feedback of client perceptions of service; and (d) not all organizational problems are primarily related to lack of information or evaluation. For example, the functions assigned to a program—remedial, preventive, developmental, and the like—are as much related to values, power, and criteria of policy choice as they are to information and knowledge.

Churchman notes in this light,

> As we delve into the deeper problems of whether the existing system is an adequate one to perform a given [function], then it is necessary to state quite clearly the gaps in our knowledge . . . instead of having a proliferation of social studies dealing with ad hoc problems that the social scientist invents, the systems approach provides a plan for social research by showing the particular kinds of problems that need to be solved in order to attain a rational allocation of resources to the [functions] of the system.[12]

That is, if you want to prevent family breakup, how do you find families at risk and get them to the settlement?

Thus the program managers have determined that their primary task is to develop clarity about program functions and then to engage in a planning process with staff to develop projections as to the specific types of clients to be served, amounts and types of service to be rendered, and expected outcomes. To support this endeavor, they need a management information system not only to assist them in making projections but also to provide information as to the extent projections are being met, the reasons for success or failure, and, where possible, suggestions on needed adaptations.

A management information system (MIS) refers to a systematic procedure for gathering and processing information to enable managers and workers to make appropriate program decisions. As such it requires information not only about discrete programs but also about an agency's adaptive ability, its interorganizational relations, its self-maintenance activities, and its financial position. An MIS is predicated on a systems view of the agency rather than a programmatic view.

The year's experience with reconnaissance research provided a number of valuable insights for development of an MIS. First, while accuracy of information is important, it is equally important not to commit vast resources of time and manpower to collecting data at a level of accuracy beyond what is needed. A judgment must be made between what is satisfactory and doable and what is ideal but unlikely to be accomplished.[13]

The crucial point is that an MIS stands or falls on staff's interest and commitment to it. There are, as noted, innumerable ways to subvert its operation. In addition, in most agencies there simply are not enough funds for hiring the personnel to man such a system. Even if there were, the necessity of staff commitment requires that they be involved in developing the system and that information requirements for particular roles be specified and built into ongoing job responsibilities. This involvement is best initiated through exploratory studies of programs carried out by staff that focus on client perceptions of service.

Second, an MIS should provide timely information. Managers and workers must specify not only what they need to know to make decisions but also when they need to know it. Time lags between asking for information and getting it should be kept at a minimum.[14]

In addition, it is important to maintain the principle in setting up an MIS that the decisions that have to be made dictate the information that must be collected. Given this principle, it is possible to focus the MIS in terms of the pressing needs or concerns of an agency. For example, there are three different levels of information needs: planning, implementation, and evaluation. While they are interrelated in practice, it is useful to separate them for purposes of conceptualizing an MIS. Each of the levels requires a somewhat different type of knowledge and information. There is no need to attempt to operationalize an MIS for all three levels at the same time.[15]

A third and crucial facet of an MIS requires more conceptual clarity. As noted, organizational goals must be specified and indicators of success established.[16] These objectives refer not only to results achieved but also to standards of worker productivity, manager performance, and agency innovation. A systems view of organizational life is required. Indices of these objectives must avoid the common problems of vagueness and imprecision as well as the opposite and equally confusing problem of reducing all complex activities to simple numbers.

Perhaps the oldest use of research in social welfare was for the social survey, "getting the facts." While this tool has waned in popularity, clearly an MIS must have baseline data if projections are to be made and changes are to be noted in agency operation and goal attainment. Such data would include status of current clients, community problems, demographic information, financing arrangements, inter- and intraorganizational problems, and estimates of efficiency and effectiveness of current operations.

While the development of an adequate MIS will take several years utilizing the above policies and procedures, experience in the demonstration project indicates that the beginning steps of developing an MIS can provide a valuable link between administrators, clients, staff, and researchers. The project's latent function has been to create an atmosphere that facilitates workers' engaging in a more deliberate and rational approach to their work as well as to stimulate initiative and increased productivity.

Workers have begun to explicate and agree on program objectives, have become more conscious of how objectives interface with everyday practice, and are attempting to make adjustments to reach agreed-on objectives. As such, agencies may profit considerably by investing resources in the development of information systems prior to the launching of more formal evaluative research.

REFERENCES

1. See, for example, Robert Weiss and Martin Rein, "The Evaluation of Broad-Aim Programs: A Cautionary Case and a Moral" in *Readings in Evaluation Research,* ed. Francis G. Caro (New York: Russell Sage Foundation, 1971).

2. Peter H. Rossi, "Testing for Success and Failure in Social Action" in *Evaluating Social Programs,* ed. Peter H. Rossi and Walter Williams (New York: Seminar Press, 1972).

3. Amitai Etzioni, "Two Approaches to Organizational Analysis: A Critique and a Suggestion," *Administrative Science Quarterly* 15 (1970):257–78.

4. For a discussion of impact models, see Edward Suchman, *Evaluative Research* (New York: Russell Sage Foundation, 1967), pp. 51–56.

5. For an analysis of how such problems can be dealt with, see Herbert Schulberg and Frank Baker, "Program Evaluation Models and the Implementation of Research Findings," *American Journal of Public Health* 58 (1968):1248–55.

6. Carol Weiss, "Alternative Models of Program Evaluation," *Social Work* 19 (1974): 675–81; and Peter Chommie and Joe Hudson, "Evaluation of Outcome and Process," *Social Work* 19 (1974):682–87.

7. Chommie and Hudson, "Evaluation of Outcome," p. 687.

8. Peter Rossi, "Evaluating Social Action Programs," *Trans-Action* 4 (1967):52–53.

9. Ibid., p. 48.

10. Robert Walker, "The Ninth Panacea: Program Evaluation," *Evaluation* 1 (1972):45–53. Walker discusses how these problems might be counteracted. This is not a difficult matter for staff to accomplish. A number of proven techniques may be cited, such as being selective as to who receives the service, reducing the volume of clients, setting propitious times when benefits are measured (such as after all the dropouts have dropped out), measuring outcomes before the client loses them, and setting goals that are quite easy to achieve.

11. For a discussion of program functions and their effect on goal formulations, see C. West Churchman, *The Systems Approach* (New York: Delta, 1968), pp. 81–103.

12. Ibid., p. 99.

13. For amplification of these points, see Saul Feldman, ed., *The Administration of Mental Health Services* (Springfield, Ill.: Charles C Thomas, 1973), pp. 120–137.

14. Ibid.

15. For a discussion of this point, see Kathy Nance and Jolie Pillsbury, "An Evaluation System for Decision Making," *Public Welfare* 34 (1976):47–51.

16. This issue is discussed in *Widening Horizons* (New York: National Council for Homemaker-Home Aide Services, 1974), pp. 54–55.

Chapter 6

An Operational Model
to Achieve Accountability for Social Work
in Health Care

Robert M. Spano, ACSW
Thomas J. Kiresuk, PhD
Sander H. Lund

ABSTRACT. This paper describes a social work accountability structure developed and implemented at the Social Service Department of University of Minnesota Hospitals. The structure is founded in a framework derived from Management by Objectives and is composed of the following elements: (a) a transaction-based Management Information System; (b) service definitions developed by the Southern Regional Educational Board; (c) problem identification and record keeping with Problem-Oriented Medical Records; and (d) outcome evaluation through Goal Attainment Scaling. The purpose of the structure is to monitor and document departmental activities, providing feedback reports to staff, management reports to the director, and summary reports to hospital administration. The structure is not a response to a particular set of organizational problems, but an attempt to develop a coherent operational model to guide departmental development, remaining responsive to future as well as current needs.

BACKGROUND AND RATIONALE

In his 1975 address to the Society of Hospital Social Service Directors meeting in Atlanta, Georgia, John Westerman, administrative director of University of Minnesota Hospitals, asserted: "The provider segment (of the health care system) which will capture consumer enthusiasm will be the one with the most clearly developed accountability system. As service recipients become more enlightened and discerning, they will be most likely to fully utilize facilities with an explicit commitment to assess their effectiveness according to meaningful public standards and to use this information . . . to continually refocus their activities on evolving human needs." "By providing a vehicle for expanding [its] role in . . . [the] delivery system," according to Westerman, the present mandate for accountability is providing social work with an opportunity to steal a march on other health care disciplines.

The legislative and regulatory background for development of accountability and quality assurance mechanisms in health care social work has been well described. In her systematic presentation of a social work peer review system, Meites (Note 1) mentions no fewer than 15 forces influencing governmental policy decisions in the direction of implementation of peer review devices; included are Medicare, Medicaid, and maternal and child health legislation, national health insurance proposals, Joint Commission on Hospital Accreditation standards, and Department of Health, Education, and Welfare licensing and certification studies. Meites points to Public Law 92-603 of 1972, the Social Security Amendment that established the Professional Standards Review Organizations (PSROs), as the backbone of the mandate for social work accountability systems. Section 1156 of this law provides for "each Professional Standards Review Organization for any area to assume . . . responsibility for review of professional activities . . . of physicians and other health care professionals." All health care practitioners are hence required to employ the same PSRO structure as is mandated for physicians, which means construction of quality assurance programs specific to health care social work based on peer review.

Implementation of quality assurance and accountability in health care social work is an idea whose time has come. It is woven into public law and professional administrative practice, and is a reflection of general public sentiment regarding economy, quality of services, and consumer protection. The mandate is not a game or management frill, but a genuine expression of the will of the American public, through their elected representatives and the sentiment of concerned professional associations. In addition, as Westerman has observed, it is a challenge and an opportunity—a challenge to put the professional standards of health care social work out where they can be examined, and an opportunity to take a greater share in the responsibility for provision of high-quality health care services.

HISTORICAL DEVELOPMENT

Components of the System

As Thomas Fuller, English writer and philosopher, once observed, "Action is the proper fruit of knowledge." This maxim has guided the effort at the University of Minnesota Hospitals Social Service Department to incorporate existing measurement and record-keeping technologies into a comprehensive accountability structure. The structure employs a framework derived from Management by Objectives and is composed of four elements: (a) identification of client problems (based on a variant of Problem-Oriented Medical Records); (b) selection of a proper social work function (according to criteria established by the Southern Regional Education Board); (c) performance of the function (monitored through a staff-effort Management Information System); and (d) assessment of outcome (based on individual goals specifically tailored to each client's problems).

Management by Objectives. The overall structure of the system is provided by Management by Objectives (MBO), which, as the name implies, is a means to administer an organization through the establishment and follow-up of time-specific goals and objectives. The technique was originally promulgated by a prominent business consultant (Drucker, 1964) and has received its widest reception in the private sector; however, in recent years MBO has also begun to attract the attention of human services administrators as well (Brady, 1973; Spano & Lund, 1976). The essential characteristic of MBO is development of a hierarchical program goal structure. At the apex of such a hierarchy is a statement of the program's overall mission; subordinate to the mission are the more concrete objectives that lead to the mission; subordinate to the objectives are specific, time-limited goals. Objectives and goals are typically derived through negotiation with concerned program staff and are modified based upon past goal attainment.

Problem-Oriented Medical Records. Developed by Weed (1969) as a means to systematize the traditional, narrative approach to medical record keeping, the Problem-Oriented Medical Record (POMR) is a vehicle for using specific client problems as the focal point for information on a case. The major components of a POMR system are: (a) a *data base* (history of the client's case, including results of examinations and tests); (b) a *problem list* (statement of initial complaints together with assessment of the case by concerned staff); (c) *plans and goals* (specific goal and associated plan for each problem); and (d) *follow-up* (progress notes and other feedback related to the problem). Although some difficulties have been reported in the implementation of POMR (Rocheleau, 1975), successful installation is typically thought to provide a more systematic and objective base for assessing quality of care and to increase the accountability of those rendering service by requiring goals and plans.

Definition of social work functions. A persistent problem in the human services has been the lack of meaningful uniform definitions of professional terms. Absence of a commonly held professional vocabulary has reduced the comparability of efforts and hindered the communication of results, thereby retarding the development of the human services as a whole. To mitigate this problem, the Southern Regional Educational Board (SREB) was commissioned by the National Institute of Mental Health to develop a manual of basic definitions germane to mental health, alcohol abuse, drug abuse, and mental retardation. The manual (Southern Regional Educational Board, 1973) provides a framework for defining human services terms according to (a) the organization providing services, (b) the staff of the organization, (c) the services provided, (d) the method of providing services, (e) the recipients of services, (f) the purposes and results of the services, and (g) the costs and revenues of the services.

Management Information System. Since the effective administration of a human services program requires knowledge of internal organizational functioning, perhaps the commonest form of program evaluation involves monitoring the amount and kinds of activities necessary for attainment of program goals. Immediate and efficient gathering, processing, and reporting of such information is the purpose of a Management Information System (MIS). The characteristics of any particular system will vary according to information needs, but in general, MIS systems typically address at least one of three topic areas: (a) client use of services (e.g., how many and what kinds of clients utilize services, why and how they utilize them, what happens to them during and after services); (b) staff allocation of time and effort (e.g., what kinds of services staff provide, how often and for how long they provide them); and (c) program allocation of material and financial resources (e.g., the costs of services and program elements, and their revenues and benefits).

Individualized Goal Attainment measurement. Although the capstone of meaningful evaluation in the human services seems to be the determination of client outcome, disagreement regarding the nature of a "good" outcome often makes this form of assessment problematic. Davis (1972, 1973) has described the development in the mental health field of a new form of outcome evaluation called Individualized Goal Attainment (IGA) measurement, wherein generalized standards of effectiveness are supplanted by criteria tailored to the needs, aspirations, and capacities of the individual recipient of services.

A prominent form of IGA measurement is Goal Attainment Scaling (Kiresuk & Sherman, 1968). In Goal Attainment Scaling, client-specific goals are scaled according to a 5-point range of possible outcomes: "Most Favorable Outcome," "More Than Expected Outcome," "Expected Outcome," "Less Than Expected Outcome," and "Most Unfavorable Outcome." At follow-up, each scale is scored according to the outcome that actually occurred, and the results from all scales are used to compute a Goal Attainment Score, which is an overall indicator of treatment effectiveness. In most applications of Goal Attainment Scaling, a score of 50.00 indicates, on the average, that the Expected Outcome levels have been exactly attained. A score under 50.00 indicates that expectations have not been met, and a score over 50.00 indicates that they have been exceeded.

Setting

The development and refinement of the elements of the accountability system occurred at two related settings in Minneapolis, Minnesota. Preliminary work took place at Hennepin County General Hospital's Mental Health Service, where the senior author was chief psychiatric social worker until 1972. It was in this organization that Goal Attainment Scaling was developed, and that the authors became familiar with an early version of the time-based Management Information System developed by Sherman (Note 2) and Saunders and Baxter (Note 3). Implementation of the accountability structure did not occur until after the senior author had left General Hospital to become the director of the Social Service Department at University of Minnesota Hospitals. It was here that the Management by Objectives procedure was initiated and that the SREB definitions of human services functions were adapted to hospital social work.

Evaluation of the System

As a vehicle to stimulate the continued development of the Social Service Department, a comprehensive accountability structure was constructed during the period 1972–1976. The purpose of this structure was to enhance program efficiency by monitoring and reporting internal processes, and to maximize effectiveness by facilitating and documenting administrative and clinical goal attainment.

The first stage in the construction of the accountability structure was implementation of Management by Objectives. Organizational goal setting was viewed as a means for rational coordination of program activities, while also affording an opportunity for orderly staff involvement in planning and evaluation. A detailed description of the MBO structure (Figure 1) and its derivation is presented elsewhere (Spano & Lund, 1976). The elements relevant to this discussion are the philosophy, the mission statement, and the program functions.

The philosophy is a systematic rendering of the values, beliefs, and assumptions that form a basis for the Social Service Department's operation, and is intended to provide the uninitiated outsider with an understanding of the program and its general context. From the philosophy the director derived a mission statement, which is a statement of the overall purpose of the program. In turn, the mission statement serves as a foundation for the development of the program functions. Program functions are the activities that must be performed if the mission is to be served. Permanent staff committees operate in each function area to establish objectives and goals. Attainment is assessed annually, and feedback is used to guide the developmental goals and objectives for the following year.

Shortly after Management by Objectives was instituted in the depart-

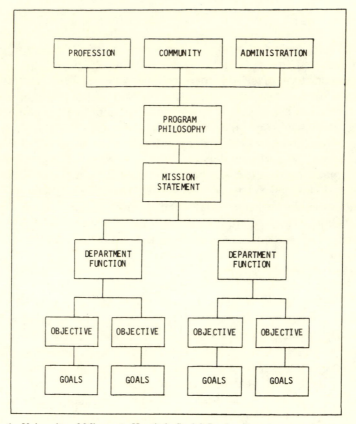

FIGURE 1. University of Minnesota Hospitals Social Service Department goal structure format.

ment a comprehensive Management Information System was implemented. The purpose of the system was creation of an information network to audit, report, and document departmental activities. Various MIS models were considered, but a time-oriented, transaction-based system was ultimately selected. In this model, staff report each professional event in their workday according to the format presented in Figure 2. All events are described according to the number of minutes expended, the hospital cost center wherein the event occurred, and the professional function performed. There are five categories of functions: (a) Individual-Oriented Services (i.e., services provided directly to clients); (b) Hospital- and Community-Oriented Services (i.e., health-related programmatic or consultation services provided to *other* organizations, individual practitioners, or members of the general public); (c) Manpower Services (i.e., educational and training activities designed to impart job-related knowledge and skills to members of the Social Service Department staff); (d) Generalizable Research (i.e., activities performed for production of scientific knowledge that may be generalized beyond the immediate situation); and (e) Intraorganization Support (i.e., activities directed toward the support, maintenance, and development of the Social Service Department).

At the present time staff are required to report activities relevant to the Individual-Oriented and Hospital- and Community-Oriented function categories, whereas reporting of activities in the Manpower, Generalizable Research, and Intraorganizational Support areas is required only during special management audits. The reason for this is that research has shown that departmental activities in these categories tend to remain stable during the year and only need to be checked periodically. Daily activity logs are stored on magnetic tape, and computer-generated feedback reports are prepared monthly for each staff person (Figure 3) and for the director. Individual staff feedback reports provide each worker with a detailed accounting of past activities, compared with the department as a whole. The reports to the director show the time expended and number of clients served by each worker in each cost center, according to the function performed and (where applicable) client problem(s).

The function codes are a feature of the system that warrants further discussion. When Management by Objectives was instituted, program functions were stated specific to the department's immediate circumstances. This facilitated development of a coherent operating structure, but proved cumbersome when it came to linking departmental activities

STAFF EFFORT ACCOUNTING SYSTEM

SOCIAL SERVICE DEPARTMENT
UNIVERSITY OF MINNESOTA HOSPITALS

Staff ID 01 — — 04   DATE 05 YR - MO - DAY 10

TIME	MODE (COST CENTER)	FUNCTION	PATIENT HOSPITAL ID	ADJUST # SEEN	PROBLEM CODE
11 — 13	14 — — — — 18	19 — 21	22 — — — — — — 28	29 30	31 32
11 — 13	14 — — — — 18	19 — 21	22 — — — — — — 28	29 30	31 32
11 — 13	14 — — — — 18	19 — 21	22 — — — — — — 28	29 30	31 32
11 — 13	14 — — — — 18	19 — 21	22 — — — — — — 28	29 30	31 32
11 — 13	14 — — — — 18	19 — 21	22 — — — — — — 28	29 30	31 32

FIGURE 2. Staff effort accounting system daily log format.

INDIVIDUAL TIME UTILIZATION REPORT
PRODUCED 2/11/76 FOR THE MONTH 1/76

INDIVIDUAL FEEDBACK REPORT

PATIENT ID NUMBER	INFORM (111-114)	INDIV COUNSEL (131-136)	GROUP COUNSEL (135-136)	CARE SERVICE (151)	RECORDS KEEPING (161-163)	CLINICAL CONSULT (221-223)	TOTAL	PROBLEM CODES
45673	0H 0M	2H 30M	1H 30M	2H 30M	5H 0M	0H 0M	10H 30M	12, 8
78865	1H 30M	4H 15M	0H 0M	0H 45M	5H 30M	0H 0M	10H 0M	7, 10
22409	0H 0M	0H 0M	10H 30M	0H 45M	1H 0M	5H 0M	16H 30M	6, 8

TOTAL NUMBER OF PATIENTS SEEN ___38___

Page 2 of 3 page report.

FIGURE 3. Staff effort accounting system individual staff feedback report (page 2 of a 3-page report).

with the functions of other human services agencies and with the overall operation of the hospital. Consequently, the idiosyncratic function statements contained in the MBO system were supplemented with standardized definitions from the vocabulary of the Southern Regional Educational Board. The function Individual-Oriented Services, for example, encompasses six kinds of activities: (a) Information, Screening, or Referral Services; (b) Problem Assessment or Evaluation; (c) Counseling Services; (d) Rehabilitation, Restoration, or Habilitation Services; (e) Care Services; and (f) Patient-Client-Related Case Preparation and Record Keeping. The category Counseling Services, to illustrate further, has six subcategories: (a) Individual Counseling; (b) Collateral Treatment or Counseling; (c) Couples Therapy; (d) Family Treatment or Counseling; (e) Group Treatment or Counseling; and (f) Milieu Therapy. As a whole, this system of definitions provides a coherent, shorthand way to document and report departmental activities.

A second important feature of the accountability structure is the standardized roster of problem codes. A major purpose of the structure is to verify the link between process activities (i.e., provision of services) and actual clinical outcomes. The means selected to accomplish this linkage was a shift in the focus of reporting from the "performance of activities" to the "solution of client problems." To this end, a list of frequently reported client problems was developed from a survey of service requests from other hospital stations and clinics. Supplemented by a set of problem definitions from Garwick and Lampman (1972), and edited for redundancy, this roster of problem categories allows staff to document the major areas of concern for each client (see Figure 4).

The completely idiosyncratic problems listed according to the Problem-Oriented Medical Records format in each patient's chart are categorized by the staff person with regard to the standard problem definitions. These problem categories are then used in three ways. First, they serve as the basis for all subsequent reporting on Social Service Department activities regarding the client's case (i.e., each transaction is documented according to the number of minutes devoted by particular staff members to performing a particular function in a particular cost center for a particular client problem category). This allows retrieval of the medical charts by psychosocial problem code, rather than by medical diagnosis. Second, the problem categories serve as the basis for development of clinical goals. Such goals, constructed according to the Goal Attainment Scaling format, serve both to guide and evaluate subsequent services.

The third use of the standard problem categories is to ensure that a basic standard of services is provided to a client. Process criteria have been developed to define the expectations of professional social work in regard to each problem category. These criteria specify the minimum set of procedures expected of a Social Service Department staff person when con-

CODE	PROBLEM	DESCRIPTION
01	ADJUSTMENT TO HEALTH PROBLEMS	Patient or family adjustment to illness, disability, dying; poor understanding of illness or treatment.
02	ANXIETY REACTION	Nervousness, anxiety attacks, tension, apprehension, anxiety hindering discharge, anxiety regarding illness or treatment.
03	BEHAVIOR PROBLEM	Temper tantrums, aggression, school troubles, acting out, sociopathic behavior, hostility, motivation, problem patient.
04	CHEMICAL USE	Patient or family alcohol problems; deliberate misuse of prescription or street drugs, referral to treatment resources.
05	CHILD ABUSE	Suspected or documented neglect, physical, psychological or sexual abuse; referrals to police or welfare.
06	CONTINUITY OF CARE	Follow-up planning, referral for home care, referral for medical or psycho-social treatment, hospitalization, planning for care.
07	DECISION-MAKING	Ambivalence, immobilized by indecision, inadequate decision making skills, need for assertiveness.
08	DEPRESSION	Sadness, withdrawal, apathy, sleep disturbance, weight loss or gain, loss of appetite, loss of ambition, lethargy, fatigue.
09	EDUCATION	Academic underachievement, school adjustment, drop-out, truancy, educational planning, referral to educational resource.
10	ENVIRONMENTAL PROBLEMS	Lacks transportation, inadequate housing, architectural barriers, under employment, poor work relations, vocational training.
11	FAMILY OR MARITAL PROBLEMS	Family or marital dysfunction, parent-child conflicts, extended family conflicts, single parent families, problem pregnancy.
12	FINANCIAL	Financial planning for medical care; financial planning for patient or family; lack of money.

Page 1 of 2 pages.

FIGURE 4. Psychosocial problem list (page 1 of a 2-page list).

fronted with a particular client problem. Figure 5 shows a portion of the process criteria developed for patients with problems in the area of interpersonal relationships and social activities. Appropriate criteria have been developed for all 20 problem categories.

The final stage in the construction of the accountability structure was initiation of a mechanism allowing assessment of effectiveness in meeting client problems. This mechanism involves taking each problem identified in a client's chart and using Kiresuk and Sherman's (1968) Goal Attainment Scaling format to specify the range of outcomes that could reasona-

SOCIAL SERVICE DEPARTMENT UNIVERSITY OF MINNESOTA HOSPITALS June, 1976 Page 1 of 3 pages.		Audit Topic:	INTERPERSONAL RELATIONSHIPS AND SOCIAL ACTIVITIES. Dependency on others; social isolation; difficulty making or keeping friends; disturbed relationships with author- ity figures; inability to meet social needs; hobbies; social life; developing interests; social group involvement
ELEMENT	**STANDARD**	**EXCEPTIONS**	**INSTRUCTIONS FOR RETRIEVAL**

Encounter Information:
  Interview patient within
  3 working days of referral or
  case finding.
	100%	Pt. refuses interview.
		Pt. discharged.
		Pt. deceased.
		Pt. transferred.
			Look for progress note or data base eval-
			uation documenting that worker had verbal
			contact with pt. within 3 days of receipt
			of referral or worker identification of
			problem.

Data Base Includes:
  Describe patient's per-
  ception of relationships
  and social situation.
	100%	Pt. refuses interview
		Pt. discharged.
		Pt. deceased.
		Pt. transferred.
			Progress note or data base evaluation de-
			scribing pt's statements about relationships
			or social situation (e.g., "I don't get out
			socially as much as I'd like.")

Describe hospital staff,
  family and active commun-
  ity personnel's perception
  of the problem.
	100%	Pt. discharged.
		Pt. deceased.
		Pt. transferred.
		Family refuses to
		cooperate.
			Progress note or data base evaluation doc-
			umenting perceptions of those contacted re:
			patient's relationships and social situation
			(e.g., FATHER: "He never seems to have any
			friends and is bored a lot.")

Document worker assessment of the problem re: relationships and social situation.	100%	Pt. discharged. Pt. deceased. Pt. transferred.	Progress note or data base evaluation in- corporating worker's impression of presence or absence of problem and judgement as to need for intervention.

Treatment Plan Justification:
  Outline plan for intervention
  in relation to the problem of
  interpersonal relationships
  and social activities.
	100%	Worker judgement that
		intervention
		unnecessary.
			Progress note or data base evaluation de-
			scribing proposed hospital-based program
			(e.g., individual or group counseling to
			improve social skills.)

FIGURE 5. Process criteria for Social Service Department clients with problems relating to interpersonal relationships and social activities (page 1 of a 3-page document).

bly occur if the client receives effective services. Goals are selected and scaled with client input, and strategies for attainment are also negotiated. Scales are constructed during the initial contact with a patient, and attainment is determined at discharge. Attainment may also be assessed periodically (to monitor progress) during a patient's hospital stay or after termination (to determine if the effects of treatment are enduring). To facilitate the goal-setting process, standardized scales are being developed for recurring problems, and formal criteria have been established to exclude from the goal-setting process certain classes of clients (e.g., clients who do not receive direct treatment; clients whose needs are so obvious and immediate as to make goal negotiation an inappropriate use of time; and clients whose stay in the hospital will be too brief to make goal setting possible).

HOW THE SYSTEM WORKS

The operation of the accountability structure is presented schematically in Figure 6. As can be seen, the sequential interaction of the elements of the structure are best described by borrowing the acronym PSRO, which in this case stands for Problems, Strategies, Reporting, Outcome. *Problems* are assessed during the development of a Problem-Oriented Medical Record data base. Individualized problems are then classified according to predetermined problem categories, and treatment *strategies* are initiated according to appropriate departmental functions. *Reporting* of both the development and implementation of the treatment strategy is done through the Management Information System, and the *outcome* of treatment is determined according to attainment of clinical goals scaled for the client during the initial interaction with the department.

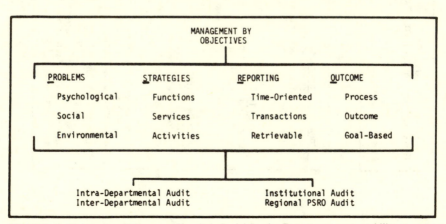

FIGURE 6. University of Minnesota Hospitals Social Service Department accountability structure.

Case Illustration

The operation of the accountability structure can best be illustrated through the presentation of a hypothetical Social Service Department case:

Mrs. Smith is a 50-year-old, married Caucasian, referred to the Social Service Department by a physician on the neurosurgical service. Her primary physical problem, persistent lower back pain, is complicated by profound depression and evidence of habituation to analgesic medication (Percodan).

The patient's initial workup was performed by a staff social worker, who proceeded according to process criteria developed for clients with needs relevant to "Physical Problems," "Drug Abuse," and/or "Depression." After the "encounter information" was collected, a data base was charted using the Problem-Oriented Medical Records format (Figure 7).

Using the data base as a starting point, a treatment plan was formulated for each of her problems. As a means to evaluate the success of the plan, the Goal Attainment Scaling format was used to develop outcome criteria related to each problem (see Figure 8). Outcomes were specified to conform to the following standards: (a) they are *realistic* (i.e., they have a reasonable probability of actually occurring, given what is known about the patient and about the past success of the prescribed treatment); (b) they are *relevant* (i.e., they are directly indicative of changes in the client's problems); and (c) they are *objective* (i.e., they are verifiable through the judgment of more than one outsider). Mrs. Smith's Goal Attainment Follow-up Guide (Figure 8) was scored when she was discharged from the neurosurgical service. As can be seen, she made significant progress in all three problem areas.

Coincident with the scoring of the follow-up guide was preparation of a Discharge Summary, (Figure 9) employing the Problem-Oriented Medical Record format to document Mrs. Smith's progress and outline future goals and actions. If Mrs. Smith continues as an outpatient client of the Social Service Department, a revised Goal Attainment Follow-up Guide will be negotiated.

COSTS OF THE SYSTEM

Start-up Costs

To prepare for the installation of Management by Objectives, a consultant was retained at a cost of $500 to provide a series of five staff training seminars. Designing and installing the Management Information System required the services of an additional consultant, whose

```
Presenting Problems:              Onset:

  1. Low Back Pain                May, 1967
  2. Drug Addiction               July, 1968
  3. Depression*                  Unknown

Problems 1 & 2:  Low Back Pain
                 Drug Addiction

  S: Patient reports severe pain in lower back and legs since accident
     at work in May, 1967.  Has had spinal fusion and laminectomy without
     much improvement.  Has been taking Percodan regularly since July,
     1968, following surgery.

  O: Patient is overweight (230 lbs).  Nurses report she lies in bed most
     of the time demanding medication.  Insurance company reports patient
     receives disability compensation of $100 per week.

  A: Chronic pain syndrome, including almost total inactivity and drug
     dependence.

  P: Admit for Chronic Pain Program to include (1) group and/or indi-
     vidual counseling, (2) physical therapy to increase activity level,
     (3) weight reduction program, and (4) detox from pain medication.

Problem 3:  Depression

  S: Patient states she feels "very low, as if nothing matters anymore."
     Has been feeling this way ever since someone drew attention to her
     weight problem.  Talks at length about not being loved by anyone;
     complains of pain all over.

  O: Patient cries daily.  Lying in bed facing wall.  Door constantly
     closed and shades drawn.  Acts lethargic and confused.

  A: Patient depressed.  Uses pain as coping mechanism.

  P: Patient agrees to daily counseling sessions with the following
     goals: (1) development of insight into pain problem, (2) learn to
     identify problems rather than to avoid them, (3) learn problem
     solving skills, (4) develop positive self image.
```

*Problems identified by team; Problem #3 handled by social worker.

FIGURE 7. Data base developed for hypothetical client of Social Service Department based upon Problem-Oriented Medical Records system procedures.

services, though donated, were valued at approximately $6,300 (42 days at $150 per day). Problem-Oriented Medical Records were already a feature of the University of Minnesota Hospitals system. Implementation of Goal Attainment Scaling necessitated a training program that cost $200.

Maintenance Costs

Maintenance costs have remained stable over the 18 months of the system's operation. Primary expenses include a $62 monthly charge for keypunching of staff activity logs and a $9 monthly charge for computer preparation of feedback reports. Two major elements have been added to the Management Information System: (a) a program to generate staff feedback reports, and (b) a revised format to accommodate client problem codes, linking them with "time expended," "function performed," "cost center," and "patient identification number." The total cost of these enhancements was $730. Investment of staff time in record keeping amounts to about 4% of all hours for all budgeted positions. This corresponds to about 10 minutes per day per staff person.

CONCLUSION

The accountability structure proposed in this paper is not a fixed response to a particular constellation of management problems, but rather is an attempt to initiate a self-renewing mechanism to accommodate unanticipated future as well as current needs. At base, the structure is an attempt to forge what Wildavsky (1972) calls a "self-evaluating organization."

Implicit in the structure are the concepts of "change," "growth," and "self-development." Numerous and frequent alterations can be expected

GOAL ATTAINMENT FOLLOW-UP GUIDE			
LEVELS OF PREDICTED ATTAINMENT	Scale: _1_ Wt.: _8_ PHYSICAL PROBLEM: Low Back Pain. Negotiated? (Yes) No	Scale: _2_ Wt.: _4_ DRUG ABUSE: Possible Addiction to Percodan. Negotiated? (Yes) No	Scale: _3_ Wt.: _10_ DEPRESSION: Refuses to Talk to People. Negotiated? Yes (No)
Most Unfavorable Outcome Thought Likely	Patient immobilized by low back pain unable to leave hospital bed.	Patient receives 3 or more injections of Percodan each day.	Patient refuses to talk to anyone but medical personnel.
Less Than Expected Success	Patient able to get out of bed, but cannot leave hospital.	Patient receives 1-2 injections of Percodan each day.	Patient talks to medical personnel and family members only.
Expected Level of Success	Patient able to leave hospital, but must wear brace whenever out of bed.	Patient receives Percodan once a week or less.	Patient talks to medical personnel, family members and personal friends.
More Than Expected Success	Patient able to leave hospital, but must wear brace 50% of time when out of bed.	Patient no longer receives Percodan (or any comparable drug) but still asks for it.	In addition to above, patient initiates conversations with new acquaintances.
Most Favorable Outcome Thought Likely	Patient able to leave hospital, and does not need to wear brace.	As above, but patient no longer asks for Percodan (or any comparable drug.)	In addition to above, patient begins to attend social functions.

Patient Name:_____   Date of Construction:_____

Hospital Number:_____   Date of Follow-up:_____

Guide Constructor:_____

FIGURE 8. Hypothetical Goal Attainment Follow-up Guide from University of Minnesota Hospitals Social Service Department's accountability structure.

PROBLEM 3:   Depression   (Problems 1 and 2 deleted for brevity.)

S: Patient has been in counseling every day during hospitalization. She now identifies the following problems, with specific goals to meet them, and actions to be undertaken to attain the goals.

Problems *	Actions	Goals
(1) Present weight is 230 lbs.	Will start behavior modification program next week; will consult surgeon regarding possible bypass.	Ideal weight 150 lbs.
(2) Needs dental work; has decay.	Will set up dental appointments starting 3/19.	Complete dental care; new dentures.
(3) Out of work; has nothing to do.	Call Department of Vocational Rehabilitation 3/19.	Complete job training program.
(4) No positive relationships with family or friends.	Stay in counseling; learn communication skills, accepting responsibility.	Be able to establish positive, enduring relationships.
(5) Despondency	Stay in counseling; learn to examine own feelings.	Be able to control feelings rather than be overwhelmed.

O: Patient is able to verbalize feelings directly. Has few complaints of pain. Has been participating actively in group and individual counseling sessions. Has worked on a schedule of activity following discharge.

A: Patient has made significant progress in all areas. (See scored Goal Attainment Follow-up Guide in progress notes.)

P: Will continue to see patient on PRN basis. Will evaluate progress after four months based on her own goals.

*Problems identified by team.

FIGURE 9. Discharge Summary developed for hypothetical client of Social Service Department. (Problems 1 and 2 were deleted for brevity.)

in the coming years in public policy, social legislation, and professional practice, and if it is to survive and prosper, the Social Service Department must adapt itself to them. For this reason, the elements of the accountability structure were selected in accordance with their capacity to adjust to changing conditions. The goal-setting and goal auditing provisions, for example, encompass what is currently known about effective delivery of social services, but also assist in the redefinition of policy and practice through the continual establishment, review, and evaluation of client and organizational goals. The same feedback potential is characteristic of the Problem-Oriented Record system, which allows documentation of the kinds of client problems handled by the service, and of the Management Information System, which keeps track of activities performed. The form of the structure, the process by which data are generated, managed, and reported, is intended to remain stable whereas the content of the information is continually renewed through the accumulation of fresh experience.

The criteria for the success of the accountability structure will be its flexibility. If, 5 years from now, the goal structure, problem list, and function definitions have not evolved from the current set, the system will have failed. If new legal, professional, and funding requirements have not been accommodated, the system will have failed. If it only produces stylish but nonfunctional reports, that are not read and not utilized in program administration and service delivery, the system will have failed. If the costs of the system become immoderate, or if it becomes another empty technological display, the system will have failed.

It is anticipated that a major new direction for the further development of the structure will be formulation of a "change technology" to assist potential utilizers in meeting the technical and organizational difficulties that sometimes accompany implementation. The impetus for this effort derives from a need for realistic and practical mechanisms to facilitate adoption, and from a recognition that the structure itself inherently combines "intentionality" (i.e., formation of future expectancies) with the effort to bring about change. Davis' (1973) formulation of the natural and necessary interaction between expectation and subsequent innovation has proved to be a most useful and unifying concept in linking the various elements of the accountability structure, and will undoubtedly serve as a catalyst for future adaptations.

REFERENCE NOTES

1. Meites, M. *One adaption of social work to a peer review system.* Unpublished manuscript, Medical Social Work Department, E. W. Sparrow Hospital, Lansing, Michigan, 1976.
2. Sherman, R. E. *Visit record system.* Unpublished manuscript, Hennepin County Mental Health Service, 1972.
3. Saunders, M., & Baxter, J. *P.E.P. system documentation.* Unpublished document, Program Evaluation Project, 1972.

REFERENCES

Brady, R. MBO goes to work in the public sector. *Harvard Business Review,* March-April, 1973.
Davis, H. R. Four ways to goal attainment: An overview. *Evaluation,* 1972, *1.*
Davis, H. R. Change and innovation. In S. Feldman (Ed.), *Administration in mental health services.* Springfield, Ill.: Charles C Thomas, 1973.
Drucker, P. *Managing for results.* New York: Harper & Row, 1964.
Garwick, G., & Lampman, S. Typical problems bringing patients to a community mental health center. *Community Mental Health Journal,* 1972, *2.*
Kiresuk, T. J., & Sherman, R. E. Goal Attainment Scaling: A general method for evaluating comprehensive community mental health programs. *Community Mental Health Journal,* 1968, *4.*
Rocheleau, B. A. *Without tears or bombast: A guide to program evaluation.* De Kalb: Northern Illinois University, Center for Governmental Studies, 1975.

Southern Regional Educational Board. *Definition of terms in mental health, alcohol abuse, and mental retardation*. Rockville, Md.: National Institute of Mental Health, 1973.

Spano, R. M., & Lund, S. H. Management by Objectives in a hospital social service unit. *Social Work in Health Care*, 1976, *1*(3), 267–276.

Weed, L. L. *Medical records, medical education, and patient care: The Problem-Oriented Record as a basic tool*. Chicago: The Press of Case Western Reserve University, 1969.

Wildavsky, A. Self-evaluating organization. *Public Administration Review*, 1972, *32*.

Chapter 7

Strategies for Information System Development

Dick J. Schoech, PhD
Lawrence L. Schkade, PhD
Raymond Sanchez Mayers, PhD

Computerization of agency information systems is proliferating rapidly as evidenced by numerous recent articles in the human service literature (Cohen, Noah, & Pauley, 1979; Elias et al., 1979; Jaffe, 1979; Schoech, 1979). Television and magazine advertisements daily expound the capabilities and low cost of computer applications, such as information systems. Although information system and computer jargon is unfamiliar, the promises and potentials are enticing. Before launching into the uncertain waters of computer systems, however, some hard basic questions should be addressed. How does a human service agency move into a computerized information system environment, i.e., develop an overall approach or strategy? What processes and tasks are involved? How would it impact agency workload, staffing, and organizational structure? What tools and skills are needed? What options are open to the agency in developing this overall strategy? And finally, are there successful and unsuccessful ways to proceed?

In addressing these questions, this article presents generalized strategies that have been derived from years of experience in developing or improving information systems in a wide range of organizations. These strategies require consideration of the information system improvement process, the accompanying organizational roles and structure, and the required tools and skills. They also require consideration of the options available to the agency in improving its information system and an awareness of the characteristics of previous successful efforts. Agencies wanting to improve their information system can benefit greatly by applying this knowledge and developing an overall information system improvement strategy appropriate to the needs of their specific agency.

79

THE INFORMATION SYSTEM IMPROVEMENT PROCESS

Every agency presently has an information system, since data is collected, stored, managed, and used in reports and for decision making. However, many manual information systems are no longer adequate to meet the increasingly complex data demands which are being placed on agencies. Often the data needed to make decisions is not collected, or if collected, it is stored in such a way that useful retrieval is extremely difficult.

Before changes in an agency information system can occur, the agency must begin to view the information it collects as a primary resource to be managed as other basic agency resources such as personnel, money, and property. Planning for the agency's information needs is a process as important as preparing the budget or anticipating personnel needs. Similarly, data collection, storage, manipulation, and retrieval require staff time and effort. A cost-benefit analysis of the information resource is advised to insure the output from the data management effort is worth the expense incurred.

The goal of an agency information management effort should be progressively to improve the existing system using available technologies and skills until the system meets the decision making needs of the agency on a cost effective basis. Achieving this goal may or may not involve computerization. For example, Figure 1 illustrates a small inexpensive manual system with many of the features of a computerized system.

The process of improving an agency information system is a major strategy consideration requiring significant agency time and effort. Figure 2 presents a sequential flowchart of the process an agency must follow to improve its information system. The process is iterative. Each step builds on and amplifies activities of the previous step. For example, the first step, preparedness and feasibility, must be given repeated consideration throughout the process.

Appendix A presents the activities involved in each step of the information system improvement process flowcharted in Figure 2. Each step begins with the planning of the goals, objectives, tasks, schedules, checkpoints, responsibilities and completion criteria. Each step ends with the documentation of all activities compiled into a report that is the basis for deciding whether to proceed to the next step. Completing this process for a relatively small agency subsystem may take more than a year, and it is important not to rush the process or take shortcuts. While going through the information system improvement process may appear to be a precise science, in actuality the movement through the process can be considered an art, and as some authors note, the state of the art in information system design is still primitive (Davis, 1974).

Figure 1. A manual data system for a small agency

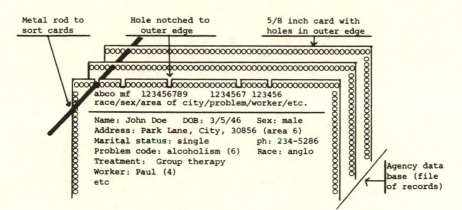

This simple manual system has some of the basic elements of an automated

system. Client data are written on a record (5X8 card) which is randomly

stored in the file of records which constitutes the agency data base. The

most frequently used data are recorded on the outside of the card by notching

the hole to the outer edge. Thus, each hole forms a key by which the data

base can be sorted using the metal rod. For example, all cards of anglo

clients would be notched to the outer edge in the "a" position above race;

all blacks in the "b" position, etc. Inserting the metal rod through the

anglo key of the data base and lifting would extract all races except anglos.

Additional sorts of the anglo cards could obtain all anglo males in a given

age group who reside in a particular area of the city, who have a specified

problem and who have been assigned to a given worker. Note that this system

is not a complete information system, for it only records, stores, sorts, and

retrieves data. A complete information system contains the people, equipment

and prodedures to collect data, perform more complex sorts and processing as

frequencies and descriptive statistics, and generate reports to meet user needs.

Each step in the information system improvement process requires
careful consideration for effective development. Agencies may emphasize different parts of the process depending on their specific situation.
For example, an agency purchasing an information system from a vendor
may skip some of the activities, especially in the design phase, because
these activities have already been completed by the vendor. However, the

Figure 2.   Flowchart of the process to improve an agency information system

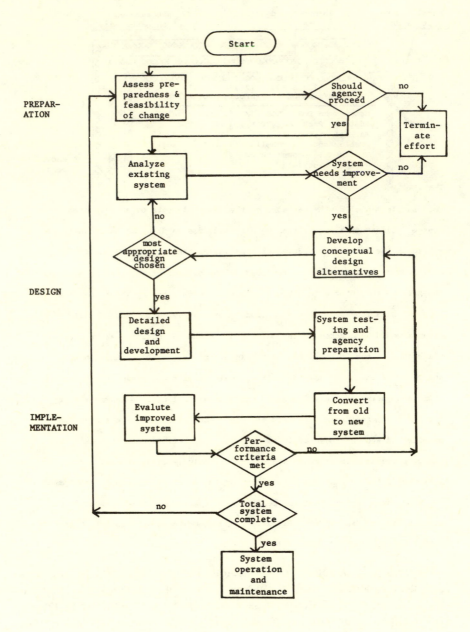

agency should compile complete documentation on all activities no matter when, where, or by whom they were completed.

The major steps in the system improvement process are described as follows.

Step 1: Assess Preparedness and Feasibility

The first step is to determine if the agency has the motivation, capacity, and opportunity to proceed. This activity involves establishing communication channels to identify the extent of support and types of concerns, and to begin the crucial dialogue whereby the agency learns to develop realistic expectations of the processes involved and the results to be obtained.

The process of improving an information system is a major undertaking which takes money, time, effort, commitment, and trust. System change cannot be forced on the agency, since the success of an information system is dependent on the accurate input of data by staff and the use of system output in decision making. The decision to proceed with the information system effort should be well thought out; however, hard facts rarely will justify the effort. Eventually the decision must be based on the belief that an improved system will be worth the time and effort expended, because it will allow the agency to better function, survive, and serve its clients.

Step 2: Analysis of the Existing System

Since data is a resource which flows through the whole organization, the study of its origin, movement through the agency, and use will involve analyzing all departmental forms and reports, data flows and procedures, as well as the decisions and goals which must be supported by data. The intent of this step is to gain an understanding of how the present system functions and to gather the information on which to base improvements. Since the existing system has evolved to meet the agency's needs, it should be a prime source of ideas for designing any new system.

Step 3: Conceptual Design

Step 3 involves the process of using the systems analysis of step 2 to develop several alternative system designs that can meet agency requirements using minimum resources. The intent of this step is to build a data model that matches or mirrors the functioning of the organization. Hardware and software options are investigated in terms of agency and design requirements, and the advantages and disadvantages of all possibilities are explored.

Step 4: Detailed Design and Development

The intent of step 4 is to translate the chosen design into a working system of data, people, procedures, logic, forms, data processing and manipulation, and equipment. Designing the data base is a technical process that involves coding and storing information to reduce inefficient and redundant data collection and processing while having maximum access and manipulation capabilities. If a computer is to be involved, the data base should be developed by someone who is knowledgeable of computer equipment. However, the usual tendency is for agencies to become over-involved in the technical aspects of the design and fail to develop other broader, integrative elements of the improved system, especially people and procedures.

Step 5: System Testing and Agency Preparation

System testing, or determining if the system performs as designed, is extremely important, because once introduced in the agency, errors are a frustrating waste of staff time and effort and threaten system credibility. The system should be tested with infrequently used data as well as routine high volume data. System testing is especially important for complex systems where many subsystems are integrated and perform core operations for the agency.

While open communication should prepare the agency for the system, certain groups such as operators, users, and others affected by the system must be made ready to accept the system once it is implemented. As with system testing, spending the necessary time and money for educating and training agency staff pays off with more trouble-free conversion and less resistance to change.

Step 6: Conversion

Conversion, step 6, is the process of moving from the old system to the new system. Since information is basic to all organizational functions, conversion means not only installing a new system, but integrating that system into the total agency structure and procedures.

Step 7: Evaluation

Evaluation involves creating a feedback loop in the information system improvement process, so system performance can be compared with design criteria and expectations. System success can be measured in several ways as the activities under step 7 in Appendix A indicate. Although evaluation is one of the last steps, it must be a consideration from the very beginning of the improvement process. Ongoing feedback is especially important in the operation and maintenance stage of the process, so the agency can continually insure that its information system meets the decision making needs of the agency on a cost-benefit basis.

Step 8: Operation, Maintenance and Modification

The intent of step 8 is to develop a smooth functioning system which continuously matches agency needs. Since no agency is static, system improvement is a never-ending process. The system must evolve and change with the agency, or it will soon become obsolete. The life of a system depends on the changes an agency experiences. Systems in highly volatile agencies may require major changes after 2–3 years, while those in very stable agencies may function well for 5–10 years with minimal change.

ACCOMPANYING ORGANIZATIONAL ROLES AND STRUCTURE

In order to improve an agency information system, the agency must be willing to create the organizational structure and to assign the responsibilities necessary for completing the process of Appendix A. Several alternative structures for moving an agency towards information system improvement are shown in Figure 3. While the structure may vary depending on how the improvement process is approached, the roles of key participants in the structure are the same whatever the structure. Information system improvement is a process involving top management, the person or department in the organization designated responsible for data and information management (the information manager), technicians and specialists, and an agency steering committee composed of department representatives, usually department heads. If one of these roles or participants is omitted, the chances of obtaining satisfactory results decreases dramatically, especially in larger organizations (Appleton, 1979).

Agency management usually consists of the executive and associate director, the agency board, and advisory committees or representatives of the parent organization. The role of agency management is to provide overall direction and to insure the effort does not falter due to a lack of resources, e.g., funds. It must not only sanction the effort, but demonstrate its commitment to go through with the process. It appoints the steering committee, adjusts work loads to insure that the effort does not simply mean more work for those involved, and insures that lines of communication are specified and kept open. Agency management must remain in control of the total effort by balancing the conflicting needs of the others involved.

Figure 3.   Possible organizational structures to improve an agency
            information system

STRUCTURE 1

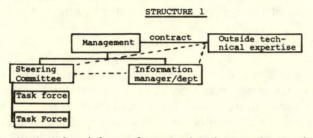

In structure 1, a balance of power exists between the steering committee
and the information manager. Disagreements are settled by top management.
Outside consultants provide technical expertise whenever needed.

STRUCTURE 2

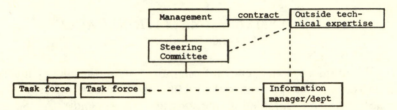

In structure 2, the information manager reports directly to the steering
committee rather than to top management. Outside consultants provide
the expertise needed.

STRUCTURE 3

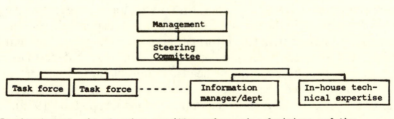

In structure 3, the steering committee makes major decisions and the
technical expertise is drawn from within the organization.

The steering committee represents the overall agency in the improvement process. Its involvement insures that the improved system meets the
needs of the overall agency. By definition, it performs an advisory role to
top management, but it may be designated to have approval authority
over certain reports or key decisions to keep top management from being
bogged down in the more routine and detailed issues which must be ad-

dressed. The composition of the steering committee may vary depending on the nature of the subsystem; e.g., line workers would be involved in the process of developing a client information subsystem. The steering committee may appoint task forces to work on special problems or issues.

The information manager/department role may be a part-time job in a small agency or a full department in a larger organization. The information manager, often called a data administrator or a management information system (MIS) director, is responsible for managing and coordinating the information system improvement effort on a day to day basis. The information manager is ultimately responsible for the training that occurs and for documentation of the total effort. The information manager should be a top level generalist manager who understands all departments of the agency as well as the technical aspects of information systems development and should have the trust of and access to top management. The information manager daily manages the information system improvement process, while the steering committee sets the overall policy and guidelines and insures that the information manager's decisions are meeting the needs of their constituent departments. For communication and coordination purposes, the information manager should be a member of the steering committee.

Technicians/specialists supply the technical expertise needed in the information system improvement effort. The source of the technicians/specialists varies depending on the sophistication of the improvement effort and the expertise available within the agency. The technician/specialist may be an outside consultant, an information system vendor, or an in-house team.

SUPPORTING TOOLS AND SKILLS

The final consideration in developing strategies for improving an information system is the acquisition and application of a variety of needed tools and skills. These supporting tools and skills are described with references that provide additional information.

Planning and Scheduling

Planning and scheduling tools are necessary for guiding the project from start to finish in an orderly fashion. These techniques include the use of Gantt, milestone, and PERT charts (Carlisle, 1976). The design of control and feedback points in the process are necessary to insure that deviation from the desired course of action is detected and handled early (Burch, Strater, & Grudnitski, 1979). Especially important is the ability to write clear, specific, and measurable objectives to guide and evaluate all processes involved.

Flowcharting

Flowcharting is the use of standardized symbols to graphically trace the flow of a series of activities (see Figure 2 for an example of a flowchart). Flowcharting graphically documents, simplifies, and illustrates the resources, logic, flows, decision points, and interactions of complex processes such as information system improvement. Standard flowchart symbols have been developed for the systems analysts and computer programmers (Burch, Strater, & Grudnitski, 1979).

Decision Tables

Decision tables or dynamic matrices which graphically illustrate complex steps of logic are used in information system analysis and design for study and communication purposes (Semprevivo, 1976). One common form of decision table is a decision tree where the trunk can be considered a decision problem and the branches are alternative solutions. Each major branch can have successive alternative or branching options (Davis, 1974).

Data Gathering Techniques

Since improving an information system may generate fears associated with technology, job displacement, job change, power changes, etc., data gathering can become a delicate process requiring skill and sensitivity. Good data gathering techniques, such as methods of observation, interviewing techniques, document analysis, questionnaire construction, and sampling methodologies are essential (Stone, 1978).

Group Problem Solving Methods

Information system development is a process involving groups, and effective group management is crucial to the effective system design and implementation. Techniques associated with such tools as brainstorming, nominal group process, delphi techniques, and conflict resolution are necessary throughout the process (Delbecq, Van de Ven, & Gustafson, 1975).

Training and Communication Skills

Communication and training skills help the changes associated with information system improvement occur smoothly. Miscommunication or lack of information can lead to rumors, fear, and resistance. Skills which help provide adequate information to all who will be affected by the system as well as skills in listening are especially important (Stewart, 1977).

OPTIONS IN INFORMATION SYSTEM IMPROVEMENT

Numerous variations or options can be considered in developing strategies for the improvement of an information system. Some of the major options are outlined below, and references that provide more details are indicated.

Extent of Automation

Often the improvement of an information system is confused with the computerization of that system. The goal of an agency with regard to data is to have a system which meets the agency information needs in an efficient and effective manner. Computerization may or may not be a part of this goal. If a computer becomes a necessity, the agency must decide whether to purchase or lease a computer or buy computer time from a service bureau.

Which Subsystems to Develop

The agency must decide which data subsystems (i.e., service data, client data, financial data, or personnel data) are presently adequate and which need improvement. Some authors suggest that a system which is very important to agency functions should be chosen for improvement first, so the benefits will be more obvious, while others recommend first improving a less crucial system in order to learn the process (Ein-Dor & Segev, 1978).

Source of Expertise

The agency must decide whether to develop the system in-house using present staff, to use a consultant to facilitate the system improvement process, to use a consulting firm to develop the improved system, or to buy a prepackaged system. This decision is obviously based on agency funds, in-house expertise and the complexity of the system desired (Paton & D'huyvetter, 1980).

The Overall Design Approach Taken

The agency must decide if subsystems should be developed independently based on immediate requirements and combined into a total system when the need arises (bottom-up approach), or if a model of the total system should be designed first and each subsystem developed as an integral part of the total system (top-down approach). Each approach has its advocates. The top-down approach makes more sense theoretically, while the bottom-up approach seems to be closer to actual practice (Ein-Dor &

Segev, 1978). A combination of both approaches is often a realistic compromise.

The Intended Users of the System

The agency must decide whether the system should address the needs of agency directors, mid-level managers, workers, or a combination of these. Different levels of the organization have different information needs (Gorry & Morton, 1971). Systems for data related to the more routine decisions of middle managers, e.g., financial data, are the easiest to design, while data supporting the complex decisions of caseworkers and agency directors requires the most sophisticated systems.

The Extent of Centralization and System Integration

Data can be collected, stored, processed, and retrieved at one central location or at numerous distributed locations. Both centralized and distributed subsystems may be independent or integrated to form one total agency system. The extent of integration varies with the number of different agency files and reporting requirements (Vickers, 1980). As files are integrated the complexity of the system increases, however the ability to obtain total agency data across programs also increases. The recommended approach is to design a system that reflects the extent of integration and centralization of the organization as a whole.

Converting from the Old to the New System

Four basic approaches can be used to convert from an old system to a new system, although a combination of approaches may also be used (Burch, Strater, & Grudnitski, 1979). The first approach is total or direct conversion, where the old system is discontinued and the new system implemented. Since this approach is abrupt, it is most suitable when the old system is significantly different from the new system and little carry over exists. The second approach, parallel conversion, involves operating the old and new system simultaneously until the new system meets predetermined performance standards. Parallel conversion allows a continuous comparison of the output of the new system with the old system. Running parallel systems is costly and it can be frustrating for staff to supply the data that the two systems require. In the third approach, modular conversion, the whole system is implemented in one section of the organization at a time, while in the fourth approach, phase-in or gradual conversion, the system is segmented and segments introduced into the total organization one at a time. Both approaches produce minimum disruption in the organization, but conversion can become a costly, frustrating, and a seemingly never ending process.

CHARACTERISTICS OF SUCCESSFUL STRATEGIES

Factors that lead to success in improving an information system are a concern of practitioners and academicians alike. The literature contains mostly testimonials rather than controlled research. Identified factors have been cited repeatedly in the literature and can be used as guides for successful information system improvement (Bowers & Bowers, 1977; Ein-Dor & Segev, 1976; Schoech & Schkade, 1980).

As indicated in the discussion of the information system improvement process, one of the major characteristics of successful systems is adequate preparation and planning. Agency processes and procedures must be formalized and quantified and major changes made before developing an information system. Involvement is also key, in that top management must show commitment and involvement by controlling the overall effort and placing the information manager in a separate high level department. Users and others affected must be kept informed and involved throughout the process, since an effective information system is ultimately dependent on its users. Developing an information system should be a gradual process with one module implemented at a time and the total process well documented. Continuity of system developers must be assured, but this is especially difficult with the scarcity and mobility of well trained staff. Finally, all persons involved must be willing to handle the extra work and frustration required if the information system is to eventually result in improved decision making in the agency.

CONCLUSION

Developing successful strategies for improving an information system requires careful consideration of the information system improvement process and the accompanying organizational roles, structure, tools, and skills. Since an information system conceptualizes and operationalizes the core processes of an agency, the time and effort to develop effective improvement strategies must be taken, because a poorly designed and implemented information system is detrimental to agency performance and results in costly revisions.

This article presents information from which an overall improvement strategy can be developed. The approach presented is not prescriptive, rather it outlines alternatives within a development framework. The most appropriate strategies are those that combine general and theoretical concepts with the real world situation the agency faces.

REFERENCES

Appleton, D. A manufacturing systems cookbook, part 3. DATAMATION, 1979, *26*(9), 130–136.

Bellerby, L., Dreyer, L., & Koroloff, N. PREPARING FOR SYSTEM IMPROVEMENT; PLANNING INFORMATION SYSTEM IMPROVEMENT; MANAGING THE DESIGN OF SYSTEM IMPROVEMENT. Portland, Oregon: Portland State U. Regional Research Institute for Human Services, MIS Curriculum Development Project, 1979–1980.

Bowers, G. E., & Bowers, M. R. CULTIVATING CLIENT INFORMATION SYSTEMS. Human Services Monograph Series No. 5. Washington, DC: U.S. Department of Health and Human Services, Project Share, June 1977.

Burch, J. G., Strater, F. R., & Grudnitski, G. INFORMATION SYSTEMS: THEORY AND PRACTICE (2nd ed.) New York: John Wiley & Sons, 1979.

Carlisle, H. M. MANAGEMENT: CONCEPTS AND SITUATIONS. Chicago: Science Research Associates, Inc. 1976.

Cohen, S. H., Noah, J. C., & Pauley, A. New ways of looking at management information systems in human service delivery. EVALUATION AND PROGRAM PLANNING, 1979, *2*, 49–58.

Davis, G. B. MANAGEMENT INFORMATION SYSTEMS: CONCEPTUAL FOUNDATIONS, STRUCTURE AND DEVELOPMENT. New York: McGraw Hill, 1974.

Delbecq, A. L., Van de Ven, A. H., & Gustafson, D. H. GROUP TECHNIQUES FOR PROGRAM PLANNING: A GUIDE TO NOMINAL GROUP AND DELPHI PROCESSES. Glenview, IL: Scott, Foresman and Co., 1975.

Ein-Dor, P., & Segev, E. MANAGING MANAGEMENT INFORMATION SYSTEMS. Lexington, MA: Lexington Books, 1978.

Elias, M. J., Dalton, J. H., Cobb, C. W., Lavoie, L., & Zlotlow, S. F. The use of computerized management information in evaluation. ADMINISTRATION IN MENTAL HEALTH, 1979, *7*(2), 148–161.

Gorry, G. A., & Morton, M. S. A framework for management information systems. SLOAN MANAGEMENT REVIEW, 1971, *13*(1), 55–70.

Jaffe, E. D. Computers in child placement planning. SOCIAL WORK, 1979, *24*, 380–385.

Paton, J. A., & D'huyvetter, P. K. AUTOMATED MANAGEMENT INFORMATION SYSTEMS FOR MENTAL HEALTH AGENCIES: A PLANNING AND ACQUISITION GUIDE. Rockville, MD.: Department of Health and Human Services, National Institute of Mental Health, Series FN No. 1, DHHS Pub No. (ADM) 80–797 (1980).

Schoech, D. J. A microcomputer based human service information system. ADMINISTRATION IN SOCIAL WORK, 1979, *3*, 423–440.

Schoech, D. J., & Schkade, L. L. What human services can learn from business about computerization. PUBLIC WELFARE, 1980, *38*(3), 18–27.

Semprevivo, P. C. SYSTEMS ANALYSIS: DEFINITION, PROCESS, AND DESIGN. Chicago: Science Research Associates, Inc., 1976.

Stewart, J. BRIDGES NOT WALLS: A BOOK ABOUT INTERPERSONAL COMMUNICATION (2nd ed.). Reading, MA: Addison-Wesley, 1977.

Stone, E. F. RESEARCH METHODS IN ORGANIZATIONAL RESEARCH. Santa Monica, CA: Goodyear Publishing Co., 1978.

Vickers, W. H. Source data processing. DATAMATION, 1980, *26*(4), 155–160.

*Appendix A: Activities in the process
of information system improvement**

STEP 1: ASSESS PREPAREDNESS AND FEASIBILITY

Communicate potential system improvement effort to all staff

Establish an agency steering committee

Define agency "preparedness and feasibility" report purpose, objectives, timetables and responsibilities

---

*For a series of workbooks designed to help an agency move through this process, see Bellerbey, Dreyer, & Koroloff, 1979–1980.

Assess commitment of key individuals to proceed, e.g., board & ex. director
Assess motivation of total agency to proceed
Assess agency expectations of system improvements
Define tentative scope and goal of overall system improvement effort
Estimate cost & benefits, and time & effort for each step of the improvement process
Estimate improved system impacts (positive & negative) on agency & personnel
Relate improvements to agency's long range goals for information management
Write preparedness and feasibility report
Decide to proceed or terminate effort

STEP 2: ANALYSIS OF EXISTING SYSTEM (SYSTEMS ANALYSIS)

Define system analysis scope, objectives, data needed, data sources, collection methods, timetables, and responsibilities
Analyze current and future data input, processing, and output operations, & requirements of each subsystem of agency, e.g., forms, reports, & files
Identify major decisions made by the agency in normal operations and the data needed to support these decisions
Analyze present and future agency goals/objectives and the data needed to move the agency toward goal achievement
Describe logical routing or flow of agency data and data processing operations
Evaluate problems with the existing system
Analyze resources for change, i.e., money, time, expertise, etc.
Review systems in other similar agencies and request information from national or state associations
Develop policy and procedural changes necessary for system improvement
Prepare systems analysis report and preliminary design ideas
Decide to proceed or terminate effort

STEP 3: CONCEPTUAL DESIGN

Define scope, goals, objectives and checkpoints of subsystems to be improved
Develop alternative conceptual designs, i.e., possible flow and management of data, records, files and processing functions to match the data needs and sources
Apply agency requirements to possible designs, i.e., required and desired data frequency, volume, quality, privacy, turn around time, use and final disposition; and information system flexibility, reliability, processing and statistical capabilities, growth potential, system life expectancy, and tie in with existing systems
Apply agency resources to designs, e.g., money, time, expertise, existing hardware and software
Translate designs into equipment configurations and specifications
Detail the advantages, disadvantages and assumptions of alternative designs

Prepare conceptual design report
Make decision to proceed or terminate effort

STEP 4: DETAILED DESIGN AND DEVELOPMENT

Select equipment for chosen design
Design and develop the data base, i.e., processing functions and procedures, program logic, file definition and structure, keys and indexes, data error checks, storage and backup mechanisms
Set up controls and technical performance standards
Design input and output forms
Code and program system
Preparing operators, users and others to receive the system
Establish user priorities, run schedules, operating logs, etc.
Prepare programming manuals, procedure manuals and instruction manuals

STEP 5: SYSTEM TESTING AND AGENCY PREPARATION

Develop and approve system performance criteria and testing plan
Test input/output logic, programming, forms, and operational procedures and practices, and the use of outputs in agency decision making
Develop and approve a training and education plan
Educate and train system operators, data users, and others affected

STEP 6: CONVERSION

Develop and approve conversion plan
Incorporate information system into agency standard operating procedures, e.g., performance appraisals, new employee orientation
Reorganize agency staff and space if necessary
Conversion of equipment, data processing, and procedures
Insure all systems and controls are working

STEP 7: EVALUATION

Compare system performance with initial system objectives
Relate benefits and costs to initial estimates
Measure agency satisfaction with the system
Determine if system outputs are used in decision making
Examine if system improved agency performance, e.g., client services

STEP 8: OPERATION, MAINTENANCE AND MODIFICATION

Develop a statement of standard operating procedures
Prepare backup and emergency plans and procedures
Complete documentation, e.g., adding to, deleting from or modifying system
Outline a procedure for system maintenance
Begin step 1 if additional subsystems are to be improved

PART III

The Role of the Department in Continuing Education of Students and Staff

Until fairly recently the education of students and staff for health care social work practice was not given a priority in social work departments. With increasing emphasis on cost containment, changing social work roles in health care, and the multi-disciplinary practice, the continuing education stance of a social work department can become crucial to its functioning and management.

As the articles by Drs. Rehr and Rosenberg point out, there are not established standards or criteria for practice and, therefore, clinical practice is not governed by any single theory of behavior. There is further evidence that what may be considered good practice can often seem to derive from good experience rather than necessarily from graduate social work training.

However, it is equally clear that with various changes and pressures occurring in the health care field, the two components of professional social work, practice and education, require open recognition of their joint responsibility to prepare students for social work. This partnership and its implications for social work practice in health care are examined in the Rehr-Rosenberg article.

But, the changes which are occurring in health care bring to the health care industry new ways of delivering health care services. Increasingly the private delivery system is beginning to penetrate the health care industry and as a result there is, as Brackett points out in his article, a bridge towards entrepreneurialism in health. His article deals with this, indicating the significance and impact on social work education for the training for students for health care and for continuing education for those already in the field. Reichert suggests that today's social workers in health practice must know how to work under various arrangements and in different settings. He suggests that social work education has not been dealing with this issue in a specific approach. He recommends that this not be dealt with in an isolated way either in the graduate school of social work or in a continuing education program. Rather, we should require research, reflection, and curriculum experimentation to keep the profession abreast of new developments in the delivery of health care services.

The final article in this section deals with social work supervision. In the context of social work supervision Cohen and Rhodes suggest that schools of social work have not been sensitive to the needs of management training, as health care social work requires. He suggests that whatever educational training programs have been designed by educators of staff development personnel have been based on assumptions which have not always reflected the most current social work practice.

Cohen and Rhodes make several suggestions in their articles based on the contemporary issues which are related to social work supervision with a specific orientation to education of social workers in health care, and for continuing education and staff development. Specific attention has been given in their article to the definition of supervision as middle management and the implications this has for education.

Abraham Lurie, PhD

Chapter 8

Today's Education
for Today's Health Care
Social Work Practice

Helen Rehr, DSW
Gary Rosenberg, PhD

Where does one look to determine whether today's education readies one for today's health care social work practice? In the very question posed, one is faced by other questions. Can we assume that a common perception of health care social work practice exists or that a common perception of social work education for health care exists? There is in the former a range of views, disparate by setting, purpose, geographic location, utilization of differential manpower, administrative predeterminations, fields of practice, and the dictation of funding resources. In the latter, there are differences not only in the philosophies of schools of social work but also in the special predilections of faculty members. In these perceptions of social work education and practice there are purposes, functions, and actions that oppose and impede each other, while a struggle to find the relationship between them continues. Yet, when we turn to the ultimate goal subscribed to by each, that is, to broaden the scope and enhance the quality of social work, it is compatible with the Statement of Purpose set by the Council on Social Work Education. That purpose is to prepare social workers with the knowledge and skills needed to assist in regard to:

—critical social ills and problems;
—developing manpower to plan, administer, or deliver efficient and effective services;
—assuring the reasonable productivity of social work services to those who pay for them, whether directly or by contributions or through taxes.

Reprinted with the permission of *Clinical Social Work Journal*, Vol. 5, No. 4, 1977, and the authors.

Embodied in the Statement of Purpose is a view of social work practice that includes a clinical base; an awareness of and planning for social ills and problems as they impinge on daily living; a differentiated use of manpower in the roles and responsibilities carried; and an inherent accountability to a number of sources for reasonable outcomes from the services offered. These are indeed responsibilities and roles which social work in health care must face.

THE NATURE OF PRACTICE

Social work in health care provides multiple services, clinical and nonclinical. Numerous roles have been identified for social workers including a social planning role, an advocacy role, a community organization role, and a research role (Kahn, 1974). We add to these a management and administrative role, as well as those of collaboration and consultation. The single largest and most demanding is the clinical role. Inherent in the enumerated roles are the issues of what are their demands and what skills, knowledge, and values are essential to meet them. These issues translate in turn into questions; for example, who should carry the role and what level of education and experience is required? For those of us in the health care field, clinical specialization rests heavily on multifunctional responsibilities and skills.

There is no question that the health care system impacts on the clinical practice of its social workers. They need knowledge of the organization of health care delivery systems, including hospitals, private and group practices, and health maintenance organizations; they must be familiar with the financing of health care as it affects the client's utilization patterns, the epidemiology of disease including social and environmental risk factors, and the effect of illness and disease on social and physical functioning. They must also have knowledge of interprofessional collaborative and team practice, and accountability measures within the system. These are in addition to the expectations in the usual Master's degree.

We believe that in the social treatment of individuals, families, and groups, there is a responsibility for securing the provision of adequate services, humanizing organizational networks by affecting the milieu of treatment and managing or coordinating the parts of the service delivery system. In the performance of multiple functions in a health care setting, we believe a social work team, consisting of many educational levels of personnel, answering to a professional MSW, is the best way to deliver social work services. The direct and indirect service responsibilities in such a scheme can be as limited or as comprehensive as the system of care will permit. Under the MSW as team leader there can be: professional assessment of the patient/family; determination of the needs and problems, and the agreed-on contracts to be worked; delegation of responsibility to appropriate personnel; the teaching of social work and other students and staff; and responsibility for administrative and professional accountability of the program. Meyer (1973) has suggested that

> manpower utilization is one of the major keys to improve quantity and thus the delivery of social services. A systems perspective permits the argument that imaginative use of deployment of manpower teams, as in the model of episodes of service when an array of competencies can be made available to clients would also enhance the quality of services. In a systems framework where concepts of input and output and of reciprocity take on meaning we can cease our unending search for cause and effect. (p. 49)

Another way of looking at the same issue is offered by Bracht (1974): "The predominance of one-to-one clinical intervention by social workers in health and mental health settings has left a short supply of professionals trained for management and coordinating and planning functions for the emerging health care system" (p. 540).

We do believe, however, that professional viability has been watered down by lowering the professional entry level from MSW to BSW. The observation we have made is that as a result of the change in educational requirement very frequently dollar availability has dictated the level of worker rather than demonstrated needs, i.e., default and economics, rather than design, have been the rationale for staffing pattern. No other profession that we know of has lowered its entry level to professional status. Rather, the trend has been toward specialization and higher educational requirements. Wherever paraprofessionals have entered the various fields, they have become assistants or aide-de-camps within the profession rather than securing professional status. Note the nursing assistant, physician assistant, and pharmacist assistant with their prescribed task determinants. At Mount Sinai Medical Center, our paraprofessionals are social health advocates and social work assistants; each group has separate definitions of tasks and in-training programs, under the direction of an MSW.

We want to comment on the status of the art of clinical practice. There are no established norms, standards, and criteria for practice. There is also question as to whether clinical practice by social workers is governed by a single theory of behavior. In the few attempts made to study practice outcomes, we see a range of theoretical principles governing the practice and yet comparable outcomes are noted among them; moreover, major differences result from the same governing principles. Things happen as a result of our practice, some results are good and some are not, and we don't know why. It is true when we examine practice we can discern good from bad (Chernesky & Lurie, 1976), yet the better practice does not always result from a specialized clinical education. Most frequently, we see "good" resulting from experience, rather than from two years of graduate social work education.

It has been suggested that ego psychology is the behavioral science to which social work should subscribe. Psychoanalytic theory, and particularly the techniques derived from that theory, provide only a small part of the knowledge necessary to do effective work, in limited periods of time, with people in states of crisis, some of whom have not asked for social work services. People who have entered settings dealing with illness do not translate their physical pains into social-psychological terms. When social workers "find" their clients, they must "market" their services, which frequently requires translating physical dysfunctioning into social functioning objectives. These social workers are rarely at the desk awaiting a client crossing a threshold, and identifying a presenting problem for professional intervention. They are most often "casefinding," developing motivation and translating their resources into achievable contracts acceptable to both client and worker. Too frequently, in social work we find a narrowly perceived clinical practice, in which overconcern with relationship and process is evident, with less interest in the client's perception of the problem-at-hand and in a shared agreement of goal. When emphasis is more on relationship than on contract we find marked differences in outcomes (Reid & Epstein, 1972; Pincus & Minahan, 1973). At Mount Sinai Medical Center when the professional stance moved to contracting, our success rate, along with client and worker satisfaction, increased (Berkman & Rehr, 1977).

Clinical social workers in health care settings also need to be taught crisis theory, social systems theory, social-ecological perspectives, and the skilled use of environmental resources, particularly useful for discharge planning and for social-health maintenance of the sick. The principles derived from such multiple perspectives allow the worker to bring to bear those pieces of theory and practice which are most relevant to the client-in-his-situation. The situation always involves other treating professionals, in order to integrate the medical and social treatment perspectives. Collaborative relationships specify the goals of care, while involving the client system in the decision-making.

According to Reid and Epstein (1972), "It is clear that no one theory of practice or series of techniques answers all needs of practicing social workers. We therefore ascribe to the idea that the social worker should "take on" a position of theoretical pluralism that enables him to utilize whatever formal theories are relevant to his purposes" (p. 30). While psychoanalytic theory has contributed much to our understanding of human behavior it is neither easily testable nor always useful in treating clients in health care settings. As a theory of human behavior, psychoanalytic theory has much to offer. As a theory which contributes to the total explanation of human behavior it leaves much to be desired. Theories of complex organizations and of social systems which address (1) the interplay among the individual, the family, the group, and their observable behaviors in sequences and hierarchies; (2) the effects of social institutions on individuals; (3) problem formulation and resolution; and (4) the effects of illness on the social contexts of the patient, need to be added to the curriculum for the social worker. In addition, the separation of theory from technique is crucial in creative social work practice. There is no one theory of human behavior any more than there is one derivative technique.

Richard Cabot (1915), in his most perceptive treatise on social work in health care settings, suggested that social work must practice within its own autonomy, separate from the medical profession. He further suggested that social work creates social programs geared to social-health maintenance. Others have continued to stress the psychosocial context of treatment in health care social work (Cannon, 1923; Bartlett, 1961; Doremus, 1976). Social work effectiveness in health care has been demonstrated in both medical and psychiatric settings by several studies (Clark, 1969; Berkman & Rehr, 1972; Weissman, 1974; Hogarty, 1974). This infusion of new knowledge to the heritage and tradition mentioned above contributes to the development of a core of social work practice in health care.

RELATIONSHIP BETWEEN PRACTICE AND EDUCATION

Schools of social work in general have failed to enhance the profession's contribution to the health care field. Both undergraduate and master's degree programs are deficient in content related to the health field and few students take advantage of supplementary courses in other professional schools (Bracht, 1974). We agree that "there is an urgent need to come to grips with the fact that the complexity of the health care system requires some added preparation at some point in the educational continuum, whether this is before or after completion of basic professional education" (Kahn, 1974, p. 76).

We believe it is premature to come to closure on the issue of specialization in clinical social work or specialization in health care in the curriculum. Whatever the specialization on the MSW level, further training will be needed for the social worker in health care. We would encourage a multi-model approach with evaluation of the results. A main issue impeding creative education is the relationship between practice and classroom teaching (Lurie, King, & Pinsky, 1977). We suggest firstly that a principle calling for joint deliberations and joint decision-making on all issues relevant to the common goal be accepted by practice and education. The implementation of this principle could be activated through any and every means, program, structure, and system as agreed to by both areas.

Educators in social work are usually professionals with little current practice orientation. Also, practitioners are not always realistic in their expectations of the educational process. There has been very little opportunity for quality practitioners to sit with quality educators to work out their differences and their agreements, and to design a curriculum integrating academic and practice areas.

We expect that a social work (MSW) graduate will bring a beginning expertise in entry skills, assessment of individuals and families, an understanding of the need for collaborative practice in the multi-disciplinary health setting, and skills in contracting and in interventions with individuals and the key social systems which affect them (i.e., families, hospital teams, etc.). We also expect that they will understand the need to frame their assessments in terms of problems which can be conceptualized in such a way as to lead to resolution (Watzlawick, Weakland, & Fisch, 1974; Haley, 1976).

We do not expect the new graduate to be aware of illness-specific knowledge, i.e., sexual dysfunction in end-stage renal disease. Nor do we expect that the recent graduate will be adept at clinical interventions in individual families and groups on the same level or with the same creative effort as an experienced practitioner.

It is evident to us that the new graduate falls short in the clinical arena of practice, particularly in assessment skills. Our evidence for believing that recent graduates are "less well trained" in assessments and intervention is the increased need for continuing education during the first 2–3 years post-master's. While a small amount of this increase may be due to a knowledge proliferation in the field, the rest is due to less emphasis on quality clinical practice skills on the master's level of education. Intra-professional and multi-professional leadership and collaborative skills are also lacking in the educational preparation of the new MSW graduate. In health care the MSW is asked to provide leadership to social work teams (MSW, BSW, assistants, advocates, etc.) as well as to provide leadership in multi-professional staff efforts. Social work education neglects these areas and concentrates on "solo" practice within a social agency framework.

Those of us in the field are appalled at the impact on our budgets of trying to ready the beginning MSW for a quality practice relevant to the client's needs in the context of the health care setting. A post-graduate "apprenticeship" of two to three years is a conservative estimate of what is needed, and is comparable to an internship or residency in medical education.

We have suggested elsewhere that local agencies of like purpose, or those in relationship to a given school, and which are so inclined, join in a combine or consortium for the purpose of developing an effective partnership with the given school. The implementing structure would allow for joint deliberation and joint decision-making by:

—giving practice representation in curriculum development, and in educational goal determination;

—making available a reservoir of resources in the field where innovative programs are underway, or where new ideas could be tested by bringing the school into the field beyond the immediate student need;

—making available the opportunity to teach appropriate concepts and theory in the appropriate locus, i.e., to broaden the concept of the campus to include the agency setting;

—making available a wider range of agency programs and activities including a range of processes and functions as learning opportunities;

—offering continuing educational opportunities developed in joint deliberations;

—permitting an exchange of staff between school and practice, on lend-lease sabbatical or planned arrangement on agreed-to objectives, to teach a session, a course, staff development etc., and allowing for valid financial and university and agency support mechanisms;

—developing a set of guidelines and expectations for experiential learning, shared with students, and made a conscious component of curriculum;

—developing standards for instructional centers and instructors, with recognition through awards of faculty rank;

—making research principles and methodology a conscious process by:

(a) the joint development of measurements for the effectiveness of education;

(b) the joint development of assessment methods of social services, their utilization patterns, their allocation, their effectiveness, their quality, and their cost allocation, with particular emphasis on professional accountability;

(c) the joint development of assessment methods of utilization of differential manpower;

(d) the joint development of studies to enhance knowledge and skills;

—making overt the costs of all aspects of the educational expectations, and jointly seeking the support mechanism;
—making available to lay groups the understanding and the knowledge relevant to achieving the common goal and to enlist appropriate lay representation in the deliberations.

None of these can effectively occur until the accrediting body for social work, The Council on Social Work Education, gives practice fair representation in its governing body and in the membership of the Delegate Assembly. We would suggest finally that the CSWE and the NASW jointly develop and sponsor regional conferences and workshops, including representation from practice and education, to deal with the issues identified. The assumption of the regional design is that it tends to have a logical relationship to issues indigenous to the area, that the working parties have the advantage of knowing each other, that the resources are known, and that the financial supports may be found in unison in the area.

We at the Mount Sinai Medical Center have entered into a first step in the design of a consortium to include the six social work departments in the Center Complex and the Hunter School of Social Work, City University of New York. The social work representatives of the six departments are faculty members in the Division of Social Work, Department of Community Medicine, Mount Sinai School of Medicine, City University of New York. The project is supported by the Mount Sinai Auxiliary Board and the Hunter School of Social Work. Its intent is to project a consortium of the departments in the Medical Center Complex and School, wherein joint deliberation and decision-making in the use of the combined resources of practice and school will prevail. In addition, at the present time, the Hunter School of Social Work has in process a Health Care Module developing curriculum for the field and for the classroom by representatives from its health agencies and from the school faculty. It is a major step in joint deliberation in curriculum development involving field and school. New projects involving Hunter and the Medical Center agencies have been planned in concert, and submitted for funding to granting agencies under mutually agreed terms.

We believe that opportunities such as those suggested will bring the two components of the profession, practice and education, into an open recognition of their joint responsibility. While this would require fundamental relearning and redefining of the roles and responsibilities of both practice and education, it would ultimately integrate the investments of both in the field of social work.

REFERENCES

Bartlett, H. *Social work practice in the health field*. New York: National Association of Social Workers, 1961.

Berkman, B., & Rehr, H. The "sick-role" cycle and the timing of social work intervention. *The Social Service Review*, 1972, *46*(4), 567–580.

Berkman, B., & Rehr, H. *Social work undertakes its own audit*. Unpublished mss., 1977.

Bracht, N. N. Health care: The largest human service system. *Social Work*, 1974, *19*(5), 532–543.

Cabot, R. *Social service and the art of healing*. New York: Moffat, Yard and Co., 1915.

Cannon, I. *Social work in hospitals*. New York: Russell Sage Foundation, 1923.

Chernesky, R., & Lurie, A. Developing a quality assurance program. *Health and Social Work*, 1976, *1*(1), 117–130.

Clark, E. Post-hospital care for chronically ill elderly patients. *Social Work*, 1969, *14*(1), 62–67.

Doremus, B. The four R's: Social diagnosis in health care. *Health and Social Work*, 1976, *1*(4), 120–137.

Haley, J. *Problem-solving therapy*. San Francisco: Jossey-Bass, 1976.

Hogarty, G. E., Goldberg, S. C., & Schooler, N. R. Drug & sociotherapy in the aftercare of schizophrenic patients, III, Adjustment of nonrelapsed patients. *Archives of General Psychiatry*, 1974, *31*, 609–618.

Kahn, E. Social service in health care. In F. P. Perlmutter, (Ed.), *A design for social work practice*. New York: Columbia University Press, 1974.

Lurie, A., King, M., & Pinsky, S. Social work education and practice. In A. Lurie and G. Rosenberg (Eds.), *Social work in mental health: A 25-year perspective*. New York: Long Island Jewish Hillside Medical Center, 1977.

Meyer, C. Direct service in new and old contexts. In A. Kahn, (Ed.), *Shaping the new social work*. New York: Columbia University Press, 1973.

Pincus, A., & Minahan, A. *Social work practice model and method*. Illinois: Peacock Publishers, 1973.

Reid, W. J., & Epstein, L. *Task centered casework*. New York: Columbia University Press, 1972.

Walzlawick, P., Weakland, J., & Fisch, R. *Change: Principles of problem formulation and problem resolution*. New York: W. W. Norton, 1974.

Weissman, M. M., Klerman, G. L., Prusoff, B. A., *et al*. Treatment effects on the social adjustment of depressed outpatients. *Archives of General Psychiatry*, 1974, *30*, 771–778.

Chapter 9

The Drift Toward Entrepreneurialism in Health and Social Welfare: Implications for Social Work Education

Kurt Reichert, PhD

ABSTRACT. Entrepreneurialism has penetrated the health care system and is increasingly manifest in social welfare in government purchase of service from voluntary agencies, in beginning competition of proprietary firms for welfare contracts, and in the spread of fee-for-service private practice. These trends, rarely discussed in a broad context, are likely to have major consequences for the future of voluntarism, for the struggle toward a comprehensive social service system, and for the values and ethics of the social work profession. Social work education should address these developments, and there is urgent need for research and broad debate.

For many years private enterprise and social welfare ideologies have coexisted in America. From the New Deal to the Great Society the federal government appeared to foster a gradual extension of services outside the market sector. Since then the balance seems to be shifting toward entrepreneurialism in ideology and in the operations of the health care and welfare systems. As Kahn points out, "Who would have predicted in 1960 that a society with increasing welfare commitments would, a decade later, be giving major attention to market models?"[1]

Most visible and most frequently reported are the private enterprise components of the health field, including the traditional entrepreneurial fee-for-service medical practice—sometimes referred to as a cottage industry—and the increasingly powerful corporate operations in insurance, drugs, construction, technical equipment, management services, and nursing home chains. Exclusive of health insurance and fee-for-service private practice, the profit-making component of United States health expenditures was 35.5 percent in 1975.[2] Major trends are increased concentration of health-related corporations; diversification of "product lines," including a recent thrust toward business operation of home health services; entry of nonhealth companies into the health field; and the growing importance of international markets.[3]

In social welfare entrepreneurial private practice has existed on a minor scale for many years, was officially sanctioned by the National Association of Social Workers (NASW) in 1964,[4] and currently involves an estimated 8,500-10,000 social workers in full- or part-time private practice.[5] The extent to which proprietary firms have entered social welfare is difficult to estimate. In some states and localities substantial inroads have been made in areas such as homemaker services, day care, rehabilitation,[6] and in institutional services for children and for the elderly. The significance here does not lie in the current number of business enterprises in social welfare but in the direction of social policy with respect to "contracting out" by government agencies. Government contracts for training, research, and demonstration have been in existence for many years. In 1964 the Economic Opportunities Act opened wide the scope of contracting for services with established and newly created agencies,[7] and the momentum toward contracting sharply increased with the decentralization of federal services under the New Federalism. Contracting out for services became acceptable practice in General Revenue Sharing (1972), in the block grants to localities under the Comprehensive Employment Training Act (1973), the Housing and Community Development Act (1974) and Title XX of the Social Security Act (1974),[8] and in many other federal programs.

Some of the literature on the pros and cons of purchase of service makes no reference to proprietary firms in social welfare. There seems to be an implied assumption that contracts would be confined to the established array of voluntary agencies.[9] However, in a searching review of purchase of service John Wedemeyer pointed out several years ago that it is "deceptively simple to fall into the trap of discussing the matter generally in the light of existing programmatic or public and private establishment structure."[10] In fact, the way is wide open for increased business operations in social welfare. As expressed by the president of Unicare Health Services, "Whenever the opportunity exists for free enterprise to operate, the private sector of the economy will mobilize its management expertise, bringing to bear the tools and knowledge previously developed in industry and elsewhere."[11] Skeptics should study developments in the health industry, or read "The Case of Proprietary Interests in Child Care" by the vice-president of the Clinicare Corporation,[12] or take note of a recent example in the author's home community, San Diego, where six out of seven bids for a homemaker services contract were made by business firms, several operating on a regional or national basis.

These and related developments of fundamental importance to social work are receiving scant attention in the social work literature. They tend to be discussed in separate rubrics, for example, in articles on private practice[13] or purchase of service,[14] and with little reference to the health field which has much comparable experience. In fact, with respect to entrepreneurial modes of service delivery we seem to be separating health and welfare into discrete worlds. Note the sharp discrepancy between strenuous NASW efforts to promote fee-for-service private practice in social work[15] and the strong NASW social policy position calling for replacement of the fee-for-service system in medicine by a "more rational, organized and efficient system of health care delivery."[16]

The drift toward entrepreneurialism probably was reinforced by the Nixon administration's general reliance on private enterprise, by the economic recession, and by the diminished governmental and voluntary support for social welfare relative to need and relative to available agency and manpower resources in the field. Business needs new markets, voluntary agencies rely heavily on purchase of service to stay alive, and individual social workers, confronted with retrenchments in agency employment, see private practice with or without third-party payments as an avenue for professional work. The explanations and justification by those directly involved are not as blunt. Business firms lean to various efficiency arguments, including economy of size, and, not unexpectedly, mention commitment to growth.[17] A guardedly worded listing of possible benefits of purchase of service from a voluntary agency standpoint includes elements such as improved opportunity for consumer choice, improved flexibility, improved management practice, encouragement of business investment in facilities, relief of government from day-to-day delivery operations resulting in greater freedom to engage in social planning.[18] Some spokesmen for private practice in social work cite existence of a market, superiority of private practice over agency practice as a service delivery mechanism (by permitting greater client autonomy and improved access to clinical social work), therapist and client freedom from bureaucratic constraints, improved therapist income, and improved prestige.[19] These varying explanations by providers require rigorous evaluation and research. As for theory to explain what may be occurring, the drift to entrepreneurialism gives credence to the radical viewpoint which holds that social welfare agencies enhance capitalist institutions,[20] a notion consistent with the view that "the most obvious function of the American health system, other than patient care, is profit making. . . . When it comes to making money the health industry is an extraordinarily well organized and efficient machine."[21]

Whatever historical or theoretical explanation one may lean to, there is much impressionistic evidence regarding possible consequences of the drift to entrepreneurialism, which should be explored before considering implications for social work education. I shall comment in a preliminary way on possible consequences for the future of voluntary agencies, for the development of comprehensive social service systems, and for the social values and ethics of the profession.

POSSIBLE CONSEQUENCES FOR VOLUNTARY AGENCIES

Even without competition from private entrepreneurs, purchase of service involves fundamental changes for voluntary agencies. "The term 'purchase' implies a market situation in which there is a buyer and seller."[22] "Prospective purchasers and suppliers must be prepared to deal in specifications, sophisticated costing techniques, and efforts to apply techniques of cost-benefit or productivity and product analysis."[23] "At contract renewal time the agencies selling services with the lesser benefits may not have their contracts renewed."[24] What this means is that the voluntary agency must engage in various forms of entrepreneurial behavior, may become increasingly dependent on government, may lose its freedom in social action or advocacy.[25]

Enter the proprietary agency, with superior cash flow capabilities and business know-how, not legitimated or supported by national standard-setting social welfare organizations, prepared to sell services packages with lowered standards and with appeal for cost-conscious decision makers. What may occur was recently exemplified in San Diego when the County Board of Supervisors awarded a day-care center contract to a proprietary firm that could make a low bid by minimizing the child development aspects of the program. When this kind of competition becomes more frequent, some voluntary agencies may be impelled to move further in the direction of proprietary agency practices and mentality, as has occurred in many parts of the health field. As an illustration, a well-known seminar for hospital executives recently announced that participants will "assess probable impact of a competitor's actions, evaluate future market potential for hospital services . . . learn how to anticipate and program for challenges by health planning bodies, analyze an action plan for maximizing their institution's influence over regulatory bodies."[26] In this kind of climate it will be difficult to salvage the best features of voluntarism in social welfare.

POSSIBLE CONSEQUENCES FOR THE DEVELOPMENT OF COMPREHENSIVE SOCIAL SERVICE SYSTEMS

Common to most proposals for the future of social welfare are broad goals for moving from the current fragmentation of services to a more coherent system, from residual to institutional conceptions of social welfare, from treatment toward prevention, from institutional racism, neglect of the poor, and other inequities toward a concern with the quality of life for all.[27] The struggle toward realization of such goals requires new forms of cooperation, greater reliance on comprehensive planning, and willingness to transcend special interests, to change systems, and to alter methodologies. Yet the ideology of entrepreneurialism emphasizes the notion that the individual decisions reached by consumers and producers will be the best decisions for the entire society. This tends to absolve entrepreneurs in the human services from examining whether and how their particular kind of effort directed at selected populations builds toward realization of more effective communitywide human service systems. For example, whatever the quality of practice by private social work practitioners with selected clienteles, the assertion that this is a superior form of service delivery[28] does not necessarily make it so for the general population any more than it has in the private practice of medicine. Any human service offered in isolation denies the reality of interdependent needs in the larger social scene.

With respect to service organizations, whether voluntary agencies or proprietary firms, entrepreneurialism accents the development of larger centralized, powerful multiservice complexes for special populations.[29] In health, for example, the most frequent type and most powerful complexes center around general hospitals and may include components such as a progressive patient care center, diagnostic and treatment center, outpatient clinics, and home care services.[30] In social welfare, multiservice complexes designed to provide more comprehensive services to a selected clientele have been developed for some time, for example, around children's institutions and homes for the elderly. The purchase of service system encourages agencies and commercial firms under strong central administration to diversify or to piece together a program from various granting sources. To be successful in the grantsmanship game, it is necessary to be prepared to get "a piece of the action" by having a drawer full of proposals ready. The immediate motives for aggregating programs into complexes range anywhere from a desire to improve services to agency survival assurance to profit maximization. The pervading overall consequence is likely to be a lessening motivation or ability to gear the organization's services to reconstruction of the overall system. Kahn alludes to this when he points out that "advocates of the market would underplay coordination and encourage competition. They do not seek to construct networks."[31] Networks that require give-and-take are threats to the continued growth of the individual entrepreneur.

According to entrepreneurial ideology, the client is the ultimate regulator of the system by his choice among alternative sources and modes of service. In actuality, he has very little freedom, as has been amply demonstrated in the health field.[32] The freedom of choice is more that of the vendor, whether private practitioner, a single function agency, or service complex. Note Piliavin's comment that private practitioners in social work could specialize in serving specific ethnic or religious groups "if they wished."[33] But the vendor's freedom is also illusory in a market in which the government has to foot the major part of the bill or insurance companies seek to maximize their profits. The stronger the forces of entrepreneurialism, the stronger, more complex, and more onerous will have to be the regulatory machinery of government which must try to bring some order out of the chaos, check abuses, and hold down costs. Since the enormous overt and hidden overhead inherent in government-regulated entrepreneurialism cannot be substantially reduced, the government's quest for cost-effectiveness, as that of the insurance companies, is bound to be focused on the services themselves. Thus the accountability industry—rapidly becoming a lucrative enterprise competing for government and insurance contracts—is likely to emphasize "hard" rather than "soft" services, short-term rather than long-term results, treatment of specific individuals rather than preventive efforts involving outreach to vulnerable populations,[34] enhancement of economic independence rather than what Kahn calls the developmental, socialization, and enrichment missions of the social services.[35] Finally, when regulation becomes the major theme of government-provider relationships, the result can be corrupt government-vendor alliances or chronic antipathy between government and vendors.[36] Both responses have greatly impeded comprehensive planning efforts in the health field. Under these and the previously mentioned circumstances, it will require protracted struggles to move toward the realization of broad social goals through reformation of the planning and delivery systems.

POSSIBLE CONSEQUENCES FOR SOCIAL VALUES AND ETHICS

Profound studies are not needed to ascertain that the values of some entrepreneurs in health and social welfare are not consistent with the interests of the people served. The daily papers have been full of reports of substantial fraud and abuse in Medicare, Medicaid, nursing homes, and other health programs, and more recently this has spread to commercial welfare programs such as daycare centers.[37] It is possible, of course, to ascribe this to human nature and to cite examples of abuses under nonprofit conditions such as in public mental hospitals. The problem, however, deserves more rigorous examination. A few years ago, the great social policy pioneer Richard Titmuss in a comprehensive study compared voluntary and commercial blood donation systems and demonstrated convincingly that commercialization of blood and donor relationships represses the expression of altruism and erodes the sense of community.[38] Titmuss's findings support the view that fraud and abuse are merely the tip of the iceberg and that the entrepreneurial system gives license to self-interest to a degree difficult to reconcile with the social values of human service.

For professionals, this kind of climate reinforces individualistic values and de-emphasizes the need for reconciling individualism with the common good. It is not to impugn the ethics of private practitioners of social work to reflect on the connection between concerns with freedom for their clients and themselves, concerns with improved income and prestige, and the fact that accountability to the community is placed below accountability to the client and the profession.[39] As Kurzman points out in his rebuttal to Levin's article on private practice, "Any attempt to separate private troubles from public issues cuts off each from the reinforcing power of the other."[40] Further, it would be presumptuous to assume that social workers are immune from the kind of ethically questionable practices in which some physicians are engaged. Some social workers contracting with nursing homes are providing no more than paper consultation, some are contracting for services in areas in which they are clearly incompetent, some seek private patients able to help them with investments, some are involved in paper nonprofit enterprises fronting for commercial operations. There is not much doubt that at this time the NASW is prepared to police unethical behavior of social workers; but is social work immune from letting its professional organization turn into a carbon copy of what David Mechanic succinctly calls the "tight knit and self-protective medical guild"?[41]

IMPLICATIONS FOR SOCIAL WORK EDUCATION

The foregoing review of possible consequences of entrepreneurialism was intended as an alert and not as an analysis of social policy alternatives. Such an analysis would have to include examination of possible benefits of entrepreneurialism and realistic strategies for accommodations with what in the foreseeable future may be irreversible trends. Enough has been said, however, to suggest that this topic deserves far greater attention than it appears to have received to date.

It is not clear how social work education now deals with this subject. Changes in national ideology and policy may receive some attention in social policy courses, but their implications for practice and for the overall outlook for practitioners and of the profession probably are addressed in a fragmented manner if at all. Although I am deeply concerned about the drift to entrepreneurialism, I am not suggesting that students be indoctrinated against entering private practice or profit-making agencies. But neither can social work education by design or by default permit convenient rationalizations. If one were to express the desirable educational objectives in a single statement, it might be something like this: Keen awareness of how the form and content of the individual social worker's practice under various arrangements and in various settings reflects and defines social policy, and a sense of accountability for populations not served or ill served equal to that for the clients served directly. With this base, if the future generation of social workers—our current students—decide to move social welfare further into the entrepreneurial arena, so be it. To the extent that they make the move without comprehending its implications, this generation of social work educators must share the burden for their lack of awareness.

Translated into curriculum terms, the issue of entrepreneurialism is not a separate subject matter to be grafted on an existing course. Rather, it has a bearing on the entire curriculum, highlighting once again the traditional problem of reconciling social change and direct service elements in the educational programs. The following specific approaches might be considered:

1. Students should be helped to develop historical and cross-national perspectives on the ways in which political, economic, and social forces affect not only broad social policies but also social work's social objectives, practice, and professional organization and strategies. Entrepreneurialism in the human services can no longer be left out as it is in some of the social policy literature in social work,[42] in contrast to the health policy literature. Neither is it sufficient to treat this only in terms of radical theory without realistic action options.

2. Students should be sensitized to value and ideological issues and be stimulated to address these in depth and in relationship to understanding social and psychological phenomena. For example, what are the relationships between self-interest and social obligations? What are the relationships between social work practice and distributive justice? In what respects may pluralism in service delivery design be viewed as a significant social value, and under what circumstances can it become an ideological screen? Is profit-making necessarily antithetical to service? What dilemmas are posed by simultaneous rejection of hierarchical aspects of the "medical model" and acceptance of its fee-for-service aspects? What bearing does market ideology have on the relationship between social workers' direct service and social change functions? Students need to learn that questions of this kind cannot be dodged, that they have to be viewed from various perspectives, that the process of lifelong learning in social work includes not only acquisition of cognitive knowledge and practice skills but a continuing alertness to social value questions.

3. Related to both of the foregoing is the student's understanding of social policy issues, particularly the often neglected issues related to the

design of comprehensive service delivery systems. What are short-term and long-range social policy options? Assuming that the penetration of the human service arena by entrepreneurialism cannot be wished away, in what ways might it be worked with? Contained? Opposed? What can be learned from the history of compromises with entrepreneurialism in the health field, such as the early efforts to allocate the territory of treatment to private practice and the territory of prevention to government, or the trade-offs embodied in Medicare or in health maintenance organizations? What are the implications of market ideology for disadvantaged populations? What are the advantages and disadvantages of market incentives for providers and consumers? What issues arise in the subsidization of voluntarism? Can entrepreneurial development of services and comprehensive planning be reconciled? How do current trends toward entrepreneurialism affect the integration of health and social welfare services? What should be the elements of a comprehensive service delivery system on the local level?

4. Social workers today require added competences which should be developed in the context of value considerations mentioned above. It is no longer tenable to teach outside of this context, for example, by offering grant writing as no more than a technical subject. Social work educators need to address the extent to which added competence dimensions such as the following should be included in the academic program and in continuing education: how to assess short-term and long-range social policy implications of one's practice; how to relate to new third-party accountability requirements and utilize research skills in a way that will enhance quality and be consistent with social objectives; how to capitalize on the entrepreneurial climate by taking a more independent stance on the job and by maximizing the system's utilization of social work services; how to develop grant applications in a way that helps to create viable new service patterns reproducible for larger populations; how to move into positions in the human services not reserved for individuals with a social work background in ways that enhance social values.

CONCLUSION

In summary and conclusion, a comment on the origin, limitations, and purpose of this paper. Some time ago, jolted by events reflecting a drift toward entrepreneurialism in social welfare, I found colleagues in practice and education who shared similar concerns. It became gradually apparent that isolated aspects of this development needed to be viewed in a broad context. A preliminary review of the literature suggested that the topic was not being given prominence in keeping with its implications for practice and education. I decided against an exhaustive study or rigorous testing of educational ideas before attempting a presentation. Instead, this paper is intended to transmit my deep concern and to urge research, reflection, and broad debate as well as curriculum experimentation in an area with profound implications for the future of social welfare and social work.

REFERENCES

1. Alfred J. Kahn, *Social Policy and Social Services* (New York: Random House, 1973), p. 148.

2. Gelvin Stevenson, "Profits in Medicine," *Health Policy Advisory Center Bulletin* 72 (September-October 1976):3.

3. Ibid., p. 17.

4. Margaret A. Golton, "Private Practice in Social Work," in *Encyclopedia of Social Work* (Washington, D.C.: National Association of Social Workers, 1971), p. 950.

5. Chauncey Alexander, *Testimony to Subcommittee on Comprehensive Coverage* (New York: Health Insurance Association of America, 1976).

6. John Wedemeyer, "Government Agencies and the Purchase of Service," in *Purchase of Care and Services in the Health and Welfare Fields* (Proceedings of the First Milwaukee Institute on a Social Welfare Issue of the Day, conducted by the University of Wisconsin-Milwaukee School of Social Welfare, 1970), p. 18.

7. Elizabeth Wickenden, "Purchase of Care and Services: Effect on Voluntary Agencies," in *Purchase of Care and Services in the Health and Welfare Fields*, p. 43.

8. Paul Terrell, "The New Federalism and Human Services: Implications for State and Local Planning and Management," mimeographed (Paper prepared for the Workshop for the Accountability and Evaluation of Social Services under P.L. 93–674, Long Beach, University of Southern California, April 27–30, 1975), pp. 3–7.

9. See, for example, Ralph M. Kramer, "Voluntary Agencies and the Use of Public Funds: Some Policy Issues," *Social Service Review* 60 (March 1966):15–26; Kenneth R. Wedel, "Government Contracting for Purchase of Service," *Social Work* 21 (March 1976):101–5.

10. Wedemeyer, "Government Agencies," p. 4.

11. Joseph Zilber, "The Case for Proprietary Interests in Health Care Delivery," in *Purchase of Care and Services in the Health and Welfare Fields*, p. 64.

12. Kent T. Wakefield, "The Case of Proprietary Interests in Child Care," in *Purchase of Care and Services in the Health and Welfare Fields*, pp. 67–71.

13. See, for example, Irving Piliavin, "Restructuring the Provision of Services," *Social Work* 13 (January 1968):34–41; Arnold M. Levin, "Private Practice Is Alive and Well," *Social Work* 21 (September 1976):356–62; Paul A. Kurzman, "Private Practice as a Social Work Function," *Social Work* 21 (September 1976):363–68.

14. See, for example, Kramer, "Voluntary Agencies"; Wedel, "Government Contracting."

15. For a summary of NASW activities with respect to practice, see Kurzman, "Private Practice," p. 366.

16. National Association of Social Workers, "Health Care," in *Public Social Policy Statements Currently in Effect* (Washington, D.C., 1975), p. 3.

17. Wakefield, "Case of Proprietary Interests," pp. 69, 70.

18. Wedemeyer, "Government Agencies," p. 17.

19. Piliavin, "Restructuring the Provision of Services"; Levin, "Private Practice."

20. Richard A. Cloward and Frances F. Piven, "The Acquiescence of Social Work," *Society* 14 (January–February 1977):55–63.

21. Barbara Ehrenreich and John Ehrenreich, *The American Health Empire: Power, Profits, and Politics* (New York: Vintage Books, 1971), p. 22.

Chapter 10

Social Work Supervision: A View Toward Leadership Style and Job Orientation in Education and Practice

Neil A. Cohen, PhD
Gary B. Rhodes, MSW

ABSTRACT. Orientations to leadership and to job are integrally related to contemporary issues in social work supervision concerning the delineation of supervisory functions and their contributions to the efficiency and effectiveness of service delivery. Data collected from supervisors in workshops and students entering a graduate school of social work regarding their orientations provide initial support for an approach to teaching and training for supervisory practice that incorporates relevant aspects of leadership and job orientations. The proposed approach, which focuses on 12 activities and tasks as essential components of effective supervision, clearly emphasizes concern for task, people, and competitive job orientation in the practice of social work supervision.

As supervision moves from its preoccupation with regulatory concerns to increased emphasis on enabling, leading, and resource development functions, the need for schools of social work to provide management training and education becomes imperative. Frequently, educational and training programs are designed by educators or staff development personnel based on assumptions about what constitutes effective practice, but with little knowledge of the attitudes and skills of the potential participants. In a profession, such as social work, where values and orientations are critical to practice behaviors, it is opportune to begin linking the structure and content of social work education and training programs with attitudes and practice orientations.

This paper presents the findings of a research study of supervisors in continuing education workshops and of beginning students in a social work master's degree program concerning their orientations to leadership style and to the job. The data are examined from the perspective of relevance to supervisory practices, education, and training.

MAJOR THEMES IN LITERATURE

Much of the literature on social work supervision has described a somewhat ethereal balance between the administrative and teaching functions (Miller, 1971, pp. 1494–1501). Little attention has been devoted to issues of leadership style, preparation and interest in supervision, or the orientation of social work supervisors to work and the job. More in-depth examination of these issues suggests that social workers are often thrust into supervisory positions because of organizational need, or the individuals' desire for more pay, or both.

Given that few supervisors have made a conscious choice to become managers (or even think of themselves as managers) and that few have had the benefits of formal or informal training, it can be assumed that few practicing supervisors and few potential supervisors have had the opportunity to examine systematically their orientations to either leadership or to work and the job.

Issues in Education and Training for Practice

Educational challenges have been numerous during the emergence of social work as a profession. Although much energy has been directed toward education for direct service, education for administration and supervision has received somewhat less persistent, directed critical attention. Currently, those involved in education and training for practice in social work administration and supervision are aware of the challenges of accountability both in efficiency and effectiveness terms. Moreover, this area of social work practice has been singled out by some as a major arena for development in the 1980s (Briar, 1974; Gruber, 1974; Turem, 1974).

At this time in the history of the profession, we can identify critical issues that have been with us in the past and whose themes linger on, as a baseline for assessing where we are and where we need to be going in graduate education, staff development, and continuing education for supervisory practice. There is general agreement that social work supervision as an organizational process is a combination of administrative and teaching functions with some additional concern for the supportive function (Kadushin, 1976). Beyond this, however, there is great divergence regarding the relative amount of emphasis to be given each role dimension. The traditional view of supervision emphasized the educational dimension defined specifically as promoting professionalism through clinical consultation and ego enhancement of workers subordinate to the supervisor (Miller, 1971). Within this tradition, the supervisor is perceived to be a super caseworker and not a middle manager. To bring more emphasis to the latter role will require definition of supervisory functions in terms of case management, managing the personal and interpersonal aspects of work, fostering client-worker-agency interdependence, and leadership techniques for upgrading the knowledge and skills of supervisees.

Another issue centers around supervision as a set of specialized skills contrasted with supervision as a representation of the "complete social worker" in the direct service arena. Educators would tend to support the former, but the reality of agency practice supports the latter (Middleman & Goldberg, 1974, pp. 153–181). The dilemma is that experience alone in the direct services is no guarantee that skills required to discharge supervisory functions effectively have been learned and/or developed.

Finally, there is the issue of one's value system and its expression in actual practice behavior. Inevitably the value base of social work distinguishes it as a profession and establishes, in principle, the vital contributions social work can make to the society. The issue, however, is the role of the supervisor in reinforcing and protecting the value system through modeling behavior rather than simply verbalizing the values that should be reflected in practice. Creative methods for resolution of this dilemma have not been forthcoming. Additionally, Perlmutter (1972, pp. 1–17), in her cogent analysis of the historical development of supervisory practice, has concluded that supervision frequently encourages and perpetuates dependence among workers while aiming to facilitate a growing independence of the clients.

Regardless of the position one takes on these issues, there can be little doubt as to the pivotal role of supervisors in social service agencies. For most workers, their supervisor is an extremely important influence. The supervisor influences how employees view their agency, how they perceive their role as employees, and how effective they are at their work (Goldstein & Sorcher, 1974; Likert, 1961). Blau and Scott (1962) concluded from their analysis of two public agencies that the supervisor is the connecting link between the formal organization and the work group. This notion of "linking" reinforces the critical role that the supervisor as middle manager can play in supporting or impeding the efficiency and effectiveness of workers and acting as an internal force for organizational development and change or organizational stagnation and routinization.

It has been formulated in theory (Argyris, 1970) and supported empirically (Hersey & Blanchard, 1969; Sorcher, Note 1) that workers respond positively to supervision that includes the supervisor (a) treating employees as individuals, (b) trusting them, (c) showing interest in their morale and motivation, (d) rewarding good work and supporting further development in weaker areas, (e) inviting and responding to their opinions on issues facing the group and/or agency, and (f) putting them at ease in interpersonal aspects of task performance.

In essence, a model for effective supervision would include skills in managing the interpersonal aspects of work as well as task performance, which would include both the quality of service delivery and training for skill enhancement.

Leadership Style

Accountability requires concern for both qualitative and quantitative aspects of performance within the context of the organization. Blake and Mouton (1969) have developed a model of organizational excellence that attempts to link theory with practice systematically. Operationally, they developed the Managerial Grid and the Managerial Grid Leadership Questionnaire to assist in linking leadership theory to understanding the behavior of managers in organizations. They contend that every person who is involved in the administration of an organization should examine his/her orientation to leadership as the first step in determining degree of consistency between orientation and actual behavior. More importantly, they see this as prerequisite to increasing one's awareness of the linkages between one's leadership style and organizational excellence.

The Managerial Grid model starts with the premise that any person working in an organization has assigned responsibilities. When these responsibilities are administrative, the person has two major concerns, regardless of whether he/she is consciously aware of them. The first concern is productivity or output, that is, the results of one's efforts and of those for whom one is administratively responsible. How much a manager thinks about results can be described as degree of concern for productivity (task performance and outcomes). Secondly, the manager thinks about fellow workers, superiors, colleagues, or those whose work he/she directs. This represents one's concern for people (the relational aspects of task performance). The relative magnitude of each concern at their interface affects the approaches that the manager uses to get results through people and interactions. Of specific importance is the proposition that the leadership orientation will influence how a manager approaches and implements strategies for integrating individual and organizational interests and needs. The approach and outcome are related to motivation, morale, task performance, and quality of service delivery.

Five major leadership styles are identified by Blake and Mouton and, when linked to management practice, suggest a number of issues that ought to be of concern to those involved in staff development and training, continuing education, or graduate level degree-oriented education for middle-management personnel. The styles represent the four extremes for task/people plus the midpoint. On a grid scale of 1 (low) to 9 (high) for task and people, a manager with a 1,1 orientation is labeled as impoverished, one with a 1,9 orientation is considered a social manager, 9,1 is labeled as a directive management style, 9,9 is a team management approach, and 5,5 is considered middle-of-the-road. Differences have been observed in the practices of managers with these differing orientations in such key areas as communications, decision making, conflict management, evaluation, and staff development.

Job Orientation

A second significant area of orientation in management practice concerns attitudes about work elements that constitute the "job" with which managers and workers are identified. Borgatta and Bohrenstedt (1971), following the tradition of Vroom (1964) and Herzberg, Mausner, and Synderman (1959), developed definitions of two sets of attitudes that seemed to be directly associated with an employee's orientation to the job: work-oriented attitudes and maintenance-oriented attitudes.

Work-oriented attitudes refer to the intrinsic satisfaction of doing a job, desire for personal development, creative activity, and assumption of responsibility. The work-oriented person wants a job that provides opportunity for originality and independence. This individual expects to have flexible hours to deal with changes in assignments and emergencies as they arise, and that evaluation will be based on actual accomplishments. A work-oriented individual is best in situation involving high risk and intense work pressure, and for this reason Borgatta and Bohrenstedt (1971) define this as a "competitiveness" orientation to the job.

Maintenance-oriented attitudes describe an individual's concern for job security and personal comfort (e.g., seniority, promotion schedules, and job routine). Also important are what Herzberg et al. (1959) call "hygienic" aspects of the job, such as lighting, ventilation, and the personality characteristics of supervisors. A maintenance-oriented person is looking for a routine job with guaranteed promotions. He/she expects a comfortable atmosphere on the job and in the surrounding community. There is also an expectation that the agency will have set policies of clearly defined values to which one can adapt one's behavior. "Conservative security" is the label given to this orientation to the job.

In brief, the most useful way to view an individual's job orientation is that it is composed of elements of both dimensions. Each individual can be characterized as tending more toward one orientation than the other. Thus, orientation to the job is not an absolute characteristic but is best defined as a point on a continuum.

Social work educators should be cognizant of the two job orientations and should teach this information as part of preparation of students for supervisory practice. Training and other organizational supports should be supplied to develop payoffs for those who have a commitment to the job, and who seek challenging, creative, and risk-taking assignments. If we are concerned about improving the quality of professional social work practice, we should begin by rewarding an individual's job orientation that most clearly matches the expected performance of a professional: self-directed, creative, responsibility-seeking—in short, competency-based practice.

RESEARCH FINDINGS

The Blake-Mouton Managerial Grid Leadership Questionnaire and the Borgatta-Bohrenstedt Job Orientation Questionnaire were administered in 1975 to 116 students entering a graduate school of social work and to a total of 88 participants in continuing education workshops on supervision. The students came from different regions of the country and brought with them a variety of experience and educational background. The workshop participants were from the mideast and southeast regions of the country and came from a variety of public and private human services organizations. Although they differed in age, experience, social work training, job responsibilities, and fields of service, the workshop participants were unified by their interest in enhancing their supervisory knowledge and skills.

One of the objectives at the workshop was to increase the participants' awareness of their own leadership style and orientation to the job. Both of the questionnaires were used to facilitate this. The newly admitted graduate students were included in the study to determine whether there were any significant differences in orientation to leadership style and job orientation between practitioners involved in supervision and individuals new to professional study. Although much research has been conducted using these instruments separately, to our knowledge no attempt has been made to determine the relationship between leadership style (i.e., task or people) and job orientation (i.e., competitiveness or conservative security) using these particular instruments.

Analysis of the Blake-Mouton Managerial Grid Leadership Questionnaire revealed that both the students and workshop participants expressed a much higher concern for people than they did for productivity. The modal score for the sample (2, task; 7, people) is illustrated in Figure 1. Blake and Mouton describe this profile as that of the Social Manager, a manager whose style is to direct more attention to staff issues and the quality of interpersonal relationships than to issues of productivity and performance.

A supervisor adopting the Social Manager style operates from the perspective that productivity is incidental to good relationships. His/her approach to supervision would be to ensure that harmonious relationships between people are established and that the work atmosphere is secure and pleasant. This individual accepts, uncritically, recommendations from subordinates, avoids conflict if possible, and if not, smoothes it over, and withholds criticism since it might make someone unhappy.

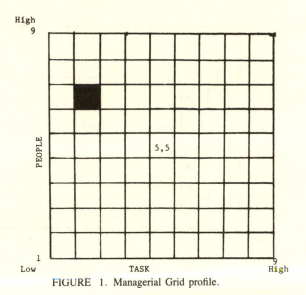

FIGURE 1. Managerial Grid profile.

Data from the Borgatta-Bohrenstedt Job Orientation Questionnaire reveal that the sample scored high on the conservative security orientation and low on the competitiveness orientation (Figure 2). When student and workshop participant scores were compared, it was found that students tended to score slightly lower on both competitiveness and conservative security.

As can be seen from Figure 2, the sample can be described as having primary concern for job security and personal comfort, interest in the job environment, and jobs with guaranteed increments and promotions. Less concern was expressed for jobs that provided opportunity for risk taking, high competition, and possibilities for creative and autonomous practice.

When the Managerial Grid and the Job Orientation results were combined, the profile of the aggregate was characterized by high concern for people and job security and low concern for task and the competitive aspects of the job.

The authors tested the strength of the relationship of the performances on the Managerial Grid Questionnaire and the Job Orientation Questionnaire by using the Pearson product-moment correlation coefficient. The correlational analyses involved four variables: competitiveness, security, task, and people. The four variables were combined into five pairs for both the workshop and student subsamples: (a) Competitiveness × Security; (b) Task × Competitiveness; (c) Task × Security; (d) People × Competitiveness; and (e) People × Security.

Correlational analysis did not reveal any statistically significant relationships among the five combinations. This outcome contradicted the original assumption that there would be a significant positive relationship

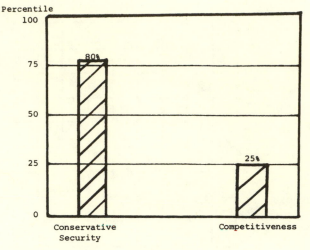

FIGURE 2. Orientation-to-job profile.

between people scores and security scores, and between task scores and competitiveness scores.

There are several possible factors that could be part of an explanation of lack of significance. First, both instruments were developed with concern for business and industrial enterprises, and the language in the attitude statements may have been inconsistent with social work terminology that would describe the same phenomena. Respondents in both groups did object to the phrasing of the Job Orientation Questionnaire and to interpretation of questionnaire items discussed by Borgatta and Bohrenstedt. This may have contributed to the lack of any discernible pattern of scores on the Job Orientation Questionnaire. Individuals scored high on both dimensions, or low on both, or a combination of high and low. Because of these inconsistencies, when Job Orientation scores were combined with Managerial Grid scores, the within differences tended to offset each other. Second, it is possible that the emphasis on competitiveness as an indicator of competency-based orientation to the job is highly inconsistent with values usually associated with the social work profession.

In spite of the lack of correlation between scores on the two questionnaires, the findings do suggest some possible concerns for social work educators and supervisors. Although we must be cautious in generalizing from data obtained from two samples that self-selected participation in either workshops or a master's degree program in social work, the trends point to primary concerns for job security (conservative security orientation) and concern for relationships (people orientation) almost to the exclusion of concern for the task. If one accepts the relationship between these orientations and the current pressures and dilemmas in social work supervision, then those involved in the teaching and training of social workers need to emphasize training and job experiences that will facilitate development of concern for task and attraction to jobs based on competent performance.

IMPLICATIONS FOR EDUCATION AND TRAINING IN SUPERVISION

Given the contemporary issues related to social work supervision, major themes in the literature, and the orientations to leadership and to job of the subjects in this study, the critical question for social work educators and staff development and training personnel in agencies is, Where do we go from here? The significance of this question is magnified by the training regulations in Title XX and Title IVA. These regulations place heavy emphasis on manpower development, with special emphasis given to skills for middle managers. These emphases reinforce our concern for education and training to increase the practice competencies of supervisors, that is, first-level middle managers.

Based on the issues, the findings of our research, and our experiences in graduate level social work education and continuing education for social work supervisors, we have developed a position on an education and training model for supervision. We start with the basic premises of andragogy which emphasize opportunities for individualized learning experiences, and we argue specifically for a model that stresses opportunities to practice skills utilization and observe the modeling of appropriate supervisory skills within a specified situational context. A carefully planned mix of didactic presentations on practice theory and research with experiential activities, including modeling by the teacher or workshop leader, is suggested as an effective approach for linking theory with practice and realigning the goodness of fit between orientations and practice behavior.

Requisite activities and task for effective supervision that take into account concern for task, for people, and for competitive job orientations have been identified as: (a) setting individual and group objectives for task allocation and implementation; (b) implementing shared decision making; (c) directing group process (including agenda building); (d) planning work and case management; (e) developing communication networks; (f) evaluating performance; (g) motivating workers; (h) case consultation and professional support; (i) team building; (j) worker and client advocacy; (k) conflict management; and (1) planned change at dyadic, team, and intergroup levels, with particular attention to coalescing separate interests into collective interests on behalf of employees and clients.

To achieve the education and training objectives suggested for more effective supervisory practice, the authors have identified and implemented the following approaches. Role playing can be helpful in developing skills in shared decision making, performance evaluation, motivating workers, consultations and professional support, and conflict management. Development exercises (specific focus on a particular supervisory or organizational process) are useful for skill development in setting objectives, agenda building, group decision making, communication, and case management. Simulations are useful for integrating specific skill components with group processes that approximate the typical situational context within which supervisors and workers practice. Furthermore, simulations can be used for developing skills in directing group processes, team building, advocacy, and planned change. In addition to providing varied opportunities to produce skill and observe the modeling of skills, these experiential activities have the added benefit of consciousness raising. This is particularly valuable in raising self-awareness of the relationship between competitive job orientation and actual practice behavior.

The final comment on the proposed model is to differentiate the packaging of the model at the graduate level from packaging for continuing education. In a graduate level curriculum it is possible to incorporate all the activities in a course on supervision that is linked in a sequence with courses on program evaluation, staff development and training, and organizational renewal. For individuals in practice, the preferred packaging would be a 2-day workshop reviewing all the activities and underlying theory and research plus practice of selected skills. Following this 2-day workshop would be a series of 1-day workshops specific to each of the 12 requisite activities and tasks. Regardless of the auspice or format, teaching and training organized around consideration for orientations as discussed above, and specification of activity and task domains for supervisory practice, should provide the much-needed impetus for educators, supervisors, and staff development personnel to meet the pressing issues of supervision defined as middle management.

REFERENCE NOTE

1. Sorcher, M. *Employee perceptions of supervisors.* Unpublished manuscript, Syracuse, New York, 1971.

REFERENCE

Argyris, C. *Intervention theory and method: A behavioral science view.* Reading, Mass.: Addison-Wesley, 1970.

PART IV

Financial Management

Financial management of social work departments in health care is only one aspect of accountability, management information and the translation of the values of social work services into dollars.

The value of social work services rests primarily on its effectiveness with the client system, its ability to demonstrate that effectiveness, its usefulness as perceived by the hospital professional and management team and its usefulness to third party payers who support the majority of social work services in health care. Financial management is therefore an important skill for social workers to acquire. It is one way in which social work can concretely contribute to the missions and goals of health care organizations since breakeven is the goal of all not-for-profit health care organizations. Rosenberg presents a number of concepts which affect the financial management of social work in health care. Volland provides an excellent example of one system of costing social work services and Stretch provides an overview of managerial functions which provide for sound fiscal budgeting. These three articles in combination provide the social work manager with examples of the applications of financial management concepts to social work practice in health care.

Gary Rosenberg, PhD

Chapter 11

Concepts in the Financial Management of of Hospital Social Work Departments

Gary Rosenberg, PhD

ABSTRACT. Concepts in the financial management of social work departments such as the utilization of cost-benefit as a way of thinking, the identification of funding sources for the department, and development of an understanding of budgetary practices are explored. Examples are offered of revenue production in in-patient and ambulatory care programs. Ideas about the contribution of social work to a hospital in an organized matrix structure are discussed. Social work can become a revenue rather than expense center by translating key functions into financial management terms.

In the financial management of the Department of Social Work, the director must (1) utilize cost-benefit as a way of thinking, (2) identify the funding supports for social work services, (3) understand the assets of various budgeting practices, (4) understand the management of revenue production on in-patient services, (5) understand the sources of revenue and revenue production in ambulatory care services, and (6) conceptualize the social work contribution to the management of the total health care organization.

When specific functions of social work can be translated into cost-benefit thinking, the contribution of our program can be understood by hospital administrators and by cost conscious physicians. By highlighting social work's revenue producing potential, and by managing expenses in a clear and honest way, the social work director can change the image of social work as a necessary expense to be kept at a minimum, in budgeting terms an expense center, to that of a department which is capable of adding income to the hospital, a revenue center. An expense center is one where the control system measures the expenses incurred but does not measure the monetary value of services. A revenue center measures both expenses and the monetary value of services (Anthony and Herzlinger, 1975).

COST-BENEFIT AS A WAY OF THINKING

Cost-benefit analysis focuses on those consequences of a program or proposal which can be estimated in quantitative and usually monetary terms. While cost-benefit can never provide a complete answer to any problem, it can be useful in objectifying aspects of decision-making and communication which have financial impacts (Anthony and Herzlinger, 1975). It can be helpful as a way of structuring thinking about social work services. At least some factors in social work programs can be reduced to quantitative terms. The resulting analysis of program narrows the areas of management judgment but does not eliminate it (Anthony and Herzlinger, 1975).

In cost-benefit terms both the costs of providing a service and the benefits accruing as a result of a service or program are put in quantitative terms. Young and Allen have provided a model of modified cost-benefit applied to adoption, which demonstrates the economic impact of charges in reimbursement structures (Young and Allen, 1977).

Collins has shown that for a cost of $1,158.50 in social work time, Denver General saved $18,402.10 in reduced length of stay. She further demonstrated that $831,120 was saved by their tax supported agencies because of social work interventions with clients (Collins, 1975). A study in Missouri on social work services in a group medical practice was seen as clearly viable from a cost-benefit criteria (Hookey et al., 1975). The necessary ingredients of cost-benefits are data on costs and the ability to translate effort and outcome into quantitative terms. Such efforts on the part of directors of social work departments will provide a clearer idea of the relationship between the costs of a service and the accrued benefits, and can gain significant allies for the efforts to maintain and expand social work services in health care.

SOURCES OF FUNDING SOCIAL WORK SERVICES

An important task for the director is to identify the sources of support from budgetary and non-budgetary sources for the direct and full costs of social work services. Direct costs are usually the amount of salary, fringe benefits, plus supplies and expenses assigned to the departmental budget. Full costs include all these direct costs as well as indirect costs such as the amount of space, overhead, and expenses of other departments which are assigned to social work on some formula basis. Most funding for social work departments in hospitals comes from the amount of the perdiem reimbursement rate assigned to social work. Some of the costs of the department may be defrayed by philanthropy and grants and others by a fee-for-service structure (billing at either cost or charges for out-patient

FINANCIAL MANAGEMENT

Table 1

	1978 Projected Costs	1978 Projected Cost per Patient Day
Routine Costs:		
"Hotel" Costs:		
Depreciation of Building and Interest	$ 862,332	$ 2.16
Depreciation of Equipment	442,290	1.11
Operation & Maintenance of Plant	2,942,802	7.36
Laundry	1,023,414	2.56
Housekeeping	2,777,449	6.95
Dietary Costs	6,406,545	16.02
Admitting & Patient Accounting	1,765,228	4.42
Administrative & General Expense related to "Hotel" Costs	1,925,060	4.81
Total "Hotel" Costs	$ 18,145,120	$ 45.39
Medical & Paramedical Costs		
Nursing (including Psychiatry)	$ 21,322,213	$ 53.33
Employee Health and Welfare	3,669,381	9.18
Employee Housing (Net of Income Recovery)	-0-	-0-
Medical Records	243,653	0.61
Social Service	2,109,882	5.28
House Staff & Clinicians	14,940,331	37.37
School of Nursing	247,138	0.61
Admitting & Patient Accounting	1,765,229	4.42
Administrative & General Expense related to Medical & Paramedical Costs	5,977,487	14.95
Total Medical & Paramedical Costs	$ 50,275,314	$ 125.75
Total Routine Costs	$ 68,420,434	$ 171.14
Ancillary Service Costs		
Operating Room	$ 13,731,210	$ 34.35
Anesthesia	1,353,025	3.38
Delivery Room	2,137,098	5.35
Radiology (Diagnostic & Therapeutic)	9,624,957	24.07
Laboratories (including EEG, EKG, Blook Bank)	16,461,119	41.17
Drugs	3,008,354	7.52
Physical Therapy	1,348,745	3.37
Inhalation Therapy	795,124	L.99
Medical Supplies	1,050,163	2.63
Recreational Therapy	758,991	1.90
Total Ancillary Service Costs	$ 50,268,786	$ 125.73
Total Inpatient Costs	$ 118,689,220	$ 296.87

services) (Nehman and Hoops, 1977; Rosenberg, 1977). The amount of per diem reimbursement assigned to social work can be calculated by the financial division and should be known by the director. An example of such a costing system is seen in Table I.

Other sources of social work funding may come from grants, allocations for special programs such as End Stage Renal Disease, Child Abuse, etc., and from non-budgetary sources such as endowments, contributions, and other funds specially set aside for the use of the social work department.

The social work department is a responsibility center—a group of people headed by a manager who is responsible for what it does (Anthony and Herzlinger, 1975). Knowledge of the sources of social work funding is essential for the social work director as the person concerned with and responsible for the planning, operating, and controlling of the day-to-day operations of the department. Such a designation is inherent in the role of director.

An important managerial function with respect to sources of funding is the development of a system of information flow on grant applications emanating from other program departments. For example, if Medicine is writing a grant, and requires social work services, the Director of social work should help plan for the provision of psychosocial services and negotiate, prior to the submission of the grant, for monies for social work time planned for in the grant. We are beyond the point where we can supply social work services without a sufficient funding base. A key role of the social work director in financial management is to make this point clear to his medical colleagues and to develop a collegial atmosphere where service grants include planning for funding of social work services.

KNOWLEDGE OF BUDGETING PRACTICES

A budget is a plan expressed in quantitative, usually monetary terms, and covers a specified time period, usually one year. Budgets are used to plan, operate, and control the social work program, and thus, are an important aspect of the director's responsibility. Budgets should include not only a statement of expenses to be incurred during the year, but also a projection of revenues that will accrue due to the effort of the social work department.

Budget philosophies generally fall into three categories: incremental, evaluative, and negotiative. Incremental budgets are those which are increased or decreased on a straight percentage basis. Usually, there is a constant increase or decrease, or there may be a constant share of the budget total e.g. if the social work budget is 5% of the hospital's budget, whatever monies are allocated for increase, social work should receive 5% of those monies. Incremental budgeting assumes services are in the proper proportion, and that future service needs reflect current allocations of financial support. This type of thinking is a way of avoiding the difficult management decisions that some services may need more support than others.

Evaluative budgets are based on benefits and costs. They are rarely used on a yearly basis. They are more frequently used for new programs or on a rotating basis for different responsibility centers every 4 to 5 years. Examples of evaluative budgets include performance budgeting, program planning, and budgeting systems such as zero-based budgeting. Most evaluative budget systems are attractive because they provide a framework for program evaluation. However, the detail and complexity of evaluative budgeting may be unnecessary and more costly than it is worth (Vignola, 1976). Such procedures are best used on some periodic basis or when a hospital or social work department is entering a new phase of development.

In negotiating budgeting the director must emphasize the role of negotiation and bargaining as opposed to evaluation. A good example of this is management by objectives (Spano and Lund, 1976). This type of budgeting is negotiative because each objective is relative and can be negotiated with the administration, physicians, and within the department. Chart I describes the budget structure and the kinds of budget and associated philosophies.

While the final accountability in budgeting remains with the director, some of the choices with respect to budgeting and the planning that accompanies budgeting, can be shared decisions with staff. Budget negotiations with hospital management is one of the appropriate issues for collaborative decision-making between social work administration and staff in social work (Hirsch and Shulman, 1976). The budgeting process can be used to educate the staff to the financial underpinnings of the program, to the costs of health care, and to revenue production issues. With staff's

CHART I

Budget Philosophy

Budget Structure

INCREMENTAL	EVALUATIVE	NEGOTIATIVE
Traditional Budget Systems	Performance Budgeting (PB)	Management by Objectives (MBO)
	Responsibility Center Budgeting (RCB)	
	1. Program, Planned Budget Systems (PPBS) 2. Zero Based Budgeting Systems (ZBB)	

increased awareness social work departments can make a vital contribution to cost containment programs, as well as to increasing revenue production. Staff also can learn that humanistic concern, skilled social work services, and proper financial management are not oppositional issues.

REVENUE PRODUCTION—INPATIENT

In most hospitals social work may not charge directly for its services to inpatients because the cost is already included in the daily charge rate. However, there are activities for which social work is responsible which do have revenue translations, i.e., cost-benefits. The director and staff need to develop a data system which tracks and categorizes activities which can be translated into revenue terms.

One example of such activities is the categories of PSRO disallowances for which social work has responsibility through its discharge planning function. Timely and skillful discharge planning and documentation of attempts to plan for patients' discharge can safeguard income to the hospital. By computing the disallowance rates in social work categories, a measure of efficiency and effectiveness can be gleaned. Actual income lost or safeguarded can be computed and compared to previous months and/or to other categories of this disallowance for which social work is not responsible. A measure of the monetary contribution of discharge planning can be computed.

Another source of in-patient revenue attributable to social work results from the concern of social work for the total psychosocial environment of the patient/family. An example is when a social worker discovers that a client/family has sources of funding for in-patient hospitalization which were not known to the admitting personnel. Keeping track of the cases where this occurs including the number of days of hospitalization and the amount of additional income which accrued because of social work effort can be translated into income production directly attributable to social work.

Social work produced revenue also emanates from the function of the community linkages. By establishing linkages between agencies and other hospitals, both organizations and their clients can benefit. At this hospital the Psychiatry in-patient census was lower than had been budgeted for. The social work director developed a program to increase admissions. Social workers contacted voluntary hospitals which did not have psychiatric services, and worked out agreements to offer patients coming to these hospital emergency rooms admission at ours. In an overcrowded publicly sponsored hospital, a liaison social worker met weekly with the staff of the other hospital to select patients who might benefit from hospitalization at our institution. This program relieved the overcrowding of the public institution and offered patients and families another choice for treatment. The patients admitted, sources of income, and number of days of hospitalization were computed; these activities resulted in additional revenue in excess of $400,000 per year attributable to the social work effort.

Many child care agencies need backup specialty care on an ambulatory care basis and hospitalization for their children at times. The development of such linkages can increase the patient census in Pediatrics. Programs have also been developed with unions. Such programs are another way of enhancing social work as a revenue producing center. These examples are illustrative of how social work functions have a direct impact in financial management terms, which is one other way of explaining the meaning of these functions to administrators in a cost-conscious environment. Some hospitals charge directly for in-patient social work services (Collins, 1978). In such hospitals the production of revenue is similar to ambulatory care revenue production.

REVENUE PRODUCTION—AMBULATORY

That social work in ambulatory care is a revenue center is a more widely held notion. In a review of the literature on social work fees, one author noted that there is "a trend towards charging fees for social work services in the medical setting in general, family practice in particular and of course in the private social worker setting" (Twersky and Cole, 1976). The relationship of costs incurred to fees charged was not explored. An example described is a fee structure related to the full cost of service in a family agency setting. The methodology is applicable to ambulatory care social work. The use of third party payments in this system resulted in an increase in the rate of fee income of approximately 900% over a three year period (Kurland, 1978).

Revenue for social work services can come from Medicaid fees for mental health services, commercial insurances, foundation support, and self-pay patients. Some commercial insurers and foundations have been willing to accept billing for social work services initially on a trial basis. For example, the Muscular Dystrophy Foundation now supports evaluations and ongoing treatment services delivered by social workers.

The key management concept for ambulatory care social work is that sources of revenue exist, and that some or all of the expenses of delivering social work can be offset by revenue production. An important ingredient necessary for the success of an ambulatory care fee-for-service program is the education of staff to the concepts of fee setting, an area of some discomfort for social workers. Social work education has not focused consistently on how social work services are supported and the relationship between funding mechanisms, worker salaries, and services to clients. In the health care industry social workers share the responsibility with other health care professionals for providing effective services at reasonable cost. Assisting clients in judicious use of their health benefits and entitlements as well as in setting fair out of pocket fees is part of the social work function. There is a value in recognizing that social work services have dollar costs and that people can and will pay to help meet them.

At our hospital there are two models for funding ambulatory care social work services. The first is when social work services are costed into the overall clinic rate in a way similar to in-patient rates. The second is a fee-for-service model, where social workers charge for interviews on a sliding scale from $10 a visit, or less if indicated, to a full cost fee of $55 a session.

THE SOCIAL WORK CONTRIBUTION TO HOSPITAL MANAGEMENT

The basic managerial functions of the social work director are those of planning, operating, and controlling the social work program in the organization. These functions can best be accomplished by a central social work department under the direction of a single social work director (Lurie and Rosenberg, 1973). The responsibility center concept gives further credence to a centralized organizational structure. The "responsibility center" is a group of people headed by a manager who is responsible for what they do (Anthony and Herzlinger, 1975).

Complex hospitals are frequently organized on a matrix management model. This system accounts for "collegial participatory decision-making structure for directing health care professionals and a hierarchial centralized decision-making structure for managing unskilled workers" (Davis and Carswell, 1977). As a professional department social work is a resource for the program departments and a responsibility center managed by a director (see Chart II).

In a matrix management model social work is a resource department to each program listed in the left hand column. The social work director is responsible for setting standards for the professional department and for providing social work resources to each program. Without a designation in management the professional social worker is deprived of the opportunity to exploit to the fullest those matters which rely on professional knowledge (Shmit, 1978). In the model depicted in Chart II social work is a member of the senior management group, the highest level management group in the hospital. Other department managers may have a reporting relationship to the members of senior management.

Because of social work expertise in the provision for and management

CHART II

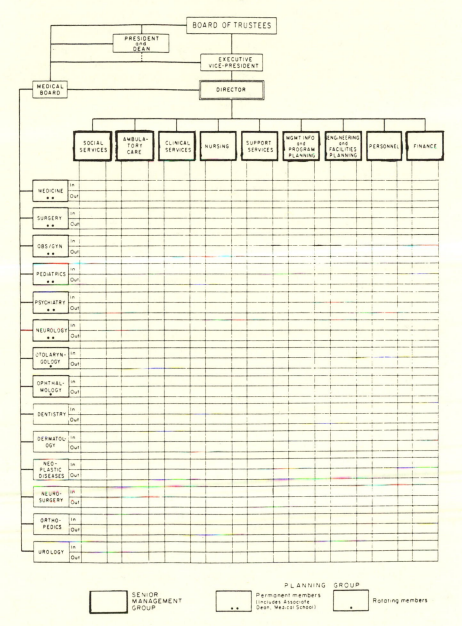

of psychosocial services, departments such as Volunteer, Patient Representative, Therapeutic Activities, and Home Care are those which could logically relate to the social work director as a member of the senior management group. This reporting relationship further strengthens the position of power occupied as the Director of Social Work and also creates a centralized management of psychosocial services. It is probable that social work can be even more influential in the provision of care to patients/families with the increasing number of functions which such a management grouping implies. Human service management is an area of social work expertise.

With a clearer contribution to the financial management of the department and the hospital, social work can forge a role in the management group of the hospital.

CONCLUSIONS

Social workers are paid from revenue sources. These need to be identified and expanded. Identifying and maximizing revenues will increase social work's ability to deliver psychosocial health services to those who can pay directly, those whose costs of care are paid through per diem methods, and those who cannot afford to pay for our services. We can defend with greater clarity and strengthen the services for the non-insured poor when we can identify our sources of revenues, and the benefits to the hospital which are accrued in serving them.

Skilled financial management ensures that the mission of social work is carried out with efficiency, and places social work in the category of a necessary, well managed, and cost efficient "caring" service department.

REFERENCES

Anthony, R. and Herzlinger, R. *Management in nonprofit organizations.* Homewood, Illinois: Richard D. Irwin, 1975.

Collins, J. "A cost-effectiveness model," in W. T. Hall & G. St. Denis (eds.), *Proceedings of Quality Assurance in Social Services in Health Programs for Mothers and Children,* Pittsburgh, 1975.

Collins, J. "A system for medicaid - medicare reimbursement for social work services." Presented at the American Public Health Association, October 19, 1978. Unpublished.

Davis, S. and Carswell, W. "The program-resource concept: A management approach for an academic medical center." *The Mount Sinai Journal of Medicine,* Vol. 44, No. 5, September/October 1977, pp. 624–632.

Hirsch, S. and Shulman, L. "Participatory governance: A model for shared decision making." *Social Work in Health Care,* Vol. 1, No. 4, Summer 1976, pp. 433–446.

Hookey, P. "The social worker as a counselor in a group medical practice." The George Warren Brown School of Social Work, St. Louis, Missouri, 1975. Unpublished.

Kurland, P. "Free systems and third-party payments in a family service agency." *Social Casework,* Vol. 59, No. 8, November 1978, pp. 560–562.

Lurie, A. and Rosenberg, G. "The current role of the hospital social work director." *Reference Article Society of Hospital Social Work Directors,* June 1973.

Neiman, D. and Hoops, A. "Can private hospitals afford social work services." *Social Work in Health Care,* Vol. *3,* No. 2, Winter 1977, pp. 175–180.

Rosenberg, G. "Comment: cost finding in hospital social work." *Social Work in Health Care,* Vol. *3,* No. 2, Winter 1977, pp. 181–186.

Shmit, D. "Professional discretion in social welfare administration." *Administration in Social Work,* Vol. *2,* No. 4, Winter 1978, pp. 439–450.

Spano, B. and Lund, S. "Management by objectives in a hospital social service unit." *Social Work in Health Care,* Vol. *1,* No. 3, Spring 1976, pp. 267–276.

Twersky, R. and Cole, W. "Social work fees in medical care." *Social Work in Health Care,* Vol. *2,* No. 1, Fall 1976, pp. 77–84.

Young, D. and Allen, B. "Benefit cost analysis in the social services: The example of adoption reimbursement." *Social Service Review,* Vol. *51,* No. 2, June 1977, pp. 249–264.

Vignola, M. L. "The latest in federal spending control zero-base budgeting." *Washington Report,* Vol. *II,* No. 8, September 1976, Washington, D.C.: American Public Welfare Association, pp. 1–4.

A Social Work Director Comments

Managing Departments of Social Work so that the delivery of quality social work services is viable for the institution is the focus of national and individual hospital concern. Dr. Rosenberg's paper is, therefore, important and timely. As this paper suggests, directors are separately and collectively attempting to educate themselves about financial management concepts in order to maximize the capacity of their departments to provide quality social work services.

A note of caution is timely. Learning fundamental concepts and applied tools from another professional field involves a careful, selective process. Dr. Rosenberg's position that social work departments should become Revenue Centers in order to gain value within the institution is, in my opinion, an example of faulty application of a management concept.

EXPENSE CENTER VERSUS REVENUE CENTER

While one can make a case, as this article does, that every group and subgroup in an organization is a responsibility center, the key for financial management rests with how each of these are specifically classified. Anthony and Herzlinger offer four such choices:

1. Expense Centers
2. Revenue Centers
3. Investment Centers
4. Mission Centers and/or Service Centers.

The primary service in health care is health/medicine. Social work services are provided to improve the quality of those health/medical services. For that reason it is appropriate for social work services to be classified and viewed as Expense Centers. Even if social work provides a service which generates revenue, I do not believe that makes the social work department a Revenue Center. While it may generate revenue which offsets the expenses incurred by the availability of social work services, it is not a Revenue Center.

Creative financial management by the social work director can take place without insisting on a reclassification that is, I believe, ill-founded and unrealistic both from the point of view of the hospital system and certainly from the point of view of external group(s) who are increasingly interested in regulating the system.

COST BENEFIT THINKING

Of greater value is the development of cost benefit thinking. This determination of the relationship between quantifiable *benefits* of the service to the full *cost* of the service uses objective data comparisons to make judgments which then become decisions of the organization. If used effectively it does, as Dr. Rosenberg indicates, narrow the margin of judgment and positively influences the support of social work services. Examples are given that effectively develop such a point of view.

The establishment of a per unit cost for social work service is basic to determine/express value as defined by the ability to meet the objectives of the organization. However, Table I, intended to explain how a unit cost can be developed, offers a total projected cost for a given period of time for social work services and also a unit (patient day) of cost for the service.

What are the components of this formula? For instance, knowing the number of patient days utilized to figure cost/patient day is essential. We also need to know what purpose such a per unit cost serves. The Financial Planning Department in this particular organization has identified a per unit cost in terms of patient days. If this fluctuates up or down over a time, what does it mean? The director will want to be able to answer this question. Such a change may be totally unrelated to the social work department and its functions. At most it represents *only* the total dollars allocated to the social work department and what portion of total dollars presumed available to the institution is committed to the social work function. The total dollars presumed available in Table I are apparently based on anticipated revenue which will be generated by providing an unknown amount of patient days. Historically, reimbursement has been based on a per patient day cost, particularly in the acute care facility. This is no longer true for all hospitals and therefore a careful development of per unit costing which includes social work and expresses comparison for interpretation is more fundamental to our knowledge than this unclear example.

BUDGETING AND MANAGEMENT BY OBJECTIVES

Financial management is possible only in direct relation to understanding of the budgetary process. The budgetary process helps identify sources of funding as well as the expenditure commitments of an organization. Knowledge of this process and its intent helps to explain how and why the organization functions. It aids the social work director in becoming proficient at competing within the organization for the scarce financial resources. Within this context, knowledge of different budgetary approaches is irrelevant. Social work directors are not usually the people deciding on how budgeting should take place. Even if they were, Management by Objectives is not a budget structure but a process by which advance planning is done. It establishes the commitment to evaluate an organization's ability to meet those objectives over a specified time. This process says that with the given amount of resources we will be able to produce something (X) which ultimately will cost a total of dollars (Y). Thus, Management by Objectives is a commitment for producing to meet an agreed-upon objective. If it were appropriately tied to the budgetary process, according to Dr. Rosenberg's scheme, it would logically fit under the evaluative box in Chart I. In my opinion, however, the content of Chart I is not relative to the financial management decisions most directors of social work departments are asked to consider.

OTHER MANAGEMENT TOOLS

Dr. Rosenberg ably identifies an information system as another tool necessary for sound financial management. However, the availability of such a system should not always lead, as he suggests, to the expression of social work services in "revenue terms." Rather, such a system should allow for the expression of a unit of productivity for social work services which gets translated into a unit of cost of quantifiable terms.

This information is essential for developing cost benefit thinking. Basic productivity/cost information leads to the ability to demonstrate a cost benefit, a cost savings, or a cost avoidance. For example, the cost of providing discharge planning services to an inpatient medical floor would have a total dollar value. The total days of unpaid services (lost revenue) saved by those services also has a total dollar value. The difference between the two totals does not become a revenue gathered by the social work department. What has occurred is a cost avoidance for the hospital: its facilities (patient beds, equipment, utilities) and staff have been utilized at a maximum by the bed being filled. A cost avoidance has taken place. No new revenue was generated. More importantly, anticipated revenue was not lost.

REVENUE ISSUES

Dr. Rosenberg and I interpret revenue differently. The ability of the social work department to increase the usage of the hospital facilities, as indicated in the article by the increase in the in-patient Psychiatry census, does not make a social work department a Revenue Center. It is an appropriate expression of the cost benefit for delivering social work services; that is, the expense(s) of providing a social work practitioner whose responsibility is to identify people who can appropriately utilize the Psychiatry facilities is valuable in meeting the high occupancy objective of the Psychiatry Department. The value to the hospital is the more effective utilization of facilities while providing quality services for appropriately needy patient populations. Such an evidence of social work capability to concurrently think in quality care and bed utilization terms elevates the department within the hospital. Such thinking is creative and essential. This does not, however, make social work service a Revenue Center.

Even though social work departments do generate revenue in Ambulatory Care Services this does not warrant its classification as a Revenue Center. As an expression of cost benefit it says that the total expenses for the service(s) is that Revenue Center are offset by revenue coming into that Center (usually from third party payers). The ability to charge for social work services does not make the social work services a Revenue Center even though it offers a way for social work to bring in revenue. As regulatory bodies look at Ambulatory Care Services, as they have been doing for inpatient hospital services, costing will be an issue. We should be able to define cost benefit, cost avoidance, and/or cost savings, developed by generating revenue, increased patient registration, reduction in missed appointments, more effective use of time through delivery of group services, and other actions.

ORGANIZATION

While I agree that a centralized organizational structure is essential for effective delivery of social work services, I do not believe that the Responsibility Center Concept is a necessary correlate. A centralized organizational structure is a management concept that is a statement of authority and reporting responsibility. It is, in part, a method of identifying accountabilities. A director of social work might be accountable to the director of the hospital and at the same time accountable to the physician chiefs of the individual hospital services. In this way the department, an Expense Center, can ''sell'' its services to each of those hospital Revenue Centers.* This accountability pattern does not reduce or imply a change in the centralized organizational concept. Here, I think that Dr. Rosenberg has confused the importance of organizational structure with the director's role as financial manager. Clarity about both is essential.

THE MANAGERIAL ATTITUDE

For social work directors to maximize their facility for financial management, it is essential, as Dr. Rosenberg suggests, to develop an understanding of cost benefit thinking. It is also essential to understand what revenues are possible to generate, what costs can be avoided, and what costs can be saved by social work services.

The development of the Uniform Reporting System (Joint Task Force, 1979), or a more refined system which expresses a unit of productivity translated into a unit of cost, will be helpful in advancing the financial management capabilities of the social work director. In the meantime judicious and thorough review of management and financial theory should continue and its application challenged for intent and usefulness.

Patricia J. Volland, LCSW, MBA

REFERENCE

The Joint Task Force on Uniform Reporting, Society for Hospital Social Work Directors and National Association of Social Workers, System for Hospital Uniform Reporting—Social Services, based on National Survey of Hospital Social Work Practice, by Claudia J. Coulton, PhD, et al, August 1979.

---

*This in fact exists at Johns Hopkins Hospital.

The Author Responds

Ms. Volland's comments offer social work directors a choice between moving in the direction suggested in my article of considering social work a revenue center or in the expense center direction suggested in her comments. Clearly, the field needs to explore both approaches.

Hospitals are organized in many different ways. The examples used in my paper illustrate a matrix management system organized on a program resource content, with social work as a resource department. The measurement of revenues or benefits accruing from social work services which are translatable into revenues can be conceptualized as part of an existing revenue center, such as Medicine or Ambulatory Care, or by conceptualizing social work as a revenue center. Both systems of capturing revenues have their advantages and disadvantages. By highlighting social work as a revenue center, the amount of revenues available as a direct result of social work productivity is easier to measure, more available to the hospital's administration, as well as to the program chairmen. When monthly financial statements list social work services as an expense and a revenue producing department, social work gains greater positive visibility.

Ms. Volland suggests that Table I fails to make the points that I wished it to make. This Chart is not an example of per unit costing. The Chart is offered as a way of assisting social work directors to understand the per-diem spread-risk insurance principle and how financial officers of hospitals assign costs to various services. In our state, social work is figured into the medical and paramedical costs under the general category of routine costs. The object of Table I is to enable social work directors to understand this per-diem insurance principle and to understand how much money is being assigned, in this in-patient per-diem rate, to social work's costs. Ms. Volland's comment that all hospitals are no longer on a per-diem reimbursement basis was a needed addition to my paper.

The second point of difference between Ms. Volland's and my viewpoint is that management by objectives is not a budget structure. Anthony and Herzlinger define a budget as a plan expressed in quantitative, usually monetary terms, and covering a specified period of time, usually one year. While management by objectives is non-monetary, it can be tied to a monetary way of doing a budget. It is a plan that can be done in one year and is linked to both evaluative budgeting as well as negotiative budgeting. The point of Chart I is that management by objectives, when linked to budget structures, not only becomes evaluative but negotiative. Objectives can be negotiated and evaluations can be performed on budgets which are negotiated. Management by objectives in a standard reference text has been listed as a type of performance budgeting (Odiorne, 1972). While Chart I may not be relevant to many social work directors' levels of responsibilities, it is likely that social work directors in the future will be called on more frequently to consider different types of budgeting structures. Knowledge of strategic processes can be useful in assisting the thinking and planning of all social work departments.

On the issue of per-unit costs, the goal of any management information system is the inclusion of per unit cost data based on a unit of productivity; I agree that our profession is beginning to move this way nationally. The problem is to develop a well conceptualized unit which is useable for financial calculation and, more importantly, for the accurate measurement of the services we provide to patients. A poorly conceptualized unit of productivity can lead to serious miscalculations and effect the provision of these services.

Ms. Volland's cogent comments have forced me to think about some positions, rethink others, and deepen my knowledge. Her ideas complement my paper and are an important contribution to the thinking on financial management in hospital social work departments.

Gary Rosenberg, PhD

REFERENCE

Odiorne, George S. *Management by objectives: A system of managerial leadership.* Pitman Publishing Company, New York, 1972, pp. 91–94.

Chapter 12

Costing for Social Work Services

Patricia J. Volland, LCSW, MBA

ABSTRACT. This paper discusses the potential for the development of a cost accounting procedure that monitors both output of service and costs while allowing for though not insuring quality of output. Such a system of costing out can help answer questions of cost effectiveness of social work services. One possible model is utilized to express the process and demonstrate potential benefits to social work services. It offers a way of defining and evaluating services with respect to standards of productivity. Necessary components of such a system are defined. It is suggested as a tool for the social work Administrator to consider as a way of clearly and effectively defining needs and defining and "marketing" the services to be provided by the department. It is presented here to encourage further exploration and refinement.

INTRODUCTION

Is it possible that a cost accounting procedure can adequately monitor both output and costs while, at the same time, allowing for quality of output? Since cost accounting procedures are a system for allocating expenses to goods or services, they are clearly not intended as a mechanism for monitoring quality. Monitoring both quality and quantity of service is necessary for insuring that service to patients does not deteriorate in these days when increased attention is focused on "levels" and "quantity" of service.

Cost accounting systems may have the capacity of helping to cost out our efforts and answer questions about the cost effectiveness of social work services. (See Appendix II-1). Since the present state of the art offers, at best, the cost of inputs and in some organizations units of output, a cost accounting system might help deal with, though it cannot totally accomplish, the analysis of the relation of costs to benefit. It can supply data on costs of providing services.

Utilizing the early efforts from one model, this paper discusses the potential for such a system. Other models are suggested. Components necessary for such a procedure are discussed. Each is discussed within the context that a social work department in a hospital is considered an "Expense Center," i.e. expenses are charged to this responsibility center without the expectation that these expenses will be balanced by offsetting revenues (Anthony and Herzlinger, 1975). An analysis of the relationship of the Social Work output to treatment objectives is considered as a potential beginning for addressing effectiveness, a possible way of relating social work service costs to a standard (Statement of Quality) of service.

MINIMAL COMPONENTS OF A COST ACCOUNTING MODEL

Before a social work department can test out the cost accounting approach, these features must be in position:

1. Identification of all expense components that make up social work costs.
2. Understanding of the current hospital system of allocation of indirect costs.
3. The establishment of an objective unit of service, probably based on time.
4. The establishment of a working standard of quality for social work service.
5. A management information system which gathers data based on the accepted standard and time unit in an ongoing manner.
6. A system which permits weighting according to defined complexity factors so that values can be assigned to tasks performed.
7. The system should have the capacity for analyzing productivity, output, with respect to outcome on which cost benefit analysis can be based.

Each of these features will be more clearly understood through the model illustrated in this discussion.

BASIS FOR A WEIGHTING SYSTEM

Throughout the health care system attempts have been made to understand the amount of time and skill necessary to diagnose and treat illness or provide appropriate health supervision. Knowledge of all component parts and their relationship to each other is basic to this understanding.

The most common method currently used is the Relative Value Unit. It is used increasingly and in various forms to identify real time and cost in relation to a specific activity. It has been tied to outcome to validate optimum effectiveness and plan for staff needs (Wood, 1976).

A comparative weighting system has numerical value assigned to each defined procedure/service. This number is based upon the relative amount of labor, supplies, and capital needed to perform the procedure. This number, then, expresses the relationship of the value one professional service/procedure has to another.

Any weighting system requires a Standard Time Unit as a basis. This Standard Time Unit is given a base numerical value (such as 10 minutes). The number of Standard Time Units necessary to provide a given procedure/service plus the amount of skill, labor, supplies, etc., necessary to perform the procedure/service are utilized to put a dollar value on the relative amount of resources or inputs to provide each service.

Such systems, inaccurate and poorly developed as they are, have been utilized by third party payors and state health commissions for the purpose of comparing the output of professional services on one health care facility with the output of another and to compare the output within a given hospital from year to year. The comparative weighting of each defined procedure/service is theoretically determined by the amount of resources required to perform a given service relative to other services. These comparisons are utilized to recommend reasonable cost and reimbursement (California Relative Value Unit Studies, 1975). The SHUR System developed by the Federal Government (as a result of Federal Anti-Fraud & Abuse Legislation) is such a system.

What is the relationship between such a weighting process and cost? Once a Standard Time Unit is established, a cost can be assigned to that unit. The total number of units necessary to provide a particular procedure/service multiplied by the cost per unit reflects the total cost for providing the procedure/service. In determining the cost for a Standard Time Unit all costs must be accounted for, including all direct and indirect (or overhead) costs and allowing for "downtime."

Such a system has value in that it measures productivity and classifies activities in relation to products or services so that the cost of the product or service can be computed. *It can also assist in determining service productivity while recognizing that these services require different proportions of necessary resources.* There are multiple factors which can contribute to this weighting process. They explain the complexity of a service/procedure. All factors that are known should be utilized to analyze and understand the procedure/service. To the extent that this is possible the actual cost of social work services provided can be determined. Expressed as a formula the equation would begin as follows:

$$\frac{\text{Total Costs for Social Work Dept.}}{\text{Total Units of Service Provided}} = \text{Cost/Unit (Butler, 1979)}$$

To maintain significant value the system must be retested and probably revised at least annually to reestablish its ability to accurately measure output. This would include a review of factors considered significant in explaining complexity and a review of the time value assigned to the base unit.

WEIGHTING PROCESS APPLIED TO SOCIAL WORK

First a Standard Time Unit is determined, for instance 1 STU = 10 minutes. It is then essential for the types of service/procedures (the chosen output) to be identified and defined. Types of service/procedures can be defined in a variety of ways: by case, visit, contact/interview, problem, number of problems, service, number of services. Any method will have value and limitations. It is a working basis, not a precise, totally dependable universal truth. To illustrate, this paper uses the Service Categories model to define a Service Package Model.

The Service Package Unit consists of activities defined in terms of the objectives of the professional process. Ten services make up the range and are defined in Appendix I. This model assumes that the service (cluster of planned activities) is the most consistently accurate indicator of time spent. Other factors (variables) must be tested over time to determine significance in relation to time spent. Other service type models might separate diagnostic and treatment services or define services by point of entry into the medical system—preadmission, intake, admission, treatment, discharge, and after-care. Whichever model is eventually chosen would have to use the standard for social work services of that department. Ultimately this should include using those factors (variables) that have been demonstrated (through study) to determine most accurately the resources necessary for providing service and assuring efficiency (Coulton et al., 1979). This would lead to the establishment of appropriate weighting factors. The cost of providing a particular service is determined by multiplying the units of output required to provide the service by the cost per unit of output. Unit cost of output, as described earlier, equals total departmental costs divided by total departmental units of output.

Based on an analysis of its own productivity standard, a particular department of social work would determine which factors should be utilized in the weighting process. The productivity standard utilized here is that incorporated in the System for Hospital Uniform Reporting (Coulton et al., 1979). This is the most widely tested standard available for the social work profession today. Utilizing a different productivity standard at this time would further require the department to proceed with extensive data collection and time studies in advance. The work of developing a reliable uniform time unit should be pursued.

In any case, each department should build in factors that recognize the possibility for differential comparison between hospitals: within each productivity standard (case, visit, contact/interview, service type, service number, problem type, problem number) the weighting would reflect the activities involved in each as they relate to total relative value of other productivity components. The selection of such factors establish the complexity of each service standard.

SERVICE PACKAGE UNIT MODEL

In order to develop a Service Package Unit Model, or any weighting system, it is first of all necessary to have an ongoing management information system which gathers relevant, objective data that is easily retrievable (Volland, 1976 and 1979). Such a system should retrieve data that identifies and defines the complexity factors as follows: service types, frequency by hospital service areas, frequency relative to the total population, the time necessary for service completion and eventually the relationship to problem type, and effectiveness (outcome) measurement in order to explain the value of the services to the patient and to the hospital.

In this system each social work service is defined and coded (Appendix I). Base weighting factors used to determine the relative value (weight) for each service category are:

1. The amount of time (number of patient/family visits) necessary for the completion of the service.
2. Location of patient at time of service contract.

Since this process is in its infancy, other factors may need to be analyzed in time, such as the complexity factors influencing need and service where data is being collected.

This model, respecting current social work practice experience, assumes that there is one service category which will best suit the problem to be dealt with as contracted. In determining the service category that most appropriately applies to each problem, consideration is given to the main objective of the service. While each of these service categories are not perfectly defined, clear understanding of the main objective of the service and consistency in applying this understanding is crucial. Analyzing data based on these service categories is functional only if that consistency is maintained.

The next step establishes the total number of patient/family visits necessary to complete this service. Weekly statistical counts, based on the social work productivity standard, i.e., patient/family visit, are collected. This total is multiplied by the current time value recognized for that hospital service area (Coulton, 1979) and correlated with the service category(s) the social worker has provided during the Service Episode. (See Appendix II-#2). An average for each service category is expected within the same hospital service area.

Knowledge of social work services most effective in dealing with problems defined by contract requires data collection, analysis, and evaluation based on the following:

1. Types of social work services available need to be classified.
2. Social work services would be analyzed by frequency of use by various hospital service areas.
3. Psycho-social classification of patient need must be matched to the social work service resource.
4. Evaluation of outcome.

Within each Service Category then, allowance must be made for complexity factors that exist in order to estimate the amount and type of social work resources that may be required. These collective factors constitute the beginning weighting process necessary to establish the relative value of each service category. To insure the continuing accuracy of the values assigned to each service category these variables would be reviewed on a regular basis.

RELATIVE COSTS FOR SERVICE PACKAGE UNIT

This information can be used in helping to establish cost of services. Such a cost accounting system can contribute to an analysis of efficiency and effectiveness of service.

Having defined each service category and the amount of time necessary for completion of this service in the particular hospital area, it is possible to explain the relative cost for each service category. Relative cost applies then to the specific resources used for each service and their relationship to each other. This becomes a numerical unit designation which expresses the relationship to the cost that one social work service bears to another.

How is this determined for social work services? The following basic formula is utilized to determine relative cost for each service category:

Relative Cost = Units of time spent × Cost per unit of time
  1. Total Time/Service Category = Pt/Family Visits × Time/Hospital Service
  2. Cost/Service Category = Total Units of Time × $ Cost per Unit of Time (See Appendix II-#3)

This relative cost should not be expected to remain constant, and it may vary from one hospital service area to another. A periodic review of these relative costs is necessary; this review should occur at least annually. Included in this review is the necessity of understanding and redefining the relative value (significant complexity components) for each service category. Basic to this, however, would be the establishment of a cost/Standard Time Unit. In determining this cost it is necessary to consider all of the indirect costs and to be sure they are all included in the unit cost. However, when first establishing a system based on Standard Time Unit, the total expenses of the department may be known without the proportion of direct and indirect expenses being known. The most accurate way of determining cost per Standard Time Unit will be to count all time per hospital service area (visit total × time value) per year and divide that number into total departmental costs for the year (Butler, 1979).

  1. Cost per Unit = Total Cost ÷ Total Units
  2. Total Units = Pt/Family Visit Total × Time Value/Visit

One cost/time Unit would be established for the department as a whole, using a constant time unit equal to 10 minutes, for example. The cost per Standard Time Unit can be checked in subsequent years by making a similar calculation at year end. Standard Time Units would continue to be counted. Total cost per Service Category then becomes possible as previously indicated. An example of this follows:

Service Category = Counseling/Illness Related
Hospital Service Area = Inpatient Medicine
Total Pt/Family Visits = 5
Time Value/Visit = 5.9 (Coulton, 1979)
Cost/Unit (10 Minutes) = $5.00 ($30/hr) (See Appendix II-#4)
Cost/Service Category = 29.5 Units × $5.00 = $147.50

A similar Service Category cost for each Service Category can then be established utilizing the same formula.

By utilizing this Service Category formula, or any other "standard" based cost accounting formula, it may be possible to establish a realistic cost, and define that cost for a given population of patients within a hospital service area. From a cost accounting point of view, this more accurately reflects the cost to the responsibility center (revenue center) where the social work service is provided and reduces the amount of overhead costs which would have to be arbitrarily allocated. It also allows the Social Work Administrator to compare "standard" social work costs and corresponding costs from one hospital service area to another. *An understanding of why these costs vary leads to maximizing service provision if analyzed carefully,* because it encourages greater efficiency in using departmental resources.

It further follows that this leads to cost effectiveness and help in analyzing the cost benefit of social services. For a given hospital, or within various hospital service areas, social work services provided can be explained in terms of efficiency and effectiveness. Quality standards would evaluate effectiveness based on the outcome of social work service. This information would also be used in the analysis and comparison of cost effectiveness for various hospital service areas. The cost benefit to patients seen in a given hospital service area can then be explained more accurately by comparing actual cost for service delivery with the degree to which the social work service has met the defined objective(s) of that area.

How will social work services be provided? Answering several questions will help Social Work administrators to determine this and to plan for ongoing service delivery.

1. What are the different social work service needs of the hospital population?
2. What variety (relative complexity) of social work service needs can be provided to the hospital population?
3. What is the most efficient workload potential per staff person to meet the needs of the hospital population?
4. How can staff be assigned to meet these population needs most effectively?
5. What is the cost of providing this social work service package to the hospital population?

A total workload expectation can be defined by determining each Service Category within that workload. Within each procedure/service "standard," a Service Category will be possible to establish relevant variables which would change the total time and skill necessary for service completion. A total workload for one staff person in one hospital service area can be established and revised by determining the variety and frequency of service categories for the population. Example # 1 expresses this relative value for each Service Category in the Workload on an Inpatient Medicine Unit.

Using the averages based on actual experience for that Hospital service

Example # 1

Service Category	Total Pt./Family Visits	Units/ Inpt.Visit	Total Time	Total Cost
1. Discharge Planning	5	5.9	29.5	$147.50
2. Counseling/Illness related	6	5.9	35.4	177.00
3. Counseling/Situational	3	5.9	17.7	88.50
4. Referral to Community	2	5.9	11.8	59.00
5. Psycho/Social Evaluation	3	5.9	17.7	88.50
6. Coordination of Services	2	5.9	11.8	59.00
7. Provision Material Help	2	5.9	11.8	59.00
8. Counseling/Psycho Social	4	5.9	23.6	118.00
9. Admission Planning	1	5.9	5.9	29.50

area, it is possible to develop a workload expectation that builds in high efficiency and effectiveness as expressed by the standard/procedure. Example # 2 builds such a workload expectation for one month. Total time available = 173 hours; this figure represents total paid time available for one full time equivalent.

For this workload example 139 of a total of 173 work hours available are utilized in providing 36 Episodes of Social Work Service. Having established such workload descriptions, the variables that impact on the complexity of the service/procedure can be utilized to explain variation and change in this standard. These variables might include the total number of problems or problem types and corresponding service categories. Population characteristics for At Risk Patients would be another added variable. More complex cases could be clearly identified based on these numbers. The variables would be rated accordingly and changes in time and, therefore, cost per service category would be identified.

POTENTIAL BENEFITS OF COSTING FOR EFFICIENCY AND EFFECTIVENESS

Having established the internal value for the Social Work "standard" and its potential for external use, consideration would more realistically be given to who should bear the allocation of the cost of such services. The choices are easy to identify:

1. For reimbursement purposes social work service is an overhead expense and charged across the board on a per patient day basis. For

Example # 2

Medicine Unit   -   31 Beds

Average LOS   -   10 Days

Average Caseload   -   36/Month

% of Pts. to Receive Social Work Services - 39%

(36 ÷ 93 patients/month)

Service Category	Total Case Episodes	Cost/ Episode	Total Time	Total Cost
1. Discharge Planning	11	147.50	324.5 (54 Hrs.)	$1622.50
2. Counseling/Illness	7	177.00	247.8 (41 Hrs.)	$1239.00
3. Counseling/Situational	3	88.50	53. (9 Hrs.)	$ 265.00
4. Referred to Community	2	59.00	23.6 (4 Hrs.)	$ 118.00
5. Psycho/Social Evaluation	2	88.50	35.4 (6 Hrs.)	$ 177.00
6. Provision Material Help	2	59.00	23.6 (4 Hrs.)	$ 118.00
7. Counseling Psycho/Social	4	118.00	94.4 (16 Hrs.)	$ 472.00
8. Admission Planning	5	29.50	29.5 (5 Hrs.)	$ 147.50
	36		831.8 (139 Hrs)	$4159.50

internal control purposes costs are charges to the revenue centers on a per patient basis where the service is actually provided.
2. Charge services equally to all patients in the hospital irrespective of the area in which the service was provided or the potential at risk patients in particular populations.
3. Attach a "charge" to the cost per patient day only for these patients who are "at risk" of having clearly defined social problems.
4. Make a charge directly to patients who receive the services.

The development of a sound cost-accounting system will assist in clarifying the efficiency and effectiveness of social work services. As third party payors recognize separate provider vendorships for the social work professional, negotiations with them could result in identifying "necessary social work services" (which would automatically be reimbursed) as well as "elective services" which patients would receive with his/her consent with corresponding responsibility for payment. This is also adaptable to costing systems designed for health maintenance organizations. In any situation the cost for social work services are specified and potential income generated by Departments of Social Work can be identified.

SUMMARY

In summary, such a system provides an opportunity for defining and evaluating procedures/services with respect to standard of productivity. It further establishes a system for costing that considers productivity relative to the benefit of the service being provided. This gives the Social Work Administrator a system with potential for defining the need, the services to be provided, and the essential supports. It provides for numerical comparison of actual costs for providing the procedures/services, in terms of value to various social work constituencies. It realistically establishes a numerical relative value between types of service within a Social Work Department. It allows for incorporation of outcome (Unit of Benefit) data for cost effective considerations. Such units of benefit focus on prevention, maintenance, and predictive treatment modes. It is limiting in that, if not carefully evaluated, it might presume that procedure/service productivity remains constant. Patient needs variability is hard to quantify. It assumes that the value of the procedure/service (in this case Social Work Service) is uniform from one health care facility to another unless facility differences are carefully specified. All of these limitations are reduced to the extent that variability factors are incorporated.

Finally, systems, if flexible, can be effective and efficient. It is wise to anticipate, given the focus on cost effectiveness and the degree of competitiveness for any kind of service contract, that the potential interrelatedness of quality and cost control through such a system will be important. Certainly this Service Package or a similar model will be attractive to the consumer because it suggests effectiveness and responsibility.

Time is the basic component. Level of complexity is established utilizing the Service Package here as an example of procedure/service "standard" setting. With vendorship status, the social work profession will have to account for the cost of services, already a definite requirement for health care professionals for the foreseeable future. Therefore, an objectively defined, output oriented costing system based on complexity of service is essential; it can be built into any social work delivery system in the future. Such data should aid in documenting that a particular social work procedure/service has contributed significantly both to the sick or disabled person's ability to use the health services and to the fulfillment of the mission of the particular program with regard to the population group served.

APPENDIX I

Service Categories

1. Patient Movement

The following 3 service categories pertain to the patient either gaining access to a Health Care Facility (clinic, hospital, or community physician or service) or continuing to receive needed health services after being discharged from a Health Care Facility. The service provided involves planning with the patient or family to achieve the specific goal implied in the title of the Service Category, namely: Admission, Discharge, or Other Health Care. Other social work services such as referrals, coordinating activities, counseling, are included in these planning activities. The essential elements in a Service Episode are assessment, problem identification, goal definition, treatment plan, and outcome evaluation.

0 – *Admission Planning*

This service category is utilized when the patient's physician has arranged inpatient admission into The Johns Hopkins Hospital, but the patient is unable to follow through because of complicating circumstances (economic, environmental, family, social). The resolution of the identified problem results in the patient's admission into the hospital.

1 – *Discharge Planning*

This service is provided to inpatients at The Johns Hopkins Hospital who have anticipated health need for post hospital care and who can utilize workers to plan for the care. The social worker with the patient family, in coordination with the hospital staff, assesses the particular situation, problems, alternatives and helps to implement the chosen plan. Alternatives include nursing home or chronic hospital placements, foster home placements, home care arrangements. This category does include counseling about such problems that impede the discharge.

2 – *Other Health Planning*

This service is provided to patients of The Johns Hopkins Hospital and is focused on a patient gaining access to a health care facility or provider to insure that they receive (physical, mental) care as needed. Results implied in this category include *outpatient nursing home* arrangements, visits with physician (private or clinic) as needed; social work service can include education about transportation resources and environmentally related health problems, how a physician and clinic assist the patient; another service provided can be the actual arranging of needed services.

2. Psychosocial Evaluation

This service is a comprehensive evaluation of a patient's psychosocial functioning and the result is a written evaluation with recommendations to be placed in the medical chart and a copy attached to the social work record. Information may be gathered directly from patient/family, from staff contacts, and the medical charts. In one or more paragraphs, the synthesis section should give clear understanding of the patient/family and should contain the analysis, weighing, and reorganization of facts, resulting in an interpretation which addresses the rationales for evaluation. Recommendations should address the staff's management of the patient as well as the social worker's plan for direct service. Problem identification should result, then in another type of service and another service episode.

3. Counseling

The counseling categories are used when the worker actively engages a patient or family to work within the context of their relationship toward resolution of specific problems that are interpersonal, intrapersonal, situational, environmental. Different modalities may be used—family, group, individual. The essential components of any social work service must be present—assessment, problem identification, goal definition, treatment plan, and outcome evaluation. The specific category selected depends upon the content of the problem.

> 4 – *Counseling—Illness:*
> The focus of problem is related to medical or psychiatric illness, including pregnancy, alcoholism, and child abuse.
> 5 – *Counseling—Psychosocial:*
> The focus is on inter or intra personal difficulties not related directly to the health situation.
> 6 – *Counseling—Situational:*
> The focus of the problem is on environmental or economic issues.

Facilitating Services

The services provided in these categories assist the patient/family in acquiring services from community agencies to alleviate clothing, shelter, etc., needs. Services that assist directly in the patient gaining access to a health care facility or provider (including health related community agencies) are appropriately recorded in the patient movement categories. The essential components of any social work services must be present; assessment, problem identification, goal definition, treatment plan, and outcome evaluation.

> 7 – *Provision of Material Help:*
> The social worker arranges directly for such concrete items as equipment, clothing, shelter, transportation, oxygen, etc. through the pa-

tient's own (medical insurance, etc.) or through hospital controlled resources (ACS grant, etc.) (exclude discharge).

8 – *Referral to Community:*

The social worker arranges for items or services to be secured through any agency in the community by either verbal or written transfer of information. Followup occurs to determine if the agency has been successful in alleviating the problem the patient was experiencing (exclude discharge).

9 – *Coordinating Services:*

The social worker acts in a liaison capacity on behalf of the patient/family. Appropriate information is exchanged between various personnel in the hospital or agencies who already know the patient or will be involved with the patient. This activity can, also, occur with agencies in the community who are already involved with the patient and working toward alleviating problems.

APPENDIX II

Definitions

(1) "Effectiveness is the degree to which what an organization does (its products and services) contribute to the accomplishment of what the organization wants to do (its goals or objectives). One could apply this to social work by saying effectiveness is the degree to which hours of patient care (units of input) provided actually contribute to better health of patients assuming this is the organization's goal. *High efficiency (a lot of output per unit of input) does not necessarily mean high effectiveness.*" (Quotation Mr. Nathaniel Butler, Business Manager, Dept. of Social Service, Massachusetts General Hospital—Spring, 1979.)

(2) Service Episode is defined as "A treatment sequence that includes case finding, assessment, problem identification, contracting, treatment, and evaluation of outcome, excludes transportation" (Recording and Reporting Manual, Dept. of Social Work, The Johns Hopkins Hospital, revised Spring, 1979.)

(3) Cost includes cost for overhead and downtime.

(4) This dollar value is selected arbitrarily for example only. It is not based on any real or known dollar value.

REFERENCES

Anthony, R. N. & Herzlinger, R. F. *Management control in non-profit organizations.* Homewood, Ill.: Richard D. Irwin, Inc., 1975, p. 22.

Butler, N. In context of conversation, Spring, 1979.

California Relative Value Studies, 5th Edition (revised). Adopted by The CMA Council, November 8, 1974. Prepared by Committee on Relative Value Studies, California Medical Association, San Francisco, 1975.

Collins, J. *A cost-effectiveness model: Proceedings quality assurance in social services in health programs for mothers and children.* March 31 - April 4, 1975, Pittsburgh, Pa. pp. 103–106.

Coulton, C. et al. *Nationwide survey of hospital social work practice.* Sponsored by the Society for Hospital Social Work Directors of the American Hospital Association and The National Association of Social Workers, 1979.

Fassett, J. D. Presented at 1974 Annual meeting Society for Social Work Directors, Atlanta, Georgia, Unpublished.

Jack, B. Social work accountability in a children and young project. *Accountability: a critical issue in social services,* Pittsburgh, Pa.

Kurzman, Paul A. Third party reimbursement. *Social Work,* 1973, *18,* pp. 11–22.

Levy, L. Financing, organization and control: the problem of implementing comprehensive community mental health services. *American Journal of Public Health,* 1969, *59*(1), pp. 40–47.

Lyon, J. G. Social services coverage in health settings: Prospects and issues. *Evaluation of social work services in community health and medical care programs. Program in public health social work.* Berkeley, Ca.: University of California, 1973, pp. 139–153.

Menn, R. L. Developing principles of cost finding for community mental health centers. *American Journal for Public Health,* 1971, *61*(8), pp. 1531–1535.

Spiro, H. R., et al. Cost finances mental health facility (III) economic issues and implications for future patterns of health care. *Journal Nervous Disorders,* 1975, *160*(4), pp. 249–54.

Vanderwall, R. W. Accountability of social services in a health program: a working model. *Accountability: A Critical Issue in Social Services,* Pittsburgh, Pa.

Vielhaber, D. P. & Irvin, N. A. Accounting for social work services in discharge planning (Preliminary results of a survey). *Proceedings quality assurance in social service in health programs for mothers and children, March 31 - April 4, 1975,* Pittsburgh, Pa., pp. 95–102.

Volland, P. J. Social work information and accountability systems in a hospital setting. *Social Work in Health Care,* 1976, *1*(3).

Volland, P. J. & German, P. "Development of an information system: a means of improving social work practice in health care. *American Journal of Public Health,* 1979, *69*(4).

Wood, C. T., MHA, & F. A. C. H. "Interrelated programs for optimum cost effectiveness in hospital management." Massachusetts Eye and Ear Infirmary. Published as part of the "Update" program on hospital management by Damon Corporation, Needham Heights, Massachusetts, 1976.

Chapter 13

Seven Key Managerial Functions of Sound Fiscal Budgeting: An Internal Management and External Accountability Perspective

John J. Stretch, PhD

ABSTRACT. This paper examines major underlying assumptions supporting the validity of seven key managerial functions as these functions are achieved and enhanced through the systematic, conscious deployment of four current budgeting strategies.

Increasingly enlightened public social policy is demanding better utilization of scarce fiscal and professional resources to meet the expanding objectives of the social environment in a complex and interdependent society. What modern human services managers need to know in substance about essential budget strategies and their increased functional utility for enhancing the objectives of human services management provide the integrating theme for the presentation.

First, it should be stated emphatically that the days of tolerating sloppy fiscal management in the human services are over (Alexander, 1977). Current accounting concepts and attendant managerial approaches which can materially enhance the range of social objectives sought by human services agencies are available now (Anthony & Herzlinger, 1975). It is a foregone conclusion that better fiscal management tools will continue to grow in influence and in force in the expanding field of human services (Slavin, 1978).

An inevitable public policy position demanding fuller accountability for both fiscal and human resource allocations authorized to engage human services issues and ameliorate social problems is highly supportive of the trend toward increased utilization of better management approaches (United Way, 1974). Currently, much attention is being devoted by leaders in the accounting profession to strengthening the conceptual models and operational tools available to support the expanding field of social service management (Financial Accounting Standards Board, 1978). Cur-

rently, Title XX funding provides growing empirical evidence for the necessity to bring better managerial competence into the service of meeting
human needs (Child Welfare League, 1978). The tools of rational management are fast becoming the hallmark of not only some of the most professionally avant garde agencies, but, more importantly, of some of the
most highly successful ones (Mogulof, 1974). To the criterion of
increasing an agency's problem relevance has been added the additional
requirement of increasing its managerial rigor (Stretch, 1978).

UNDERPINNING ASSUMPTIONS

Resources are viewed as scarce and constrained (American Institute of
Management, 1973). There are never enough of the resources of time,
personnel, and technology to fulfill all of the legitimate wants and aspirations of people—nor will there ever be (Garfinkel, 1974).

Resources must therefore be utilized effectively to achieve clear policy
objectives. Resources must also be used efficiently in order to insure that
maximum benefits are obtained through social services from a rationally
justified combination of resources reflecting minimum costs.

The scarce resource assumption provides a realistic management focus. A useful workable administrative framework for justifying human
services growth through sound resources deployment emerges.

Other key assumptions which underlie the usefulness of resource budgeting strategies as developed and justified in this paper are:

1. Rational planning translated into operationally sound management
   approaches must be further engaged by human services managers in
   order to provide both increased rigor and added relevance to the
   human services field.
2. Conceptualizing resources as scarce increases both the range and
   depth of commitment towards their effective and efficient
   utilization.
3. Increasing accountability through public policy mechanisms is inevitable and, in both the short and long run, is extremely healthy
   for the continued growth and expansion of human services.
4. Budgeting strategies are very important administrative tools for
   operationalizing sound management activities currently required
   for directing responsible and responsive human services enterprises. Without minimal acceptance of these underlying assumptions, the fiscal budgeting approaches as management tools have
   little justification or ultimate usefulness.

One additional corollary should be added by way of a value statement.
Increasing managerial expertise in the field of human services will pro-

vide added rigor to both target and justify resource utilization better, and in no substantive way will hinder the progress for people being sought through expanding social goals (Briar, 1974).

Managerial tools and techniques should not erroneously be made to take the place of substantive progress (Gruber, 1974). Methodologies, no matter how potentially powerful, should not be allowed to assume a primary importance which overshadows substantive issues of policy development and program design which flow from a continual questioning of the mission, goals, and objectives to be pursued by human services organizations. A perspective of substance over technique should be maintained throughout the discussion to follow. Simply put, we in the human services should continually examine and question what we want for the people we serve—why we want these objectives and why they are socially important—before we become overly captive by how to best achieve them (United Way of St. Louis, 1977). A substantive perspective on social progress does not deny the utility of parallel conceptual and methodological tools to aid us in the quest of relevant objectives; it only seeks to put methods in their proper place—as servant not as master (Reid, 1974).

Human services practitioners need not therefore unduly fear sound management if they understand the basis of management as fundamentally instrumental (Weissman, 1973). The most powerful ally of the human services is still unfilled human need and potential. Better meeting these needs should be the guiding objective of all human services managerial strategies (Rosenberg & Brody, 1974).

SEVEN BASIC OBJECTIVES OF BUDGETING

In this section we shall set forth seven basic managerial objectives in the field of human services to be supported by four current budgeting strategies. Each budget strategy is briefly described in terms of the key management functions it serves. The four strategies considered are line item budgeting, functional budgeting, program budgeting, and zero-base budgeting.

A few of these objectives may at first reading appear a bit unfamiliar to some managers in the human services field. The human services administrator should feel more at ease with the basic managerial concepts presented after the full context and application of these fiscal concepts and the functions they serve are presented. The degree to which one function takes priority or precedence over another is first, often a matter of managerial style, and second, dependent on the particular set of administrative responsibilities that the human services manager has to deal with at the time.

The seven key functions as conceptualized by the author are, in the order discussed: controlling, allocating, monitoring, prioritizing, evaluating, planning, and programming. If properly executed, these key functions could provide a foundation for additional integration of modern fiscal tools to meet basic human service goals.

Controlling: The First Management Function

The first, and in the judgment of the author the most important, of the seven basic managerial functions to be served by any sound budgeting strategy is increasing the degree of managerial control. Increasing the span of effective and efficient management control means increasing the ability of the key administrator and his/her delegated management team to have the capacity to direct and determine the quality and amount of activities to be supported through a given budgetary decision.

Resources cannot be allowed to escape the direct control of the relevant management system (Henke, 1977). At all times central management must be able to put its finger on what type of resources and what amount of the resource pool is being channelled to what purposes in the organization (Drucker, 1977).

If the manager does not have the capacity to answer key questions of this type, he/she has no clear fiscal operational control. Without such control the ability to direct fiscal resources through sound management is meaningless (United Way, 1974).

Control is paramount. The first and foremost objective to be served by any sound budget system is resource control. A human service agency that has no knowledge of how, why, and where fiscal and human resources are deployed, is in deep trouble managerially.

An agency which has this capacity operationally and is effectively utilizing sound accounting principles to enhance resource control is in a good basic position to discharge both its internal managerial responsibilities and its external accountability responsibilities (United Way, 1975).

It was principally to insure the responsible fulfilling of the dual objectives of sound internal fiscal management and creditable external fiscal accountability that the currently most used and widely accepted budgetary strategy, the line item expenditure budget, was developed.

The line item expenditure budget approach allows for a very tight degree of managerial control over each major significant resource item allocated through the budget decision process. The main feature and advantage of the line item budget approach is its reliance on explicit categories of expenditures to insure justification. Suffice it to say that when human services managers usually think of "the budget," they are most probably thinking of the typical item-by-item line control budget where such key expenditure categories as personnel, rent, utilities, and so forth, are explicitly defined and authorized in terms of what can be spent on each line item.

By extending the control function which targets and justifies the organization's activities, several allied and equally important functions served by sound budgeting come into focus. The allied functions which closely tie into the control function are the management functions of allocating, monitoring, and evaluating.

The Allocation Function of Management

Resources must be allocated by someone through some process. Allocation is a conscious, systems-justified managerial process heavily dependent on current and projected considerations linked through program objectives to achieve overall goals. Allocation supports the central function of managerial control. Sound allocation procedures increase the span of managerial control.

Resources should be allocated on the basis of an explicit, conscious, rational, systems-integrative approach to achieve the mission, goals, and objectives of the agency (United Way, 1972). Ideally, there should be in place a clearly explicit or, if this is not possible, at the least a generally agreed on accountability expectation that out of several possible allocation patterns currently available to the manager, the pattern finally selected will achieve the organizational goals and objectives of the human services agency in the most effective and efficient way. A specific budgetary strategy which makes the total allocation process highly explicit and at the same time operationally most feasible has been incorporated in the zero-base approach to budgeting (Pyhrr, 1973). In substance zero-base budgeting (ZBB by acronym designation) focuses intermediate as well as top levels of decision makers in an organization on justifying their program allocation decision patterns when presented with alternative program approaches to achieve organizational goals and objectives. The ZBB approach is an attempt to force key managers to make explicit what level of output will be associated with what level of budgeted resources allocated.

The Management Function of Monitoring

Next to be considered is the monitoring function of budgeting. Every well-run and responsive organization must know if it is on or off course within given critical parameters of its basic operations. The function of useful, intelligent feedback is performed through the monitoring function of management.

As controlled fiscal expenditures are justified and allocated, there must be a corresponding capacity in the hands of key management to track the outcomes of resource decisions. Management must be able to take corrective action when necessary, if resources are poorly used or unwisely expended. The monitoring function when enhanced by budget authority is usually served well if the agency has in place and is actually using in its management decisions processes relevant data generated by a good management information system (MIS) (O'Brien, 1970). As part of the central MIS, the budget subsector of the nonprofit organization should be tracked internally by a series of accepted accounting practices, such as voucher controls and explicit expenditure rules designed for the purpose of monitoring on a daily, monthly, or quarterly basis what resources are going where and with what overall results (National Institute of Mental Health, 1971).

What conceptual and operational changes may be called for in the accounting profession to adequately provide the quantity and quality of information required by the users of financial statements in non-business organizations is now concerning the financial accounting standards board. A full discussion of the complexities currently under review would take us afield of this paper. But the main thrust of the type of information given high priority is pertinent here. Four major categories of information which financial statements should provide are:

1. Financial viability—these data would supply information that indicates the organization's ability to continue to provide the services for which it exists.
2. Fiscal compliance—these data would indicate that spending mandates and regulations have been fairly complied with and that fiscal resources have been used for intended purposes.
3. Management performance—these data would justify managerial decisions on how well money was spent to achieve objectives.
4. Cost of services provided—these data would shed light on unit costs, standard budgets for services expenditures, and variances associated with shifts in quality and quantity of services (Anthony, 1978).

In addition to tighter existing fund accounting standards which have been also under conceptual and operational review, program budgeting as an additional management strategy is closely allied with the objective of effective monitoring of fiscal and human resources as these are targeted to achieve program objectives. Program budgeting considers expenditures in light of the major program components operative in the human service agency's mix of services. Program budgeting has been found to be a useful management tool in monitoring the effect of key allocation decisions as these affect the level of program quality. Program budgeting is essentially output oriented. A program budget is constructed by regrouping all line item expenditures into their respective program areas. For example, the line items of personnel, rent and utilities would be regrouped according to some rational formula of direct and indirect cost factors to reflect the various agency programs that these resources support (Ramanathan, 1978).

Prioritizing as a Management Function

The management function of prioritizing can best be served through a conscious systems-orientation in which management uses explicit, integrated, rational planning, coupled with zero-base techniques, and program budgeting mechanisms to rank order key activities (Knezevich, 1973). The necessity to set realizable priorities again flows from the fundamental assumption that managerially, resources should always be viewed as scarce. We cannot do everything we want at the same time. Setting priorities which are rationally justified and at the same time can realistically direct scarce resources to highly productive ends is a basic justification for any budgeting process.

Recently there is a renewal of interest in United Way agencies to look at priority needs studies. Priority needs studies held promise in the early 1960s for combining professional and community leadership judgments toward a concensus of where United Way limited resources should flow for serving a given community (United Way, 1974). Priority needs studies fell out of favor by the end of the 1960s chiefly because they proved to be methodologically cumbersome and, probably more importantly, because by themselves priority needs studies could not deliver the easy decision making outputs that they initially promised to do.

The standard approach most often employed in a priority needs study was to develop a series of rating scales which captured major value dimensions associated with the problem areas to be addressed. A representative cross section of professional and community leadership used these ratings to develop funding priorities. Value ratings tended to cluster at given points to reflect a community's commitment to a range of problem areas. These value clusters were then systematically translated through the rating and ranking process into program priorities which in turn were to help determine levels of funding.

Priority-needs assessment techniques also seem to be gaining renewed support in the field of mental health. Needs assessment data used to form budget priorities is again becoming a focus of renewed interest in both the planning and management fields (Neigher, Hanner, & Landsberger, 1977).

This renewed interest from a budgeting perspective is readily understandable to management. In reality, the budgeted amount actually assigned to deal with a given problem area becomes the acid test of how great a given priority is perceived by community and professional leadership.

The Evaluation Function

In the author's judgment, a little explicitly recognized but nonetheless important management function inherent in the fiscal budgeting process is evaluation. Evaluation through the budget making decision process is an assessment tool that most managers use wisely and widely. Budgeting decisions are usually not viewed as explicitly evaluative (Tripodi, Fellin, & Epstein, 1973).

If a program as budgeted is not meeting its objectives, then there is or should be a corrective budgetary decision to insure that it does. The corrective budgetary decision may take the form of dropping the program, of redesigning it, or if undersupported, of materially increasing the pool of existing resources available to it. The management function served by this explicit budgetary decision is that of program evaluation (Elkin & Vorwaller, in Seidler & Seidler, 1975).

In the context of management responsibility, the focus here is to what degree it is reasonable for the administrator to hold the program accountable for achieving the desired objective within the framework of the resources it has been allocated (Weiss, 1972). If it is administratively reasonable to hold the program accountable, then the function of management evaluation is engaged. If the resources allocated through the budget process are not producing the desired program effects, corrective administrative action is mandatory. The literature on evaluation often assigns this important management function to the specialized area of evaluation research (Sze & Hopps, 1974). It is often overlooked in evaluation research designs that many programs, however, have no chance of achieving even minimal objectives when budgeted resources are not minimally adequate. The management function of evaluation of program success by explicit budget analysis is not the prevalent way the evaluation literature approaches the issue of program success.

A managerially oriented approach to program effectiveness should stress feasible cost/benefit criteria (United Way, 1972). The major idea here is that programs are justified to the extent that they provide benefits for clients who make use of them and by serving clients well for the community that supports them. Benefits, however, are not free; they entail costs. Costs are in turn justified by the quality and quantity of benefits they make possible. Resources become costs when they are allocated to given programs (Vargo, 1977). Ultimately, however, it is the manager who is held accountable for efficiency and effectiveness of resource allocation decisions. It is the manager who must finally translate program evaluative outcomes into realistic budget decisions so that the staff gets what is required to do the job.

The Planning and Programming Functions

We shall discuss briefly two additional management functions inherent in the fiscal budgeting process—planning and programming. Planning and programming functions, although analytically separate and operationally distinct from each other, from a managerial perspective will be discussed together as they are both ultimately dependent on one another. The mutual dependence comes about because planning decisions loop back to influence current and future planning approaches. Planning and programming management functions in turn flow out of and back into budget decisions. The end product is a set of funded priorities (United Way, 1972).

The management literature dealing with planning and programming activities is extensive (Haimann & Scott, 1974). Current areas of renewed interest for human services administrators are the resurgence of formal planning and programming methodologies such as Planning, Programming and Budgeting Systems (PPBS) (National Institute of Mental Health, 1976), and the continually found usefulness of Management by Objective (MBO). These efforts seek to insure effective and efficient planning through rational resource utilization designs. The emerging attention of human services agencies managers to aspects of functional budgeting serves these ends. When constructing a functional budget, all activities of the agency are categorized into the major functions they serve. In human services agencies, there are usually two—direct service functions and supportive functions. Supportive functions allow direct services to be carried out, and all of the activities performed by management would fall under the support function. It is useful at times to determine what amount of agency resources are flowing into direct services for people and what amount of agency resources are being used for support of these services. If service functions are low, it may be hard to justify large expenditures for administrative overhead.

In the functional budgeting framework, planning activities for most agencies would fall under the general function of administrative support, whereas operationalized planning, when it becomes translated into actually funded agency programs, would then fall under the function of agency service operations (United Way, 1974).

It should further be stressed that the planning function in management cannot be viewed operationally as removed, abstract, and exclusively administrative. Good planning must involve both program staff and management if it is to ultimately be translatable into sound agency programs (Kahn, 1969). New budget opportunities brought about by budgetary increases or required budgetary constraints brought about by budgetary cuts makes necessary planning alternative approaches to meeting the major goals and key objectives of the agency. A budget can thus be viewed as a resource map which brings into clear definition managerial and service objectives grounded in sound planning. Useful techniques found in budgeting approaches enhance decision making within this perspective (Pattillo, 1977).

SUMMARY

This paper has conceptualized and developed seven managerial functions. These key administrative functions are supported and enhanced through the four current budget strategies available to human services administrators. Critical assumptions which underlie the justification for the seven management functions were made explicit. A major argument of the paper was that the growing demand for greater managerial expertise to support both sound internal management and increased public accountability requirements is having and will continue to have a salutary effect on the sound development of human services. An integrating theme has been that increased attention to nonbusiness entities in general and to human services agencies in particular by the accounting profession is producing a much greater range of conceptual strategies and operational tools to help target and attain the objectives and goals of social development.

REFERENCES

Akana, P. *Some thoughts on planning.* Alexandria, Va: United Way of America, 1977.

Alexander, C. Management of human service organizations. *Encyclopedia of Social Work,* Vol. 11, pp. 844–849. New York: National Association of Social Workers, 1977.

Anderson, W., Frieden, B., & Murphy, M. (Eds.), *Managing human services.* Washington, D.C.: International City Management Association, 1977.

Anthony, R. *Financial accounting in nonbusiness organizations.* Stamford, Conn.: Financial Standards Accounting Board, 1978.

Anthony, R., & Herzlinger, R. *Management control in non-profit organizations.* Homewood, Ill.: Richard D. Irwin, 1976.

American Institute of Management. What is management?, Cited in P. E. Connor, *Dimensions in modern management.* Atlanta: Houghton Mifflin, 1973, pp. 22–27.

Brager, G., & McLaughlin, M. *Training social welfare managers.* New York: Columbia University Press, 1978.

Briar, S. The future of social work. *Social Work,* 1974, *19,* 514–518.

Brody, R., & Krailo, H., An approach to reviewing the effectiveness of programs. *Social Work,* 1978, *23,* 226–232.

Child Welfare League of America. Hecht Institute for State Child Welfare Planning. *Manual 1: Finding federal money for children, Title XX and other programs.* Washington, D.C., 1976.

Child Welfare League of America. Hecht Institute for Child Welfare Planning. *Manual 2: Obtaining federal money for children, Title XX and other programs.* Washington, D.C., 1978.

Child Welfare League of America. Hecht Institute for State Child Welfare Planning. *Manual 3: Audit-proof contracting for federal money for children. Title XX and other programs.* Washington, D.C., 1978.

Child Welfare League of America. Hecht Institute for State Child Welfare Planning. *Manual 4: Managing federal money for children, Title XX and other programs*. Washington, D.C., 1978.

Drucker, P. F. *New demands on top management*. Third Annual Distinguished Guest Lecture Program, St. Louis University School of Business and Administration, May 17, 1977.

Elkin, R., & Vorwaller, D. Evaluating the effectiveness of social services. In L. Seidler & L. Seidler, *Social accounting*. Los Angeles: Melville, 1975, pp. 410–425.

Financial Accounting Standards Board. *FASB discussion memorandum: An analysis of issues related to a conceptual framework for financial accounting and reporting: Objectives of financial reporting by nonbusiness organizations*. Stamford, Conn., 1978.

Garfinkel, E. The economics of social welfare programs. *Social Work*, 1974, *19*, 596–606.

Gruber, M. Total administration. *Social Work*, 1974, *19*, 625–637.

Haimann, T., & Scott, W. *Management in the modern organizations*. Atlanta: Houghton Mifflin, 1974.

Hellriegel, D., & Slocum, J. *Organizational behavior contingency views*. New York: West Publishing Co., 1976.

Henke, E. *Accounting for non-profit organizations*. Belmont, Calif.: Wadsworth, 1977.

Kahn, A. *Theory and practice of social planning*. New York: Russell Sage, 1969.

Knezevich, S. *Program budgeting*. Berkeley, Calif.: McCutchan, 1973.

Lyden, F., & Miller, E. (Eds.), *Planning, programming, and budgeting: A system's approach to management*. Chicago: Markham, 1972.

Magulof, M. Future funding of social services. *Social Work*, 1974, *19*, 607–614.

National Institute of Mental Health, *Accounting guidelines for mental health centers and related facilities*. Rockville, Md., 1971.

National Institute of Mental Health. *Cost-finding and rate-setting for community mental health centers*, Rockville, Md., 1976.

Neigher, W., Hammer, R., & Landsberg, G. *Emerging developments in mental health program evaluation*. New York: Argold, 1977.

O'Brien, J. *Management information systems*. New York: Nostrand Reinhold, 1970.

Pattillo, J. *Zero-base budgeting: A planning, resource allocation, and control tool*. New York: National Association of Accountants, 1977.

Pyhrr, P. *Zero-base budgeting*. New York: John Wiley and Sons, 1973.

Ramanathan, K. *Introduction to management controls in human service organizations*. Seattle: University of Washington, 1978.

Reid, W. Developments in the use of organized data. *Social Work*, 1974, *19*, 585–595.

Reinherz, H., et al. Training in accountability: A social work mandate. *Health and Social Work*, 1977, *2*, 42–56.

Rosenberg, M., & Brody, R. *Systems serving people*. Cleveland: Case Western Reserve University Press, 1974.

Schieff, M., & Lewin, A. (Eds.), *Behavioral aspects of accounting*. Englewood, N.J.: Prentice-Hall, 1974.

Slavin, S. (Ed.) *Social administration*. New York: The Haworth Press, 1978.

Stretch, J. Increasing accountability for human services administrators. *Social Casework*, 1978, *59*, 323–329.

Tripodi, T., Fellin, P., & Epstein, I. *Differential social program evaluation*. Itasca, Ill.: F. E. Peacock, 1978.

Turem, J. The call for a management stance. *Social Work*, 1974, *19*, 615–624.

United Way of America. *Budgeting*. Alexandria, Va., 1975.

United Way of America. *The painful necessity of choice*. Alexandria, Va., 1974.

United Way of America. *A PPBS approach to budgeting human service programs in the United Way*. Alexandria, Va., 1972.

United Way of America. *UWASIS II*. Alexandria, Va., 1976.

United Way of America. *Accounting and financial reporting*. Alexandria, Va., 1974.

United Way of Greater St. Louis. *Management evaluation manual*. St. Louis, 1977.

Vargo, R. *Readings in governmental and non-profit accounting*. Belmont, Calif.: Wadsworth, 1977.

Weiss, C. *Evaluation research*. Englewood Cliffs, N.J.: Prentice Hall, 1972.

Weissman, H. *Overcoming mismanagement in the human service professions*. San Francisco: Jossey-Bass, 1973.

PART V

The Role of the Department in Staff Evaluation and Continuing Education

During periods of budgetary constraints staffing patterns and performance evaluations become crucial issues. Aside from the impetus generated by fiscal policies, developing a reasonable staffing approach and evaluating job performance are two of the most significant aspects of social work administration in health care.

Realistic staffing patterns have proven to be a very complex issue. There are so many factors involved in arriving at the assignment and use of social work manpower that formulae no matter how well constructed cannot possibly meet all of the contingencies that have been foreseen. And yet an approach to the assignment of manpower becomes important and even if it were not for the immediacy of fiscal constraints and staffing patterns represent a major challenge to any social work administrator.

The first article in this chapter reflects the dilemmas and the issues that have to be confronted in developing a rationale for a staffing pattern. The article includes suggested formulae which can be used under certain restricted circumstances. But, as Lurie has indicated, there needs to be room for variation from a suggested formula depending upon many factors. Nevertheless, the attempt is extremely important and as such can lead the reader into areas of greater specificity in dealing with the challenge for justifying a reasonable staffing pattern.

One of the variables involved in the use of social work manpower resources is the setting of organizational goals. This, too, can be a very difficult assignment and Yankey and Coulton have developed models which can help in contributing to development of organizational goals. The paper suggests that these models can be used also as a basis of evaluating the behavior of employees. The article deals with conflicts, particularly in welfare agencies, when the performance of professionals as determined by their goals may be in conflict with the goals of the agencies.

The recognition that this conflict exists is in itself an important concept for administrators to recognize. But, dealing with it and particularly evaluating staff performance in the light of this conflict can become complex, particularly for social workers. The professional social worker is trained to respect the client's right of self determination and in some measure begins to apply that right to his own organizational behavior. And yet, for an organization to survive, the organization must have the loyalty of its members in contributing to the goals which the organization seeks to achieve.

The issues raised by these conflicts are dealt with by Yankey and Coulton and the implications, particularly for social welfare organizations, are highlighted.

The final article by Robert Spano in this section is more specific in dealing with performance appraisal in a hospital social service setting. In this article the authors describe a staff performance appraisal system that has been developed and implemented at the University of Minnesota Hospital. The specificity of the information which can be obtained and used to evaluate performance measured against the criteria developed by those making the evaluation of the employee is impressive.

This movement toward an objective appraisal as opposed to the traditional social work narrative must be given serious consideration, particularly as we move into a computer age. The article describes the model as the final element of a comprehensive accountability system and reflects a sophisticated approach as an addition to the supervisory process which has been traditionally thought to be one of the important contributions of social work in the behavioral field. As we move away from some of our traditional social work methodologies it is important to replace them with other tested models and Spano's article does this in a reflective manner.

Abraham Lurie, PhD

Chapter 14

Staffing Patterns:
Issues and Program Implications
for Health Care Agencies

Abraham Lurie, PhD

ABSTRACT. Unsolved staffing pattern issues are viewed in the current context of funding pressures, third party payment, and management necessity for program and cost projections. Relevant factors are mustered for consideration with their implications. Use of differentiated skill levels and response as well as development of departmental services mandate are considered. The author also shares his experientially derived thoughts on staff ratio to certain institutional assignments.

HISTORIC PERSPECTIVES AND CRITERIA

The publication and circulation of surveys describing manpower utilization and staffing patterns of social workers in medical and psychiatric settings attest to the profession's long-standing concern with this issue. The Hollinghead New Haven study,[1] a study of social work in general practice in England called the Derby scheme;[2] Tessie Berkman's study of the use of psychiatric social work in mental health clinics and hospitals in the United States; National Association of Social Workers (NASW) publication, "Utilization of Personnel in Social Work"; the United Hospital Fund Metropolitan Regional Medical Program devoted to social work manpower and knowledge in relation to critical illness; the work of Briggs and Barker regarding the differential use of social work manpower, and a subsequent report by Briggs and Glick dealing with manpower research in social work education; and Herman Shepard's recent review of Social Work Departments in New York City hospitals have each grappled with aspects of this difficult administrative issue.

These studies have yielded interesting findings: that 55 to 65% of all patients admitted to general hospitals require some psychosocial intervention; that "bed size is only one factor which determines the number of staff in a hospital social service department;"[3-8] that one full-time professional social worker can service between 50 and 60 patients in a long-term care facility;[9-10] and that there is increasing need of social work intervention. Yet one is left with the uneasy feeling that staffing patterns are frequently dependent upon subjectivity and sometimes whimsy.

Among criteria which have been utilized but are now viewed with skepticism are size of case load, number of hospital beds, nature of the program, and interview count. These variables are significant but not conclusive. Although hard data would be welcome, we know that some issues do not lend themselves to precise, data-based solution.

Realistically, staffing patterns can be discussed only in terms of knowledge and function. Specifically, staffing in social work departments is related to the mission of the department within a health agency structure and the professional knowledge necessary to perform that mission.

COMPELLING CONTEMPORARY ISSUES

Why then is it important for social work to look again at staffing patterns? Each dollar now spent for social work, as for other services, is subject to increasingly vigorous and critical examination. The justification of requests for staff on the basis of human need couched in psychosocial terms, is a reasonable but not always persuasive argument. But, there are other reasons besides increasing costs and the limitation of resources why analysis of staffing patterns in health settings has become critical. One is the influence of third party payors such as insurance companies, Medicaid, and Medicare. Constraints from other funding sources must be considered. Labor organizations are a limiting factor in the prerogatives of management as it pertains to staffing. Contractual arrangements between labor organizations and with third party payors require specificity in costs and services.

The result is a demand for quantification and the correlation of staff functions to goals and mandated responsibilities. Depending on the vantage point from which it is being observed, every discipline is either suffering or benefiting from pressure to define its value and to justify its manpower requirements. Administration is not the *bete noire*. On the contrary, it is to the advantage of every discipline as well as the public that the highest levels of administrative echelons be held accountable for decisions affecting staffing and for quality of service. Quality assurance and responsible deployment of professional resources are inextricably bound together.

Peer review systems mandated for social work managers in health settings are another push toward explicit definition and measurement with respect to staffing patterns, knowledge content, use of differential levels of manpower, and criteria for measuring outcomes.

IMPACT OF LEVELS OF EDUCATION AND SKILL ON PLANNING

Twenty-five years ago the basic levels of social workers were masters of social work (MSW) differentiated on the basis of setting, i.e., medical, psychiatric, family services, or group work agencies. Now the entry degree into the professional field has been defined by our professional and educational collegial bodies as the bachelors degree. Several levels of potential social work manpower below the bachelors degree have been developed. While descriptions for social work tasks are still being developed for these levels, doctoral programs in social work have been burgeoning. Whereas in the past there have been limited numbers of workers in other than MSW categories.

Now there are increasing numbers in many classifications with a variety of skill and experiences and a confusing array of functions and roles. In addition to the 7,387 MSW graduates in 1972-1973 there were approximately 8,000 bachelor (social work) graduates and 112 doctorates of social work, DSW. (Statistics edited by Dr. Lillian Ripple and Dr. Ralph Dolgoff, Council of Social Work Education.)

Regulatory bodies are playing an increasingly significant role in influencing staffing patterns. For example, an operational and planning model for abortion services in New York City includes suggested staffing pattern for social workers. This pattern was developed by Mark Mandell, a health analyst with the Office of Program Analysis of the New York City Health and Hospitals Corporation, we assume, in consultation with others.[11] Such models, whether born of wisdom or fiscal caprice, can have the power of government sanction. As they can be tied to funding, they become a particularly important influence. Hence, the necessity for guidelines and standards derived from professional competence and available to government bodies or institutions inaugurating social work programs.

The number of hospitals throughout the country that have social work services has increased from 27% (1970) to about 50% (1974), almost double the number. This rapid increase, particularly in small hospitals, requires the establishment of priorities and staffing patterns. Many hospitals are starting-up programs either with consultants or with one- or two-person departments and on the basis of experience plan to expand the service as the need is demonstrated. Guidelines which can be used as a basis for staffing are important to beginning social work administrators.

UNRESOLVED PRACTICE ISSUES

Internal professional issues having to do with staffing concern the delivery of effective service for patient and family care by staff at multilevels of skill. Questions to be asked and, as soon as possible answered are:

(1) What are our minimum expectations of recent social work graduates, or of social work graduates with varying levels of experience?

(2) How should they be used in the health setting?

(3) What kinds of tasks should they perform?

(4) Who should supervise them?

(5) What should be the nature of this supervision and for how long?

Staffing patterns will be affected by the resolution of these issues. Before offering some specific guideline suggestions, several caveats are in order. While specificity is needed in all settings, the "formula" for one health setting will not necessarily apply to the needs of other settings even though they may be similar. We must seek out the commonality and the variables. Determination of staff requirements must be made in relation to goals. Hence, the necessity to grapple with these issues:

(1) What are the clearly explicated departmental goals or functions?

(2) In what area should social work be strengthened?

(3) What are the present and developing priorities and how are they related to the department's function?

(4) Which clientele shall the department serve, and at what level of intervention?

(5) Should social work service be limited to crisis intervention?

(6) Which cases should be continued after discharge and which referred to other agencies?

(7) Should the service be psycho intensive, concrete intensive, or a combination of both?

PROGRAM CONSIDERATIONS

Social workers employed as primary therapists may not be able to carry as many "cases" as those involved in offering concrete services so that the treatment goals become an important factor in determining staff ratios. Social workers with heavy programs, systems, or milieu responsibilities may not be able to define work load in case units, but in population units.

Another issue strongly influencing staffing patterns are educational offerings, both formal and informal, designated as departmental functions. If social workers are to be used in educating others (social work students, physicians, occupational and physical therapists, nurses, and ward clerks) then social workers with certain requisite education and experience must be used. Upgrading social work skills (in-service education) also requires an allotment of time and this, too, needs to be determined in advance for a reasonable staffing pattern to be developed. Education cannot be viewed as formal classroom teaching since so much informal interaction and educating of residents, interns, housestaff, nurses, and others occurs in the patient areas.

Another area is research.

(1) What will be the thrust and level of the research endeavor?

(2) Should it be evaluative or basic, interdisciplinary or departmental?

These will influence staff assignments and the level of staff, as well as expectations. It can be argued that research should not have any priority and that the objective is to establish services for direct patient and family care. However, the professional commitment to progress through inquiry is reenforced by external calls for cost-effectiveness and quality assurance. When quality control is mandated by the regulatory agencies then the relationship of manpower to quality control and outcome measurement is legitimized. To evaluate effectiveness of social work service necessitates research.

The time and staffing implications of community development and organization responsibilities is a growing consideration. In the health setting, community planning and prevention of physical and social breakdown are becoming parallel responsibilities to assessment and treatment. If participation with viable social action groups and liaison community groups are of concern to health organizations, as they should be, then allowance must be made for staff time.[12] Such tasks should be done mainly with skilled social work manpower.

Another manpower factor is the pressure of minority groups to use health settings to meet employment as well as other "nonhealth" community needs. These influences pose constraints and set precedents that influence deployment and utilization of social work manpower.

A relatively new issue is the practitioner's perception of appropriate task and production expectations. How can social work tasks be organized to give workers maximum professional satisfaction and stimulation? If staffing patterns are unrealistic and case loads unmanageable, the work requirement becomes so difficult that the investment of the worker will be diminished. The effort will be to survive, not to become involved in an emotional and energy debilitating effort. Ideally, departmental administration and staff form consensus around expectation. Unless this grows out of reasonable expectations and understanding of task components, workers may form their own priorities system based on minimal performance rather than professional and departmental commitment.

Essential to establishing staffing patterns is task definition. This involves setting the parameters of function and role of the worker. Depending on the definition, these determinants will influence the number of staff and administrative structure of the department. Several guidelines can be suggested. The social work task should be specific enough to make possible evaluation of goals and the means for achieving these goals. The goals and processes of the department should be accepted formally by hospital administration. Different levels of performance expectation will determine specific staffing patterns. If specific tasks are defined in terms of principally concrete functions which may involve only minimal or routine judgement and do not require any creativity, then this task should be performed by a lesser trained and experienced person than an MSW.

REVIEW OF QUALIFYING FACTORS

Before venturing some explicit formulations which may have common application, it is important to make clear that: at best, numbers represent guidelines rather than rules to be followed dogmatically; the number of variables which influence staffing patterns are so numerous that it would be most unwise to assume that the suggestions made would be valid in all types of settings; and the most obvious danger is that numbers can be used to justify minimal or maximal expectations, depending on the observer.

In summary, factors that must be taken into account in developing staffing patterns are:

(1) The nature of the service.

(2) The quality of the service expected.

(3) The educational and experiential background of the social worker.

(4) The population which the health setting serves, i.e., ethnic minority, low income, middle class, etc.

(5) The location of patients, that is, whether it is an inpatient or outpatient service.

(6) The nature of the illness and treatment, psychiatric, general medical, surgical service, or pediatrics.

(7) Whether the social worker represents the primary care person or is adjunctive or supplementary to other services.

(8) The level of care, chronic versus acute.

(9) The number of outpatient clinics manned by social workers.

(10) The extent of outreach into the community.

(11) The educational role of the department, intra and extramurally.

(12) The ordering of priorities in terms of professional, administrative economical needs.

STUDIES ABOUT TIME AND NUMBERS

From our experience the amount of time that social workers will spend in direct patient care will vary depending on the nature of the service. At the Long Island Jewish-Hillside Medical Center, which includes a variety of hospital settings (an acute hospital, a general hospital, a psychiatric, and a chronic care unit) we have logged that amount of time spent in social work activities which we have defined as those activities specifically related to social work tasks such as face-to-face and telephone interviews, including patient, family, and collateral contacts.

In a recently completed study we found that social work staff in the medical center was spending approximately 55% of an eight-hour day in direct social work activity. Six percent, relatively little time, was spent in staff development, four percent in research activities, and only two percent in student training activities. Approximately seven percent of social work staff time is spent in supervision and 12% on paper work. Meetings consumed 11% of staff time (although half were related directly to patient care) and the remainder two to three percent was spent on miscellaneous activities.[13]

These figures varied depending on whether it was psychiatric or medical service. Nevertheless the average of 55% (and if we include the six percent of meeting time directed to patient care then the average becomes 61%) seems to fall within the generally accepted guideline that has been followed in apportioning staff time; namely about one hour of supportive time for every hour spent in direct patient care. It is encouraging that the findings of this, the third study of its kind which has been done at Long Island Jewish-Hillside Medical Center during a fifteen-year period, show that productivity has increased (from 53% to at least 59%). The amount of time workers are spending in direct patient care, despite apparent increasing administrative demands, is greater than shown in previous surveys.

These results are in accordance with the estimate which was given by the nine hospitals reporting in the Shepard study which showed that between 65% and 74% of social work time was given to direct services.

While obviously more refined data needs to be gathered the indication is that social workers in health settings, or at least in hospitals for which we have data, are spending 60% or more of their time in direct service.

RECOMMENDATIONS

On the assumption that social workers should be spending between 60% to 70% of time in direct service contact we recommend:

For a 60 bed acute medical or surgical unit, 2 MSWs and 1 BSW or paraprofessional as an acceptable staffing pattern.

For high risk groups in medical inpatient settings such as pediatric (catastrophic), cancer, cardiac, surgery, and geriatric wards, 1 MSW for each 25 patients.

For general medical/surgical outpatient department we estimate that 10,000 patients generate 35,000 visits of which 85% would require psychosocial services. We recommend 3 MSWs and 3 BSWs for each 10,000 patients. We recognize that specialty clinic care poses extra demands on social work service in comparison with primary care clinics and the estimate given represents an average.

For specialty clinics, specific patterns based on time and quality control should be developed. As an example and relying mainly on the work of Mandell previously cited, 100% of the patients requesting abortions could be referred for social work services and social workers could accept 15 to 22 abortion patients per week. He suggests that social workers plan to see 25% more patients that actually receive abortions to reach this maximal case load. However, at one of our hospitals, social workers work with groups of patients and the numbers of patients referred can be increased.

The experience of our emergency room leads us to believe that for every 30,000 visits per annum, 3 full-time MSWs on staggered shifts need to be employed to cover evenings and weekends.

We can make the assumption that 100% of a psychiatric inpatient population has the potential need for some social work intervention from the point of referral to discharge planning. This is in contrast to the Hollinghead study where the psychosocial intervention need for patients in a general hospital was found to be 64%.

In a psychiatric inpatient unit in which the social workers have specific therapy responsibilities, we would assign 2 social workers for a 20 patient unit which includes working with the families and the milieu. For a psychiatric inpatient unit in which a number of disciplines in addition to social work have responsibility for therapy, 2 social workers for 24 inpatient bed unit should be adequate. For outpatient psychiatric clinics the recommendation would be for 1 MSW for each 30 patients.

One problem area in staffing patterns covers the use of the BSW. The differential between the use of undergraduate degree social workers as opposed to those with MSW needs continued study and evaluation. An empirical guideline suggests that all psychosocial assessments be initially made by an MSW. For every four to seven MSWs on staff one BSW can be used to increase to a maximum the professional input of MSW. There are indeed useful and critical functions which the undergraduate social workers can perform: interviewing for financial evaluations, arranging alternate care, developing certain liaison relationships with community agencies, initiating and completing nursing home referrals, serving as advocates for patients and families who are entitled to various benefits as yet not received, and for experienced BSWs counseling responsibilities under the supervision of MSWs. A large proportion of undergraduates could seriously dilute and jeopardize the quality of social work care. We would seriously question the use of BSWs to replace MSWs and whether the motive was for quality care or simply for economic purposes. And we would note, too, that where and when this has been done, it often is in those services affecting patients of low income or ethnic minorities who have nonprestigious diseases.

The amount of social work time devoted to management policy planning and supervision will be a variable. Size of staff becomes a factor; the larger the hospital the greater the time needed for these functions. The size of the social work administrative staff is dependent on the diversity and complexity of the services and varies considerably from hospital to hospital.

Another problem area which requires study is the ratio of supervisory staff to practitioners. This ratio will be determined by the level and intensity of supervision needed and on supervisory staff available. For example, group supervision instead of individual supervision may be used. Again, as a general guideline, supervisors should be responsible for the supervision of eight to ten MSWs; assistant supervisors, or senior workers from two to four staff which could include a combination of two to four MSWs and/or BSWs, or paraprofessionals. However, assistant supervisors or senior workers should carry a case load in addition to their supervisory responsibility.

Any numbers game is subject to risk. The several studies which have been cited and which pinpoint the amount of time spent by social workers in designated social work activities indicate a surprising degree of concordance. This would suggest that despite the lack of "hard data," the empirical method which social workers have used for years has validity. It is heartening to note that even though we have been able only to estimate, we appear to be more accurate than we may have supposed. Judging from the data we now have, it is clear that even though we need to tighten up many of our activities, to continue to examine our productivity, to maintain and to improve the quality of our services, the use of social work manpower has been closer to expectations than we had dared to hope. We cannot afford to rest on our laurels because of the need to use ourselves and our staff even more productively and to provide better services to patients and their families. Realistic staffing patterns for social work is good management, good administration, and most important, is essential if we are to deliver quality care to patients and their families.

REFERENCES

1. Duff, Raymond S., and Hollinghead, August D. *Sickness and Society*. New York: Harper and Row, 1968.

2. Cooper, Brian. "Social Work in General Practice: The Derby Scheme." *The Lancet 1* (1971):541.

3. Berkman, Tessie. *Practice of Psychiatric Social Workers in Psychiatric Hospitals and Clinics*. New York: American Association of Psychiatric Social Workers, 1953.

4. National Association of Social Workers. *Utilization of Personnel in Social Work*. New York: NASW, 1962.

5. United Hospital Fund of New York (N.Y. Metropolitan Regional Program). *Development of Social Work Manpower and Knowledge in Relation to Critical Illness—A Report*. New York: UHF-NY 1968.

6. Barker, Robert L., and Briggs, Thomas L. *Differential Use of Social Work Manpower*. New York: National Association of Social Workers, 1968.

7. Briggs, Thomas L., and Glick, Lester. *Manpower Research in Undergraduate Social Work Curriculum Building*. Washington, D.C.: Education Service, Department of Medicine and Surgery, Veterans Administration, 1971.

8. Shepard, Herman. *Report of Study of Social Service Departments in Major Hospitals in New York City*. New York: Hospital for Joint Diseases, March 1973.

9. Brady, Elaine. *The Social Worker's Guide for Long Term Care Facilities*. Rockville, MD.: National Institute of Mental Health, 1974.

10. Coalition of Professional Social Workers in Long Term Care Facilities. *Guidelines for Social Worker Service in Long Term Care Facilities*. Revised edition. New York: CPSWLTCF, 1975.

11. Mandell, Mark D. "An Operational and Planning Staffing Model for First and Second Trimester Abortion Services." *Americal Journal of Public Health* 64 (1974):8.

12. Lurie, Abraham, and Rosenberg, Gary. "Problems in Community Organization for Community Mental Health." *Hospital and Community Psychiatry* 23 (1972):350–353.

13. Chernesky, Roslyn, and Lurie, Abraham. "The Functional Analysis Study: A First Step in Quality Assurance." *Social Work in Health Care* 1 (1975–76):213–223.

Chapter 15

Promoting Contributions to Organizational Goals: Alternative Models

John A. Yankey, PhD
Claudia J. Coulton, PhD

ABSTRACT. A perennial issue confronting administrators is the degree to which employees' behavior should be directed to assure attainment of organizational goals. This issue takes on an even more complex dimension when the organization is a professional organization. Individual professional goals can come into conflict with organizational goals. This conflict can be evidenced in many social welfare organizations. The administrative response to this issue will be determined to some extent by implicit theoretical assumptions about how professionals' behaviors are regulated and what shapes professionals' activities toward the attainment of organizational goals. Two theoretical models purported to explain the control of performance in professional organizations are analyzed. The first model emphasizes the concepts of selection and socialization. The second model emphasizes organizational processes, structure, and evaluation of performance. An assessment of the two models reveals that the second model provides a more complete, general, and empirically supported approach for understanding the control of performance in professional organizations. The implications of this model for social welfare agencies are highlighted.

To what degree is it important for employees of an organization to behave in ways which will enhance organizational goals? This question is one which has historically confronted administrators of all organizations, public and private, large and small. There is general agreement that to survive, an organization must insure that its members engage in some behaviors that contribute to organizational goals. The issue then becomes one of determining a strategy for controlling or directing behaviors toward such goals.

This strategy determination takes on more complex dimensions when the organization is a professional organization. As used here, a professional organization is one in which professionals constitute both the production component and administrative line structure. The professional in such an organization is a worker who is formally trained to produce, preserve, communicate, and apply specialized knowledge (Heyderbrand, 1973).

Using this set of definitions, many social welfare agencies can be seen as professional organizations. Such organizational settings place considerable emphasis upon individual autonomy, collegial decision-making, and accomplishment of personal goals. These emphases can place employees in conflict with organizational goals. What, then, is the strategy employed by administrators to insure that employees engage in behaviors contributing to organizational goals? How can performance be controlled or directed to produce the desired results?

The strategy chosen by any organization will depend upon implicit theoretical assumptions about (1) how the professional's behavior is regulated; and (2) what shapes a professional's activities toward the attainment of organizational goals. The success of the strategy will depend upon the validity and power of theory on which it is based. Two theoretical models can be identified which purport to explain the control of performance in professional organizations. As used here, control of performance refers to the extent to which members' task behavior meets organizational normative criteria (Thibaut & Kelly, 1959). A task is any activity or set of activities carried out by a person or persons to attain an organizational goal.

ALTERNATIVE EXPLANATIONS

The first model has been extracted from the discussions of Blau (1956), Goss (1961), Etzioni (1964), Wilensky (1964), and Goode (1957). In general, this model begins with the concept of selection. Professional organizations are seen as recruiting and selecting members who will perform as required automatically. This tendency to perform as required is a result of the socialization process that occurs within training programs, professional schools, and through formal and informal professional associations. This socialization process results in the internalization of a set of beliefs and values which are consistent with professional norms. These norms affect members' beliefs about the desired results of their activities and about the causal relationships between these results and the procedures and activities in which these professionals engage. In addition to internalized beliefs and values, behavior is controlled by the fact that violation of professional norms results in negative sanctions being applied by informal or formal professional associations. Conversely, compliance with norms results in the applications of positive sanctions through these same professional structures.

This model is diagrammatically represented in Figure 1. The arrows represent postulated cause-effect relationships. The major concepts in the model are:

1. *Degree of selectivity* is the extent to which an organization selects members who are expected to perform as required for the achievement of organizational goals. Selection is based on certain credentials.

2. *Extent of socialization* refers to the degree to which persons have been exposed to the norms of the professions, usually occurring in professional schools and associations. An indicator of this concept is frequently the amount of professional training members have had or their membership and involvement in professional associations.

3. *Extent of internalization of beliefs and values* refers to the extent to which persons have incorporated the norms of the profession into their cognitive structure as beliefs and values. To operationalize this concept, it would be necessary to identify the norms of a profession, derive their manifestations in beliefs and values of individuals, and determine the extent to which individuals in a given organization had incorporated these into their cognitive structures.

4. *Extent to which sanctions are applied* refers to those sanctions applied by formal or informal professional associations for compliance with or violations of professional norms. An indicator of sanctions applied are the actions taken by formal or informal professional associations intended to reward or punish members.

5. *Degree of control of task performance* is the extent to which members' task performance meets normative criteria of the organization. This reflects an organization's implicit and explicit criteria for the performance of tasks and the extent to which members' task behavior conforms to these criteria.

This model suggests that these concepts would be related in several ways. First, the more selective the organization in recruitment of members, the greater the effects of the professional socialization process will be on them. Second, the greater the exposure to socialization processes, the more the members can be expected to have internalized professional beliefs and values. Third, internalization will also be affected by the extent to which professional sanctions are applied for violation of and compliance with professional norms. Finally, since it is assumed that professional goals and organizational goals are equivalent, the application of professional sanctions and the internalization of professional norms will result in the control of members' performance within the organization.

The second model to be described is derived from studies by Dornbush and Scott (1975), Thompson (1967), Friedson (1970), and Heyderbrand

Figure 1

MODEL 1 OF CONTROL OF PERFORMANCE IN PROFESSIONAL ORGANIZATIONS

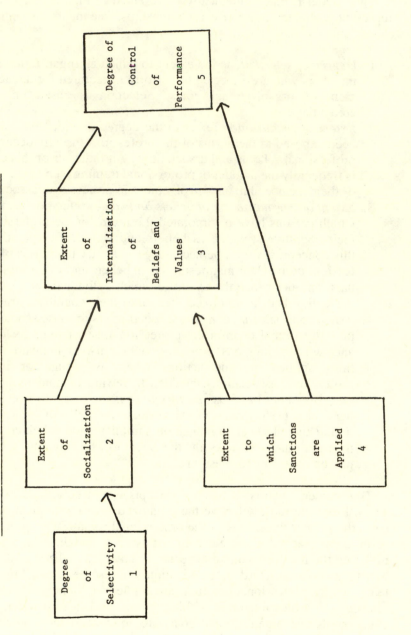

(1973). It starts with the assumption that all organizations, including professional organizations, are rational; that is, their activities are determined by their beliefs about what causes desired results (Thompson, 1967). Rationality requires that the task performance of members be controlled so as to contribute to these results. Therefore, organizations develop structure and processes to maximize this control by conducting implicit or explicit evaluation of members' performance.

Evaluation is the general process of judging the worthwhileness of an activity (Suchman, 1967). The performance of members of professional organizations is evaluated according to organizational normative criteria. If the findings of evaluations affect the distribution of valued sanctions and if members believe that the evaluation procedures are valid, the task performance of those subject to the evaluation is affected. To the extent that the evaluation criteria reflect the performance necessary for the achievement of organizational goals, control of task performance will be achieved.

Figure 2 represents this model. It assumes that the organization is rational and therefore undertakes evaluation. Numerous concepts in this model require definition:

1. *Degree of control of task performance,* as in Model 1, is the degree to which members' task performance meets the organization's normative criteria.
2. *Belief that effort is related to evaluation findings* is defined as the extent to which a member perceives that the direction and level of his efforts on a task are positively related to the level of evaluation he receives. In the concrete situation, this means that a person does or does not believe that if he works hard, he can obtain a positive evaluation.
3. *Extent to which evaluation is perceived as valid* is the perception that levels of performance are accurately judged and that higher levels of performance actually receive higher evaluations. In other words, does the person believe that the evaluation procedures will measure his true performance?
4. *Extent to which task is visible* is the extent to which the evaluator can directly observe the participant in the performance of his task or the outcomes produced by those performances.
5. *Extent to which performance is measurable* refers to the presence or absence of instruments or procedures which assign values (quantitative or qualitative) to aspects of performance.
6. *Extent to which inputs are uniform* refers to the constancy of the characteristics of the "raw material" on which tasks are to be performed.

7. *Extent of knowledge about cause and effect* refers to the extent to which there is certainty about what actions produce what outcomes.
8. *Extent of crystallization about desired outcomes* refers to the degree to which there is consensus about and specification of desired outcomes.
9. *Degree of professionalism* is the extent to which members of an organization display attitudes which are associated with professionals (e.g., use of the professional association as reference group, belief in service to the public, sense of calling to the field, autonomy) (Hall, 1967).
10. *Belief that evaluation is related to sanctions* refers to the extent to which members perceive that evaluation findings will affect the distribution of rewards and punishments.
11. *Extent to which the evaluator controls valued sanctions* refers to the degree to which the evaluator can influence the distribution of rewards and punishments which are valued by members.
12. *The position of the evaluator in the organizational hierarchy* refers to his formal position within the organization.
13. *The position of the evaluator in the professional hierarchy* refers to his prestige within the profession.

The model represented in Figure 2 suggests a series of relationships among these concepts. First, the amount of control an organization has over its members' performance will increase if: 1) the members believe that more effort on their part will result in a better evaluation; and 2) they believe that the evaluation findings will affect the way that important sanctions are distributed. On the other hand, the higher the degree of professionalization, the lower the amount of control over performance will be.

Second, if evaluations are believed to be valid, members are more likely to believe that increased effort will result in a better evaluation. Evaluations will be seen as more valid if: 1) the quality of tasks carried out is actually measurable; 2) the task is visible; 3) the "raw materials" on which the task is performed are uniform; 4) there is confirmed knowledge about what members' actions will produce desired outcomes; and 5) there is agreement about what outcomes are desirable. On the other hand, the degree of professionalism in an organization is likely to be higher when inputs are not uniform, where there is uncertainty about cause and effect, and where there is uncertainty about desired outcomes.

Finally, members of organizations will expect evaluation to result in the distribution of important sanctions only when the evaluator is in a position to control such sanctions. The evaluator's degree of control will depend upon his position in both the professional and organizational hierarchies.

Figure 2

MODEL 2 OF CONTROL OF PERFORMANCE IN PROFESSIONAL ORGANIZATIONS

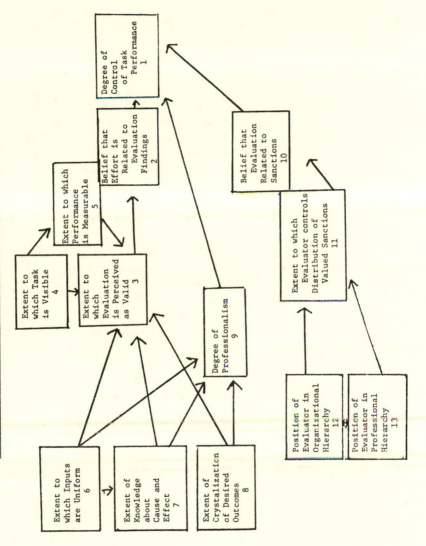

ASSESSMENT OF THE MODELS

As stated earlier, an organization will be more successful in achieving its goal if its strategy for controlling its members is based on a valid and powerful theory. These two models can be compared on the fullness and richness of their explanatory power and on how well they reflect the real work of professional organizations, especially social welfare agencies.

Model 1 seems to provide less explanation and understanding than Model 2. It is difficult to see, for example, how sanctions are to be applied by the professional group without some systematic method of evaluating task performance. It is more likely that these evaluation processes occur but are informal and/or implicit. If this is so, they should appear in the model to facilitate understanding and prediction. Conversely, Model 2 makes evaluation explicit and allows the characteristics of the organizational tasks and the evaluations to vary. This allows these concepts to help explain the degree of control of members' task performance.

The process by which internalization of professional beliefs and values influences behavior is not explicated in Model 1. There is some evidence, however, that this hypothesized relationship between professional beliefs and values and behavior may not be consistent with empirical findings. Further, there are questions in general about the extent to which beliefs and values actually determine human behavior (e.g., Deutsher, 1970).

The consistency of Model 1 with empirical findings is also problematic with regard to the notion that sanctions are applied by professional associations when members' performance is inconsistent with professional norms and values. Formal negative sanctions are seldom applied by professional associations and there is some evidence that such associations function to protect professionals from such influences. For example, compare the number of times physicians are censured by the American Medical Association to the number of malpractice suits or claims fraud investigations. Informal sanctions may be applied, but these are more likely to be applied for noncompliance in socio-emotional rather than instrumental performance (Friedson, 1967).

Finally, Model 1 assumes that the mechanism of selectivity assures that the goals of members are consistent with organizational goals. This automatic goal congruency between professionals and the organizations that employ them does not seem to be supported by empirical findings (Gouldner, 1957; Chatterjee & Ginter, 1972, 1973). In fact, one study found that many members of a professional organization, while giving lip service to organizational goals, were actually individual goal maximizers (Bozeman & McAlpine, 1977).

Model 2 explains control of task performance at a more general level; that is, it is not limited to professional organizations. In professional organizations certain concepts in the model are likely, however, to take a narrow range of values, thus affecting the degree of control of task performance. For example, degree of professionalism is likely to have a high value in professional organizations. Since this is hypothesized to have a negative relationship with degree of control, other things being equal, a higher quantity of professionalism would be associated with a lower quantity of control. Likewise, uniformity of input, extent of knowledge of cause and effect, and crystallization of desired outcomes have a negative relationship with professionalism. This suggests that in professional organizations inputs will be less uniform, there will be major gaps in knowledge about cause and effect, and there will be many different opinions about the desired results. Task visibility and performance measurability, which have positive relationships with validity of evaluation, are also likely to be limited in professional organizations. This suggests that in order to achieve more control over task performance in professional organizations, these and other variables must be manipulated toward levels at which they will make this control possible.

In addition to its greater generality and fuller explanatory power, there seems to be more empirical evidence to support the relationships among concepts identified in Model 2. There is evidence that the degree of control over task performance is positively related to the belief that effort and sanctions are related to evaluation (Dornbush & Scott, 1975; Hind et al., 1974). There is evidence that the degree of professionalism in an organization is negatively related to the acceptance of authority (Simon, 1976; Scott, 1975; Goss, 1961). There is also evidence that the nature of the tasks being evaluated is related to the degree of control of task performance (Thompson, 1967; Dornbush & Scott, 1975). In addition, there is evidence that the extent to which distribution of sanctions is determined by evaluation findings is related to degree of control of task performance (Hind, 1974). Finally, there is evidence that positions in organizations differ in the number and types of sanctions they can control (Bendex, 1956).

In summary, Model 2 seems to provide a more complete, general, and empirically supported model for understanding the control of performance in professional organizations. Complete confidence in the model would, of course, require much further testing. Also, it would have to be established that it explains behavior in schools of social work as it has been demonstrated to do in other university departments and secondary schools.

IMPLICATIONS

Social welfare agencies seem to implicitly accept one or the other of these models when establishing procedures to promote employee contributions to organizational goals. If they do this while guided by an inaccurate model, they are not likely to be successful.

From the foregoing assessment of the models, Model 2 seems to provide a more complete, general, and empirically supported framework for understanding the control of performance in professional organizations. If it were assumed that this model is actually a better description of reality, what does this suggest for social welfare agencies? Such agencies are unique organizations in many ways. First, they seldom work with uniform inputs as there is wide variation among clients entering the agencies. Second, there is only limited knowledge about what procedures will produce the desired results. For example, there is only beginning knowledge about what interventions or services are most likely to produce specific outcomes. Third, there is not always agreement about what outcomes are desired. Fourth, some of the tasks performed by professionals are often difficult to measure and observe. Many professionals perform in privacy of an office where only the consumers observe the process. Procedures to quantify social workers' performances are in the beginning stages of development with many questions being raised about their validity.

Finally, in professional social work organizations there may be multiple sources of valued sanctions, many of which are not under the control of the evaluator. For example, money, prestige, and power are distributed both within and outside organizations. Further, even within organizations, they are not usually controlled solely by the evaluator whose status in the professional hierarchy may not be commensurate with his status in the organizational hierarchy.

In order for social welfare agencies to move toward Model 2, several things must occur. First, there must be increased agreement about the desired characteristics of the organization's outcomes (i.e., goals) and increased knowledge about how to produce such outcomes. Second, those tasks that must be performed to produce these agreed upon products must be made observable and measurable. Third, members of the organization must believe that their performance will be objectively and accurately assessed. Fourth, employees must believe that "good" performance will result in the receipt of valued sanctions. Fifth, evaluators must occupy top positions in both the professional and organizational hierarchy.

Of course, it could be argued that control of performance is not desirable in a professional organization. It is not known just how much of an organization's resources must go into organizational goal achievement in order for that organization to survive. However, if a social welfare agency does perceive the need to control performance to some extent, it will be more successful if it is guided by a model that is a more accurate and complete representation of reality. It would be somewhat ironic for such agencies, desirous of legitimating themselves through increasing their scientific base, to have their administrative practices based on a conceptual model whose lack of empirical support would itself obviate such legitimation.

REFERENCES

Bendix, R. *Work and authority in industry*. New York: Wiley, 1956.

Blau, P. *Bureaucracy in modern society*. New York: Random House, 1956.

Bozeman, B. & McAlpine, W. Goals and bureaucratic decision making. *Human Relations*, 1977, *30*, 417–429.

Chatterjee, P., & Ginter, D. Commitment to work among public welfare workers, *Public Welfare*, 1972, *30*, 53–58.

Deutsher, I. Words and deeds. In W. Filstead (Ed.), *Qualitative methodology*. Chicago: Markham, 1970.

Dornbush, S., & Scott, R. *Evaluation and the exercise of authority*. San Francisco: Jossey-Bass, 1975.

Etzioni, A. *Modern organizations*. Englewood Cliffs: Prentice-Hall, 1964.

Friedson, E. D. Professions, bureaucracy, client services. In W. Rosengren & M. Lefton (Eds.), *Organizations and clients*. Columbus: Merrill, 1970.

Goode, W. Community within a community: The professions. *American Sociological Review*, 1957, *22*, 194–205.

Goss, M. Influence and authority among physicians in an outpatient clinic. *American Sociological Review*, 1961, *26*, 39–50.

Gouldner, A. Cosmopolitans and locals: Toward an analysis of latent social roles. *Administrative Science Quarterly*, 1957, *12*, 461–478.

Hall, R. Organizational considerations in the professional-organizational relationships. *Administrative Science Quarterly*, 1967, *12*, 461–478.

Heyderbrand, W. *Comparative organizations*. Englewood Cliffs: Prentice-Hall, 1973.

Hind, R., Dornbush, S., & Scott, R. A theory of evaluation applied to a university faculty. *Sociology of Education*, 1974, *47*, 114–128.

Scott, W. R. Reactions to supervision in heteronomous professional organizations. *Administrative Science Quarterly*, 1965, *10*, 65–81.

Simon, H. *Administrative behavior*. New York: Free Press, 1976.

Suchman, E. *Evaluative research*. New York: Russell Sage Foundation, 1967.

Thibaut, J. W. & Kelley, H. H. *The social psychology of groups*. New York: Wiley, 1959.

Thompson, J. *Organizations in action*. New York: McGraw-Hill, 1967.

Wilenskey, H. The professionalization of everyone. *American Journal of Sociology*, 1964, *70*, 137–158.

Chapter 16

Performance Appraisal in a Hospital Social Service Department

Robert M. Spano, ACSW

ABSTRACT. An attempt is made to design and install a measurable approach to staff performance and appraisal. The model represents the final element of a comprehensive accountability system that appears to be both timely and necessary for social workers in health care. Contributions to the system have been made by the management staff of the department.

INTRODUCTION

The elusiveness of a meaningful measure of "quality of performance," and the importance of personnel appraisal in terms of organizational as well as staff well-being, have meant that one of the most difficult and sensitive tasks in human service administration is performance evaluation. Despite its importance, however, and particularly in the human services, performance appraisal is commonly regarded as a relatively artificial and unfulfilling process, unrelated either to staff need for useful "knowledge of results" feedback or organizational need for maximization of effectiveness and efficiency.

Current Practice

A recent study by Weite (1980) has reported on performance appraisal practices in 196 private social service agencies. Forty-five percent of the agencies used narrative statements as their primary mode of evaluation for professional staff, 30% used rating scales completed by a worker's supervisor, and 25% used an outcome or results-oriented approach (e.g., negotiation of observable goals between worker and supervisor). The primary purpose of performance appraisal in nearly half of the agencies (49%) was staff performance improvement, while 29% used it for personnel decision-making (e.g., promotion, discharge, wage change). Fifteen percent used it for promotion from probationary status, and 7% used it for staff training and development. In concluding his article, Weite notes:

A discrepancy appears to exist between the primary purpose of performance appraisal and the method or technique used to accomplish this purpose. The essay and rating scale methods frequently involve minimal input from the supervisee and often fail to identify specific prescriptions for improved performance. The results-oriented approach to appraisal, if properly utilized, as when supervisor and supervisee jointly determine goals to be accomplished, may be a more effective approach for accomplishing the purpose of performance appraisal, i.e., improving performance.

Objective

The objective of this article is to describe a staff performance appraisal system that has been developed and implemented at the Social Service Department of University of Minnesota Hospitals. Recognizing the weaknesses of traditional approaches, which essentially rely on either supervisor narrative descriptions of staff or of ratings of staff according to standard checklists, the University of Minnesota structure is founded upon principles thought to optimize both the meaning and rigor of staff accountability assessment. These are:

Participation. The system provides for systematic staff involvement in the development or shaping of the criteria by which personal performance is to be evaluated. This involves negotiating personal goals related to the mission of the organization, arriving at statistical criteria to assess level of effort, and weighting importance of activities in organizational function areas.

Feedback. The system provides for periodic feedback to staff regarding progress toward stated performance criteria. Such feedback is provided on a formal basis in bi-monthly supervisor-supervisee conferences, as well as informally whenever a staff member wishes to check and see how (s)he is doing.

Flexibility. To help assure maximum relevance and credibility, performance criteria are shaped and individualized to reflect the diverse professional interests and organizational responsibilities of staff. As is described above, this flexibility is particularly manifest in the unstructured nature of the goals which may be set, and in the range of options available in specifying effort criteria and weighting areas of activity.

Comparability. Although criteria are shaped and tailored to individual specifications, the same basic structure of criteria applies to all. This permits comparison of performance between and among staff.

Multiple Input. Assessment of performance is based upon input from a variety of sources, and is not merely based upon supervisor descriptions or ratings. Among the kinds of information which may be included as performance criteria are: (1) personal staff goals, (2) client outcomes, (3) audits of clinical records, (4) results from the department's management information system, and (5) evaluations of actual staff interactions with clients.

Comprehensiveness. As is implied above, the system attempts to capture information relevant to all significant aspects of a worker's job, including the outcome, process and level of effort of performance.

Relevance. The system is explicitly linked to the mission and functions of the social service department, and conforms to the reporting requirements and information needs of the larger hospital system.

Rewards. The system attempts to link staff performance outcomes to immediate consequences in the department. Possible sanctions for performance include changes in pay, promotion or demotion, changes in assignment and termination.

Ease of Operation. The system operates within the existing budget constraints of the department and attempts to be neither burdensome nor obtrusive to staff.

SETTING

The setting for the staff performance appraisal system is the Social Service Department of University of Minnesota Hospitals. Founded in 1909, the department currently employs 26 full-time MSWs and one case aide, and provides a full range of services to the hospitals' patients and their families. In 1980, 14,427 clients received direct services from the department.

Accountability System

A recent addition to the department has been a comprehensive accountability structure (Spano and Lund, 1976; Spano, Kiresuk and Lund, 1977; and Spano and Lund, 1980). Derived from a framework based on Management by Objectives, the system is composed of the following elements: (1) a transaction-based and time-oriented management information system, (2) client problem identification and clinical record-keeping with Problem Oriented Medical Records, (3) service provision standards grounded in definitions provided by the Southern Regional Educational Board, and (4) goal-oriented outcome evaluation. The purpose of the accountability structure is to monitor and document department activities, providing feedback reports to staff, management reports to the director, and summary reports to hospital administration.

Implementation of Performance Appraisal

Consistent with the department's philosophy that organizational change should be undertaken with maximal participation of those affected, the performance appraisal system was implemented incrementally over a one year period in order to permit successive modifications to meet staff needs. The prototype for the system was developed by a committee, chaired by the director, of departmental supervisors. The prototype was presented to staff, revised to meet their suggestions, implemented on a trial basis, revised according to this experience, and finally, implemented on an operational basis as is described in this article.

PERFORMANCE CRITERIA

On the date of their anniversary review, individual staff meet with their supervisor to evaluate their performance for the past year and to negotiate criteria by which their work in the future is to be assessed. Criteria are negotiated in each of the five function areas specified by the department's mission structure:

1. "Direct Services": Clinical work with the hospital patients and their families.
2. "Hospital and Community": Consultation or education services provided to health care professionals outside the department.
3. "Manpower and Training": Personal or professional development activities to enhance staff skills.
4. "Research and Publication": Activities intended to develop and communicate useful professional knowledge.
5. "Social Service Department Activity": Administrative activities within the department.

Each function category contains a set of criteria. These are used to evaluate staff members' professional activities, and serve as a basis for decisions regarding merit pay raises, promotions and special assignments. The rating levels conform with civil service guidelines: (1) unsatisfactory, (2) marginal, (3) satisfactory, (4) superior, and (5) outstanding.

The criteria from which these ratings are determined are of two varieties: (1) those which, when accomplished, give the person a "satisfactory" rating, and (2) those which, when a "satisfactory" rating has been received, give the worker a "superior" rating. Staff not accomplishing satisfactory levels are rated "marginal" or "unsatisfactory," depending upon the number of criteria they have achieved. "Outstanding" ratings are a subjective judgment of the director, as informed by recommendations from the supervisor of a staff person who has received a superior rating. An outstanding rating is intended to recognize extraordinary performance which has significant impact on the community or upon the profession of health care social work. To date, no staff person has been recommended for an overall rating of outstanding. However, letters of recommendation have been sent to a number of staff for their outstanding work or achievements in particular projects or committee assignments. Supervisors have consentually agreed that an outstanding rating should be a rare event.

Function Category 1: "Direct Services"

Criteria for "Satisfactory" Rating. There are five criteria which serve as the basis for a satisfactory rating in the function category "direct services." The forms for evaluating these criteria are displayed in Figure 1 and Figure 2.

The first criterion is the percent of effort expended by a staff person in the direct services area. The exact figure for each staff person is arrived at through negotiation between a staff person and his/her supervisor. The information necessary to assess attainment of the criterion is obtained from the department's management information system, described earlier. Called the "Staff Effort and Accounting System (SEAS)," the basis of the system is staff reporting of the amount of time they devote each day to performing specific professional activities related to defined departmental functions. The basis for developing and evaluating the first criterion is the ratio of the time reported devoted to direct services to the time devoted to all other activities (including time devoted to no specific departmental or professional activities at all).

The second direct services criterion, also based on the previous year's average for department and individual, is number of clients seen by a worker. Once again, this figure is negotiated between worker and supervisor, and information necessary to access attainment is obtained from SEAS.

The third criterion is a "satisfactory" rating on at least three of four charts submitted by a worker for audit to determine the degree of compliance with departmental performance standards for record keeping and service provision. As part of the department's continuing accountability effort, such standards have been developed pertinent to each of 25 categories of client problems. (Spano and Lund, 1980) As can be seen in Figure 1, audit assessments are targeted to four areas: (1) data base assessment, (2) problem identification, (3) treatment plan, and (4) implementation of plan. All four areas must show documentation of compliance for the chart as a whole to be rated "satisfactory."

The fourth criterion is an assessment of worker interviewing skills with an actual client. A minimum of two tapes, audiovisual or observed interviews, are required. Standards of evaluation include: (1) clarity of purpose, (2) maintenance of focus, (3) collection of relevant information, and (4) provision of relevant information. Evaluations are conducted by randomly selected peers of a worker.

FIGURE 1

U N I V E R S I T Y   O F   M I N N E S O T A   H O S P I T A L S

S O C I A L   S E R V I C E   D E P A R T M E N T

A N N U A L   P E R F O R M A N C E   R E V I E W   F O R M

DATE (YEAR): _____

NAME: _____

FUNCTION CATEGORY I: DIRECT SERVICE

CRITERIA FOR ACHIEVING SATISFACTORY RATING (LEVEL 3)

CRITERIA 1. PERCENT OF EFFORT (MONTHLY AVERAGE)

AVERAGE FOR INDIVIDUAL LAST YEAR (SEAS): _____% DEPARTMENTAL AVERAGE (SEAS) _____%

INDIVIDUALLY NEGOTIATED PERCENT OF EFFORT PROJECTED FOR PERFORMANCE YEAR _____%

ACTUAL PERCENT OF EFFORT ACHIEVED DURING PERFORMANCE YEAR (SEAS) _____%

CONTRACT ACHIEVED	CONTRACT NOT ACHIEVED

CRITERIA 2: NUMBER OF PATIENTS SEEN (MONTHLY AVERAGE)

AVERAGE FOR INDIVIDUAL LAST YEAR (SEAS) #_____ DEPARTMENTAL AVERAGE (SEAS) _____#

INDIVIDUALLY NEGOTIATED NUMBER OF PATIENTS TO BE SEEN (PROJECTED) #_____

ACTUAL AVERAGE NUMBER OF PATIENTS SEEN DURING PERFORMANCE YEAR (SEAS) #_____

CONTRACT ACHIEVED	CONTRACT NOT ACHIEVED

CRITERIA 3: CHART AUDIT: (MINIMUM OF 4 SUBMITTED, MINIMUM OF 3 IN COMPLIANCE)

CHART #	DATA BASE ASSESSMENT	PROBLEM IDENTIFICATION	TREATMENT PLAN	IMPLIMENTATION OF PLAN	AUDITOR
1					
2					
3					
4					
5					

NUMBER OF CHARTS
IN COMPLIANCE

CRITERIA 4: INTERVIEWING SKILLS: (MINIMUM OF 2 TAPES, AUDIO-VISUALS, OR OBSERVED INTERVIEWS IN COMPLIANCE)

T	AV	OI	CLARITY OF PURPOSE	MAINTAINS FOCUS	OBTAINS RELEVANT INFORMATION	PROVIDES RELEVANT INFORMATION	REVIEWER
1							
2							
3							

NUMBER OF INTERVIEWS
IN COMPLIANCE

CRITERIA 5: OUTCOME STATED IN CHART FOR THE CASES REVIEWED IN AUDIT.

YES ☐   NO ☐

207

FIGURE 2

A N N U A L   P E R F O R M A N C E   R E V I E W   F O R M

DATE (YEAR): _____

NAME: _____

FUNCTION CATEGORY I: DIRECT SERVICE (CONTINUED)

CRITERIA FOR ACHIEVING SUPERIOR RATING (LEVEL 4)

(AT LEAST 2 OF THE FOLLOWING NEED TO BE ACHIEVED)

CRITERIA 1. HAS BEEN INVOLVED IN PLANNING/DEVELOPING SPECIFIC PROGRAMS IN CLINICAL
AREA.

<u>YES</u>   <u>NO</u>

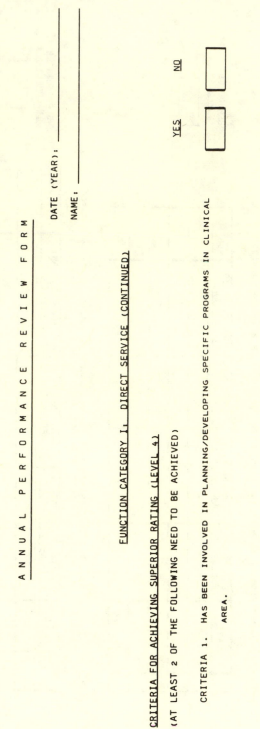

CRITERIA 2.   HAS TAKEN PRIMARY RESPONSIBILITY IN DEVELOPING AND IMPLEMENTING A

TREATMENT APPROACH FOR SPECIFIC CLIENT POPULATION.

CRITERIA 3.   CHART AUDIT SHOWS USE OF GOAL-ORIENTED APPROACH IN AT LEAST 2 CASES.

CRITERIA 4.   HAS DEVELOPED AND ACHIEVED AT LEAST ONE GOAL WITH EXPECTED OR BETTER

OUTCOME.

COMMENTS OR MENTION OF ADDITIONAL ACHIEVEMENTS:

NEGOTIATED WEIGHT FOR FUNCTION CATEGORY

LEVEL OR PERFORMANCE FOR FUNCTION CATEGORY

The fifth criterion, also assessed during the chart audit process, is specification of a statement of "expected outcome" for each problem listed for a client. This helps assure that staff are orienting themselves to solving problems, rather than merely providing services.

Criteria for Superior Rating. Assuming that a worker has met the criteria for a satisfactory rating, a worker is considered "superior" if, in addition, at least two of the following criteria have been met: (1) the worker has been in the planning or development of specific service programs in relevant clinical areas, (2) the worker has taken primary responsibility in developing and implementing a treatment approach for a specific client population, (3) the chart audit demonstrates that the worker has employed a goal-oriented treatment approach for at least two clients, (4) the worker has developed and achieved at least one professional development goal with an expected or better than expected outcome. More information about the process of scaling goals for staff will be provided in a subsequent section.

Function Category 2: "Hospital and Community"

Criteria for Satisfactory Rating. There are two criteria for achieving a satisfactory rating in the function category of "hospital and community" activities (see Figure 3). The first of these is the percent of effort expended in health-related programmatic or consultant services to other organizations (including hospital units), individual practitioners or members of the general public. Attainment of the criteria is monitored through the SEA System. The second criterion is documentation that a worker contributes to the orientation of new health team members.

Criteria for Superior Rating. In order to receive a "superior" designation, a worker must satisfy both of the criteria for a "satisfactory" rating as well as at least two of the following: (1) documentation of hospital activities outside the department, (2) documentation of professional or community activities, (3) provision of at least one inservice program to medical, nursing or allied health personnel, (4) provision of at least one educational program to community agencies or professionals, (5) development and attainment of at least one relevant professional development goal at the expected or better than expected level.

Function Category 3: "Manpower and Training"

Criteria for Satisfactory Rating. There are four criteria for achieving a "satisfactory" rating in this function (see Figure 4). These are: (1) schedules a minimum of alternate month individual supervisory conferences and shows evidence of preparation for them, (2) makes appropriate use of intradepartmental clinical consultant, (3) provides recognized intradepartmental clinical consultation, and (4) attends all staff development programs required by the department.

Criteria for Superior Rating. A "superior" rating in manpower and training is received if all the requirements for a satisfactory rating are satisfied and in addition at least two of the following are accomplished: (1) the worker holds a clinical faculty appointment or participates in training of students from a graduate school of social work, (2) the worker participates in the ongoing professional development activities of the department, (3) the worker attends professional conferences, symposiums or workshops, (4) the worker has developed and achieved at least one relevant professional development goal related to manpower and training.

Function Category 4: "Research and Publication"

Criteria for Satisfactory Rating. There are no criteria for satisfactory rating in this function category. Since hospital policy prevents staff from engaging in research activities during normal working hours, it is not appropriate to apply the criteria to staff who choose not to involve themselves in research or publication activities. Nevertheless, the Social Service Department does support this function and recognizes the need to reward relevant staff effort. Funding for research is sought from external sources only.

Criteria for Superior Rating. As can be seen in Figure 5, to attain a "superior" rating, at least one of the following criteria needs to be achieved: (1) the worker has completed at least a draft of an article relevant to social work health care, (2) the worker has engaged in individual or collective research within or outside the department, (3) the worker has developed and achieved at least one relevant professional development goal relevant to the production and dissemination of professional knowledge.

Function Category 5: "Social Service Department Activities"

Criteria for Satisfactory Rating. There are six criteria for receiving a "satisfactory" rating regarding departmental administrative responsibilities. As can be seen in Figure 6, these are: (1) attendance at all departmental administrative staff meetings, (2) observance of deadlines in submitting required reports, survey requests, committee assignments and special departmental projects, (3) timely submission of required data for SEAS monitoring, (4) provision of prompt and appropriate service in response to requests from internal and external sources, (5) demonstration of knowledge and compliance with departmental and hospital policies, procedures and work rules, and (6) demonstration of professional behavior in keeping with departmental standards and the code of ethics of NASW.

FIGURE 3

A N N U A L   P E R F O R M A N C E   R E V I E W   F O R M

DATE (YEAR): _____

NAME: _____

FUNCTION CATEGORY II: HOSPITAL AND COMMUNITY ACTIVITIES

CRITERIA FOR ACHIEVING SATISFACTORY RATING (LEVEL 3)

CRITERIA 1. PERCENT OF EFFORT: (MONTHLY AVERAGE)

AVERAGE FOR INDIVIDUAL LAST YEAR (SEAS) _____ %   DEPARTMENTAL AVERAGE (SEAS) _____ %

INDIVIDUALLY NEGOTIATED PERCENT OF EFFORT PROJECTED FOR NEXT YEAR _____ %

ACTUAL PERCENT OF EFFORT ACHIEVED DURING PERFORMANCE YEAR (SEAS) _____ %

CRITERIA 2. CONTRIBUTES TO THE ORIENTATION OF NEW HEALTH TEAM MEMBERS.

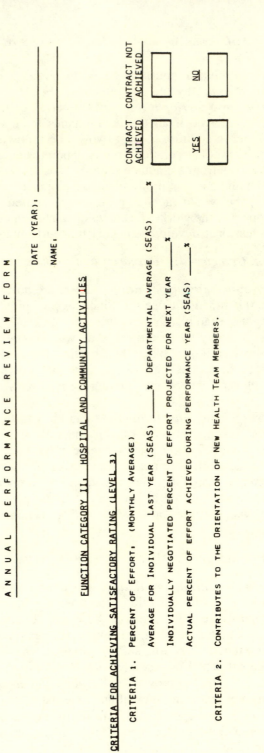

CONTRACT ACHIEVED   CONTRACT NOT ACHIEVED

YES ☐   NO ☐

CRITERIA FOR ACHIEVING SUPERIOR RATING (LEVEL 4)

(AT LEAST 2 OF THE FOLLOWING NEED TO BE ACHIEVED)

YES   NO

CRITERIA 1. DOCUMENTATION OF HOSPITAL-WIDE ACTIVITIES.

CRITERIA 2. DOCUMENTATION OF PROFESSIONAL AND/OR COMMUNITY ACTIVITIES.

CRITERIA 3. PROVIDES AT LEAST ONE INSERVICE PROGRAM TO MEDICAL/NURSING/ALLIED HEALTH
PROFESSIONALS, INCLUDING BUT NOT LIMITED TO PSYCHOSOCIAL ASPECTS OF ILLNESS.

CRITERIA 4. PROVIDES AT LEAST ONE EDUCATIONAL PROGRAM TO COMMUNITY AGENCIES AND
PROFESSIONALS.

CRITERIA 5. HAS DEVELOPED AND ACHIEVED AT LEAST ONE GOAL WITH EXPECTED OR BETTER OUTCOME.

COMMENTS OR MENTION OF ADDITIONAL ACHIEVEMENTS.

NEGOTIATED WEIGHT FOR FUNCTION CATEGORY   LEVEL OF PERFORMANCE FOR FUNCTION CATEGORY

FIGURE 4

A N N U A L   P E R F O R M A N C E   R E V I E W   F O R M

DATE (YEAR): _____

NAME: _____

FUNCTION CATEGORY III, MANPOWER AND TRAINING

CRITERIA FOR ACHIEVING SATISFACTORY RATING (LEVEL 3)

	YES	NO
CRITERIA 1. SCHEDULES A MINIMUM OF ALTERNATE MONTH INDIVIDUAL SUPERVISORY CONVERENCES AND SHOWS EVIDENCE OF PREPARATION FOR THEM.	☐	☐
CRITERIA 2. MAKES APPROPRIATE USE OF INTRADEPARTMENTAL CLINICAL CONSULTATION AS NEGOTIATED WITH SUPERVISOR.	☐	☐
CRITERIA 3. PROVIDES RECOGNIZED INTRADEPARTMENTAL CLINICAL CONSULTATION AS NEGOTIATED WITH SUPERVISOR.	☐	☐
CRITERIA 4. ATTENDS ALL STAFF DEVELOPMENT PROGRAMS REQUIRED BY THE DEPARTMENT.	☐	☐

CRITERIA FOR ACHIEVING SUPERIOR RATING (LEVEL 4)

(AT LEAST 2 OF THE FOLLOWING NEED TO BE ACHIEVED)

YES   NO

CRITERIA 1. HOLDS A CLINICAL FACULTY APPOINTMENT OR PARTICIPATES IN TRAINING OF STUDENTS
FROM A GRADUATE SCHOOL OF SOCIAL WORK.

CRITERIA 2. PARTICIPATES IN THE ONGOING, OPTIONAL STAFF DEVELOPMENT ACTIVITIES OF THIS
DEPARTMENT.

CRITERIA 3. ATTENDS PROFESSIONAL CONFERENCES, SYMPOSIUMS, OR WORKSHOPS.

CRITERIA 4. HAS DEVELOPED AND ACHIEVED AT LEAST ONE GOAL WITH EXPECTED OR BETTER OUTCOME.

COMMENTS OR MENTION OF ADDITIONAL ACHIEVEMENTS.

NEGOTIATED WEIGHT FOR FUNCTION CATEGORY

LEVEL OF PERFORMANCE FOR FUNCTION CATEGORY

215

FIGURE 5

A N N U A L P E R F O R M A N C E R E V I E W F O R M

DATE (YEAR): _____

NAME: _____

FUNCTION CATEGORY IV: RESEARCH AND PUBLICATION

CRITERIA FOR ACHIEVING SATISFACTORY RATING (LEVEL 3)

    NONE REQUIRED.

CRITERIA FOR ACHIEVING SUPERIOR RATING (LEVEL 4)

(AT LEAST ONE OF THE FOLLOWING NEED TO BE ACHIEVED)

    CRITERIA 1. HAS COMPLETED AT LEAST A DRAFT OF AN ARTICLE RELEVANT TO SOCIAL WORK/

             HEALTH CARE.

YES ☐   NO ☐

CRITERIA 2. HAS PUBLISHED ARTICLE OR ARTICLES RELEVANT TO SOCIAL WORK/HEALTH CARE.

CRITERIA 3. ENGAGES IN INDIVIDUAL OR COLLABORATIVE INTER/INTRADEPARTMENTAL RESEARCH
PROJECTS AND DOCUMENTS ACTIVITY.

CRITERIA 4. HAS DEVELOPED AND ACHIEVED AT LEAST ONE GOAL WITH EXPECTED OR BETTER
OUTCOME.

COMMENTS OR MENTION OF ADDITIONAL ACHIEVEMENTS.

NEGOTIATED WEIGHT FOR FUNCTION CATEGORY

LEVEL OF PERFORMANCE FOR FUNCTION CATEGORY

217

FIGURE 6

A N N U A L   P E R F O R M A N C E   R E V I E W   F O R M

DATE (YEAR): _____

NAME: _____

FUNCTION CATEGORY V, SOCIAL SERVICE DEPARTMENT ACTIVITY

CRITERIA FOR ACCIEVING SATISFACTORY RATING (LEVEL 3)

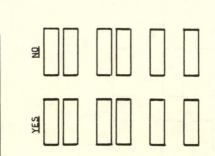

	YES	NO
CRITERIA 1. ATTENDS ALL DEPARTMENTAL ADMINISTRATIVE STAFF MEETINGS UNLESS OFFICIALLY EXCUSED.	☐	☐
CRITERIA 2. MEETS DEADLINES IN SUBMITTING REPORTS, SURVEY REQUESTS, COMMITTEE ASSIGNMENTS, AND SPECIAL DEPARTMENTAL PROJECTS.	☐	☐
CRITERIA 3. SUBMITS REQUIRED STATISTICS CONSISTENTLY, APPROPRIATELY, AND PROMPTLY.	☐	☐
CRITERIA 4. PROVIDES PROMPT AND APPROPRIATE SERVICE IN RESPONSE TO REQUESTS FROM INTERNAL AND EXTERNAL SOURCES.	☐	☐
CRITERIA 5. DEMONSTRATES CONSISTENT PROFESSIONAL BEHAVIOR AND ATTITUDES IN KEEPING WITH DEPARTMENTAL STANDARDS AND MISSION.	☐	☐
CRITERIA 6. DEMONSTRATES KNOWLEDGE OF AND COMPLIANCE WITH DEPARTMENTAL AND HOSPITAL POLICIES, PROCEDURES AND WORK RULES.	☐	☐

CRITERIA FOR ACHIEVING SUPERIOR RATING (LEVEL 4)

(AT LEAST ONE OF THE FOLLOWING NEED TO BE ACHIEVED)

	YES	NO
CRITERIA 1. PARTICIPATES IN CONSTRUCTION AND COMPLETION OF YEARLY DEPARTMENTAL GOALS AND OBJECTIVES.	☐	☐
CRITERIA 2. DEMONSTRATES LEADERSHIP IN DEPARTMENTAL ACTIVITIES BY CHAIRING COMMITTEES OR COMPLETING SPECIAL ASSIGNMENTS.	☐	☐
CRITERIA 3. HAS DEVELOPED AND ACHIEVED AT LEAST ONE GOAL WITH EXPECTED OR BETTER OUTCOME.	☐	☐

COMMENTS OR MENTION OF ADDITIONAL ACHIEVEMENTS.

NEGOTIATED WEIGHT FOR FUNCTION CATEGORY ☐

LEVEL OF PERFORMANCE FOR FUNCTION CATEGORY ☐

Criteria for Superior Rating. To receive a rating of "superior," in addition to meeting all of the "satisfactory" level requirements, at least one of the following must be accomplished: (1) participation in construction and completion of yearly departmental goals and objectives, (2) demonstration of leadership in departmental activities by chairing committees or completing special assignments, (3) development and achievement of at least one professional development goal relevant to departmental administration.

GOAL SETTING

A vehicle for assuring maximal individualization of performance criteria is specification of worker outcome goals in pertinent function categories. Paralleling the Management by Objectives process used for planning and administration of the department as a whole, this appraisal technique permits a staff person to determine performance goals based upon their job responsibilities. Such goals, determined collaboratively between supervisor and supervisee, then serve as part of the ultimate performance appraisal.

As shown in Figure 7, the basis for performance goal setting in the department is Goal Attainment Scaling (Kiresuk and Sherman, 1968). In Goal Attainment Scaling, goals are scaled according to a five-point range of possible outcomes: "Best Possible Outcome," "More Than Expected Outcome," "Expected Outcome," "Less Than Expected Outcome," and "Most Unfavorable Outcome." A range of outcomes permits evaluation and reward of performance that exceeds expectations.

The process of goal scaling occurs in the following way. Workers wishing to state goals for themselves meet with their supervisor to indicate the relevant function area and to describe the nature of their intent. If the supervisor agrees that the goal is pertinent to the worker's role and responsibilities, the two parties negotiate to set an "Expected Outcome" which is realistic, relevant and measurable. Once the expected outcome is established, the other four levels are completed, so the scale represents an exhaustive and mutually exclusive range of possible outcomes. Assessment of attainment usually occurs on a worker's anniversary review date.

PERFORMANCE SCORES

The form displayed in Figure 8 is the mechanism to determine the performance scores for each worker. Subscores are calculated for each function category, and these are summed to determine the overall value. Substances are composed of a weight and a function category rating. A weight is a value indicating the relative emphasis a department function is

FIGURE 7

UNIVERSITY OF MINNESOTA HOSPITALS
SOCIAL SERVICE DEPARTMENT

ANNUAL PERFORMANCE REVIEW

NAME: _____   DATE: _____

FUNCTION CATEGORY: I   II   III   IV   V
                         (Circle One)

OBJECTIVE:

LEAST DESIRED OUTCOME 1	
LESS THAN EXPECTED OUTCOME 2.	
EXPECTED OUTCOME 3	
BETTER THAN EXPECTED OUTCOME 4	
BEST POSSIBLE OUTCOME 5	

CURRENT LEVEL:

NEGOTIATED COMPLETION DATE: _____   ACTUAL COMPLETION DATE: _____

ACTUAL OUTCOME STATEMENT	(If different from above)

LEVEL ACHEIVED: 1   2   3   4   5
                     (Circle One)

221

FIGURE 8

UNIVERSITY OF MINNESOTA HOSPITALS
SOCIAL SERVICE DEPARTMENT

Performance Rating Form

NAME: _____   TITLE: _____

RATER'S NAME: _____   DATE: _____

FUNCTION CATEGORY	WEIGHT	LEVEL OF PERFORMANCE					FINAL SCORE
		1	2	3	4	5	
DIRECT SERVICES							
HOSPITAL/ COMMUNITY							
MANPOWER/ TRAINING							
RESEARCH							
DEPARTMENTAL							
						TOTAL SCORE	

WEIGHT × RATING = FINAL SCORE FOR EACH FUNCTION

SCORING KEY Level of Performance	Range
1	from 0 - 1.49
2	from 1.50 - 2.49
3	from 2.50 - 3.49
4	from 3.50 - 4.99
5	5.0

WEIGHT KEY RANGES BY FUNCTION	
Function	Range of %
I	40 - 80%
II	1 - 20%
III	1 - 20%
IV	0 - 5%
V	1 - 15%
	(Total must = 100%)

accorded for a worker. Weights are negotiated with a worker's supervisor. The ranges of permissible weights in each function category, reflecting the approximate amount of time devoted by a worker to that function, are presented below:

FUNCTION	RANGE OF PERCENT
1. Direct Services	40 to 80%
2. Hospital and Community	1 to 20%
3. Manpower and Training	1 to 20%
4. Research and Publication	0 to 5%
5. Social Service Department	1 to 15%

Weights must total 100% for an individual worker. Although, as one would expect, the system requires greatest emphasis be placed on direct services, it is sufficiently flexible to reflect work done in other function areas, and thus is sensitive to differences in staff work assignments and professional interests.

The score for each function category is obtained by multiplying its weight times the score for that category. For example, a person who has accomplished the five "satisfactory" criteria required in direct service work, and in addition has been involved in developing a specific clinical program and has also utilized a goal-oriented treatment approach in at least two of their audited cases, would receive a four, or "superior," rating. If a weight of 65% had been decided upon between worker and supervisor for "direct services," one would multiply four times .65 and obtain 2.60 as the score for that function category. Scores achieved in each function category are summed, and the total is located in the scoring key range displayed below to find the worker's overall rating.

LEVEL OF PERFORMANCE	RANGE
1. "Unsatisfactory"	0 to 1.49
2. "Marginal"	1.50 to 2.49
3. "Satisfactory"	2.50 to 3.49
4. "Superior"	3.50 to 4.99
5. "Outstanding"	5.00, plus supervisor's recommendation and director's concurrence.

CONCLUSION

Initially implemented in 1979, the system has been operational for nearly three years without significant modification. Such change as has occurred has been devoted to streamlining the operating procedures and making definitions of quality more precise and explicit. As expected, the performance criteria definitions have afforded staff with significant flexibility for work achievement beyond the satisfactory level, and construction of individualized goals in each program function area has helped to individualize performance criteria to accommodate differences in worker programmatic assignments, professional growth needs and career goals.

Contracting ahead for the performance period assures both staff and supervisor that the negotiations are binding. Neither party can make unilateral decisions concerning the contract. Performance ratings are based on level of achievement, and, so far as can be determined, tend not to be influenced by personality characteristics or by any other differences that may exist in the supervisor-supervisee relationship. To this point, no significant conflict has been reported or observed regarding either the construction of goals or their follow-up scoring. Should such conflict arise, it would be mediated by the director of the department. One benefit of the system has been enhanced uniformity in the evaluation standards of the individual supervisors. This has been the result of the formal definitions of performance in each function category.

Overall, new staff tend to achieve a "satisfactory" or "marginal" level of performance. This is due in part to the complexities of the University setting, as well as the difficulty involved in adjusting to the clinical and administrative demands of their new positions. Experienced staff, on the other hand, tend to achieve a "superior" level of performance. This uniformity in ratings is not surprising. The department attracts high quality staff people and it is expected that most will perform at a superior level. Those who consistently score at the satisfactory level or below tend to leave the department.

Candidates for employment in the department are informed of its administrative structure, style of management, reporting system and staff appraisal element as they become serious prospects for staff positions. Those whose philosophies and values are compatible with the direction of the department are offered employment. For those who accept positions, a significant investment is made to provide inservice orientation, including individualized supervision and availability of a "new staff" support group. Such support groups are focused on organizational issues, interprofessional relationship problems, case problems and ways to cope with isolation and social work identification in a health care setting. Integral to this process is orientation and practice with the staff appraisal system. Most new staff become competent in the operation of the system after a brief training session.

Informal observation and staff report indicates that the system has had a positive impact on organizational performance. The most popular feature of the system is the negotiated individualization of performance criteria. This appears to enhance motivation and permits staff to organize their efforts toward outcomes which are both personally and organizationally relevant.

A problem yet to be faced is the introduction of descriptors of quality of treatment to complement the quantitative criteria that have served for the past three years. Preliminary work has been done and a list of possible descriptors of quality have been identified by a staff committee. These will be incorporated into the system in the coming year.

Both staff and hospital administration have responded positively. Beyond some initial "performance anxiety," staff have shown no resistance to the system and presently treat it as a routine element of their professional responsibilities. At the administrative level, the system has been accepted by both the campus and hospital personnel departments as replacement for their own performance appraisal procedures.

As a whole, the system represents the culminating component of a comprehensive accountability system that has taken more than seven years to construct. Implementation of the system gives the department the capacity to assess and evaluate performance at the staff, as well as the client and program level.

REFERENCES

Kiresuk, Thomas J. and Robert E. Sherman. "Goal Attainment Scaling: A General Method for Evaluating Comprehensive Community Mental Health Programs," *Community Mental Health Journal*, 4, 1968, 443–453.

Spano, Robert M. and Sander H. Lund. "Management by Objectives in a Hospital Social Service Department," *Social Work in Health Care*, 1(3), 1976, 267–276.

Spano, Robert M., Thomas J. Kiresuk and Sander H. Lund. "An Operational Model to Achieve Accountability in Social Work," *Social Work in Health Care*, 3(2), 1977, 123–141.

Spano, Robert M. and Sander H. Lund. "Accountability, Evaluation and Quality Assurance in a Hospital Social Service Department," *Quality Review Bulletin*, October, 1980, 14–19.

Wiehe, Vernon R. "Current Practices in Performance Appraisal," *Administration in Social Work*, 4(3), 1980, 1–7.

PART VI

Social Work Manager as Innovator

The health care industry is experiencing changes in every facet of its structure and at a more rapid rate than ever before. Changes produce crises which create obstacles in the execution of functions which may have been laboriously defined. New disciplines have emerged because of the different problems and dilemmas with which health care institutions and agencies have to cope.

Such phenomena as burn-out, unionism, multi-hospital systems, and free standing clinics are manifestations of the various changes which are occurring. The issues which social work managers face are to continue to function well within the understood parameters of social work function and by revised definition to assume new responsibilities. If social work as indeed any service or function under rapidly changing conditions is to survive, innovation must become a significant aspect of the social work manager's role.

In this respect Dr. Nacman's article on using crisis as opportunities for innovation is a particularly useful statement. It is important to understand the nature of crisis and to recognize that such situations may bring opportunities for innovation. Crisis forces mobilization of energies and ingenuity is put to the test. It is possible to use the crisis, as Dr. Nacman indicates, to provide opportunities for change which under stable circumstances are not as conducive for innovation.

Developing innovative programs requires an adventuresome spirit which poses risk. On the other hand, the results of an innovative pattern can expand the parameters of social work function and bring to the social work administrator the image of one who is prepared to embark on unknown areas and is a developer of programs. The article by Starr, Ellis and Oka describes the use of a patient attitude survey in a small health clinic which was subsequently made the basis for change in a delivery system which had positive results for the consumers of the service and the professional staff. In this instance the process was based on client feedback and the process developed by the social work department reflected an innovative approach. But more important, the results, complementary to the professional staff, also reflected some weaknesses which needed improvement and which subsequently were made. There was a risk because it might well have been that the results of the survey could have shown negative results, but again it is the administrator who takes risks, particularly in areas of administrative ambiguity, who makes possible the potential to develop leadership and expand areas of functioning. The third paper deals with developing a social work designed humanistic program which enhances patient care by establishing a human relations program. The importance of this paper is that it demonstrates that innovative programs can be developed in small as well as in large health care agencies. Perhaps even more significant is the nature of this survey because it indicates that it is possible for small as well as a large staff to devote time to direct practice evaluation with concomitant benefits to the social work staff involved in such evaluation efforts and many benefits as well for members of other professional staff. As a result, the expertise and credibility of a social work staff, regardless of size, is enhanced.

The future developments in health care will depend largely upon innovative practice, particularly in those areas which in the past have been most vulnerable to budgetary constraints. Good innovative practice based on sound social work techniques and knowledge can improve the prestige of social work practice and make its usefulness known to much larger areas of professional interest. The social work manager should be a creative person who is prepared to take risks and is willing and able to establish new programs.

Abraham Lurie, PhD

Chapter 17

Social Work Designs
a Humanistic Program
to Enhance Patient Care

James J. McNamara, DSW

ABSTRACT. This article is a description and evaluation of the University of Utah Medical Center's effort to enhance patient care through the establishment of a hospital staff human relations program. The program, focused on select hospital staff, aimed at greater staff awareness and sensitivity to the problems and needs of patients resulting from hospitalization. Because of the positive initial response, the program has been extended and has become a major staff development and education project. This program was presented by a team of social workers and represented a new contribution to the health care system by social work.

Among the more perplexing problems facing hospitals today are increased demands for immediate attention to efforts promoting enhanced patient care. The professional and consumer literature is replete with an exposé of patient protest regarding the delivery of hospital care ranging from dissatisfaction with rooms and food to complaints of inadequate parking facilities and high costs. Most notable among the barrage of accusations by patients is the consistent and overwhelming request to be treated humanely.[1]

The following material is a description and evaluation of a human relations program established at the University of Utah Medical Center to improve patient care. The program, developed by a team of social workers, was designed to heighten staff awareness of and sensitivity to the problems and needs of patients resulting from hospitalization.

BACKGROUND OF PATIENT CARE

During the latter years of the past century, the provision of health care was a comparatively simple process. The family physician was responsible for the medical and health needs but was also involved in problems of

daily living encountered by an individual or family. This relative simplic-
ity resulted from the limited technical and scientific knowledge regarding
disease, leaving the physician with little more than a personal approach to
illness.

The first half of the 20th century, however, brought about a rapid increase in scientific developments that has vastly complicated the practice
of medicine. The modern physician has been forced to expand his medical and scientific horizons to the degree that his ability to recognize and
to deal with patients' problems of daily living has declined drastically.

This rapid change has coincided with the developing behavioral sciences which have contributed to a greater understanding of the individual,
his behavior, and, particularly, his reactions to illness.

Despite the tremendous strides, the system of health care has been
wracked with problems from rising costs to increased expectations of the
consumer population. Of particular note is the current philosophy that patient care should be extended beyond the medical process to encompass
treatment directed to the total patient, involving social, emotional, and
cultural considerations.

The implementation of this philosophy has continued to prove difficult
for administrators, physicians, and others because they have limited training for such tasks, and physical and biological components receive ultimate attention. As the hospital emerges as the "center" for delivery of
health care, it assumes the great responsibility for providing quality, comprehensive, accessible, and total care to the individual patient.

IMPACT OF ILLNESS

The experience of illness may be viewed by an individual as an attack
by a hostile and unknown force, requiring the relinquishment of control
of certain activities normally under one's command. Illness affects family
economics by entailing additional costs, by loss of income, and often by
creating burdensome indebtedness. It frequently imposes inconveniences
and hardships on others and sometimes means separation from house and
family. Illness is usually accompanied by problems and changes in the
family, forcing adjustments if the patient is to improve or recover. For all
families there are anxieties, changed plans, and shifts in relationship that
require recognition and skilled resolve. For many there are severe economic problems and inadequacies in the physical setup of the home, all of
which mean hardship. Illness often necessitates enduring a series of bewildering and frightening medical procedures at the hands of unknown
and impersonal experts. The whole experience of illness and care may stir
up fears of inadequacy, mutilation, and possible annihilation.[2]

The individual who becomes sick is confronted with an entirely new set of expectations and assumes different patterns of behavior in carrying out the role of the patient. His illness, his reactions to the experience of pain, to the physician, and to others comprise a series of different, yet important reactions. Furthermore, the highly scientific nature of medical diagnosis and treatment is beyond the full understanding of the average patient.

The impact of an illness upon a patient depends upon a number of factors, including the nature of the illness, the treatment received, and the character of the person. Recognizing multiple variables that may influence the effects an illness has upon a person, we must seek an understanding that will have positive impact containing ingredients of expressed concern for the dignity of the individual.

Patients, too, would like to find assistance for problems in the medical delivery system. Many realize, of course, that there can be no solution to some of their problems, but seek for staff to recognize them as individual persons, to show interest in and sympathetic understanding of their difficulties, and to make their medical experience as little frustrating and tedious as possible.

It has been stressed that the personal relationship between the patient and staff is an essential part of treatment. Yet the most frequent complaint made by patients about institutional care is the impersonal relationships and the fact that the patient, as an individual, often feels lost in the big health machine.[3]

Compounding the problems facing hospitals are the built-in conflicts that exist in any agency or organization—conflicts related to functional imperatives contained within all organizational systems. Within the hospital system, professional units develop different values and norms of behavior. Each professional staff will be differently oriented because of particular responsibilities, resulting in a conflict in functioning orientation. Disagreements among various units often are found and may be blamed on professional jealousy or professional differences. Again, these disagreements create potential for catching the patient in a staff conflict situation.[4]

DEVELOPMENT OF THE HUMAN RELATIONS PROGRAM

The impetus for increased positive concern for patients at the University of Utah Medical Center was provided by the dean of the college of medicine, whose expressed goal has been to provide optimal delivery of health care with a primary focus on meeting the patient's total needs. The dean presented this challenge to the Medical Board which in turn instructed officials from hospital administration and the college of medicine to design and implement a program to enhance patient care. Program proposals were solicited from several sources, and the program selected was the one developed by a team of social workers. The team members were social work educators with considerable clinical practice experience and familiarity with institutional programs and related problems of health care delivery. The team worked from the onset of planning through the actual program presentation. The theoretical framework used to develop the program was that of organizational development. A course of planned change was attempted through the "conscious utilization and application of knowledge as an instrument or tool for modifying patterns and institutions of practice."[5] By selecting leaders from among the hospital staff, a normative, reeducative program was developed that was designed to release and foster growth in the individuals who were key persons in the system to be changed.[5]

PROGRAM PLANNING

The early deliberations by the faculty team involved many hours in developing a curriculum to achieve the medical center's objectives. From the early discussions there appeared to be general agreement by the faculty team that the hospital setting was unique, complex, and involved tremendous expertise in the delivery of health services. In collaboration with the officials from the medical center and the faculty team, there evolved a dialogue around development of a meaningful human relations program directed toward enhanced patient care. From these discussions, a primary focus was placed on problems encountered by patients in the health care delivery system. The review of the literature and research data supported much of the early deliberations and provided the basis for ultimate program direction. It was recognized, for example, that patients undergo significant change resulting from hospitalization and often react to the accompanying stress in a variety of ways that hinder or complicate care. Another noteworthy area, supported by research, pointed to accounts of conflictual staff encounters resulting in less than favorable care, much less harmonious team effort. Finally, there was pronounced support for consideration of the essential ingredients of effective communications as perhaps the most crucial area in the discussions. A significant portion of problems in the health care delivery system appeared to be related to "poor communication" involving staff and patient.[6]

Around this knowledge of supportive research and the atmosphere of mutual understanding between medical center representatives and the faculty team, the challenge and innovative potential became obvious, and the program began to take shape; as a result of extensive deliberations it was agreed that major portions of the program should be devoted to the following broad content areas: (a) change as an integral part of hospitalization; (b) behavioral reactions of patients to the stress of hospitalization; (c) the ingredients of effective communication, which was deemed the foundation of the helping process; and (d) the issue of conflict, particularly as it related to intrastaff relationships and the ultimate effect on the patient.

In addition to planning the content to be taught, the format of the program and the specific learning experience were considered at length. It was agreed that didactic sessions were essential to teach the basic content. It was also agreed that experiential learning opportunities were necessary to assist participants in translating concepts into the desired terminal behavior. To accomplish the latter, the decision was made to follow didactic presentations with small-group activities that would provide the opportunities for informal discussion and for the participants to apply the concepts in such activities as communication exercises in pairs, sending and receiving messages, role playing in conflictual situations, and communicating until shared meanings were reached.

It was also agreed that small groups would be limited to 12 members to provide experiential opportunities for all participants. Each group would have one of the four teaching staff as a leader, who would also provide additional learning opportunities through modeling the desired terminal behaviors. For didactic sessions the participants would meet as a total group. Thus it was concluded that 48 participants would be the optimal size, permitting four small groups of 12 each. It was also decided that 2 days would be the minimal time required to accomplish the objectives and that the 2nd day would be 1 week following the 1st to permit participants to digest and to experiment with concepts and skills taught on the 1st day.

Certain administrative considerations had significant importance in the planning for the initial program. Selection of personnel for participation was made by service directors at the request of medical center administration. The major criterion of selection was key personnel who had high patient interaction or considerable supervisory responsibility.[7] Selected as participants were key staff working in the emergency room, outpatient department, admitting-discharge office, and numerous other crucial areas wherein the volume of patients served was large and contact by personnel frequent. Also selected were high-level administrative staff familiar with the hospital program and capable of rendering judgments as to the merits of the Human Relations Program in enhancing patient care. The selection process resulted in representation from 22 of 27 major services. The largest number of participants (41%) came from the professional services areas including nursing, pharmacy, administration, and social work. The remaining participants represented were secretarial, business, technical, and volunteer services. The physician group was excluded because of scheduling problems, but there was strong agreement on the need for training among this group as well.

Another important consideration of the planning effort was the provision of a follow-up session. The faculty decided on a 3-month period, allowing participants an opportunity to make operational specific techniques and skills presented in the program. The follow-up session was designed for a 2-hour period wherein small groups could reconvene and discuss areas of success or concern with the faculty team.

Another noteworthy aspect of planning revolved around the evaluation component. The presentation of the first 2-day workshop was considered a pilot program representing a trial-and-error period during which new approaches could be tried out flexibly with a view toward later revision. The evaluation, which provided an opportunity for research and learning from the experience, consisted of three questionnaires given to participants before the presentation, at the conclusion of the sessions, and 3 months later for follow-up.

PROGRAM CONTENT

The following is a summary of the program content. It highlights only major aspects, as it is impossible to incorporate all the material of the 2-day workshop in this article. As noted, the program focused on four major content areas, which were taught through didactic presentations and small-group sessions.

Change as an Integral Part of Illness and Hospitalization

The didactic session pointed out that change resulting from illness or accident is unpredictable and that the change may affect individuals or significant others in widely different ways. Adaptations to changes such as those involved in the family disruption caused by hospitalization are not made easily. Too much change can cause harmful effects, but change may also provide potential for growth and improvement. The need for medical care is an example of unplanned change, which is stress producing. What the patient brings to a stress situation includes existing patterns of thinking, coping patterns, differing levels of anxiety and emotionality. Change is both planned and unplanned, and hospitalization requires channeling unplanned change into planned change. Most important is understanding a patient's resistance to change, a chronic reality within the hospital setting. The small-group session allowed participants to examine change in personal, meaningful self-examination shared among the group members.

Behavioral Reactions to Stress

The didactic lecture dealt with internal conflicts, unknowns, fears, and role changes. Patients under the stress of hospitalization struggle with a fine balance between trust and mistrust of others, denial or acceptance of illness, along with fears of the unknown or uncertainties as to their capacity to handle problems. Family patterns and stability are often modified with role substitutions and shifting parenting, causing complicated problems.

In addition, the patient must adapt to a hospital social structure, rules, patterns, and procedures that require adjustment and orientation. Patients are often placed in situations wherein guidelines of appropriate behavior are unclear and may even lose social function. The hospital, at best, is a radical departure from customary environments, and a variety of reactions to the stress of illness can be anticipated.

In the small-group session on reactions to stress, participants were asked to recall crises in their own lives involving stress. Participants then shared their experiences. Discussion centered on the varied nature of stresses revealed and individualized patterns of coping with stress.

Ingredients of Effective Communication

The didactic session emphasized communication as the crucial component in the hospital system. Often staff blame poor communication on the patient, failing to realize that the patient is in unfamiliar surroundings. Special emphasis was placed on the essential qualities of effective communication, namely, warmth, basic respect for others, empathy, and genuineness. Styles of communication were discussed across conventional, manipulative, speculative, and open forms. Finally, the importance of developing listening skills that enable the creation of a positive atmosphere for communication was stressed. The small-group sessions involved several exercises wherein participants were given task sheets for developing and practicing both listening and communication skills.

Dealing with Conflict

Human institutions of all types are constantly dealing with problems of conflict, rivalry, and tension. Conflict flows largely from the apprehensions and threats to security. In hospitals rifts may exist among a host of professionals and contain the seeds of strife that may ultimately affect the patient. The hospital setting is a highly sensitive area because of high patient interaction wherein the staff build up feelings of antagonism resulting in tension toward the patient or his family. The points of tension prevail daily in hospitals, but the tension can be reduced by solid management and human relations training for the hospital staff. The small-group sessions involved participants in tasks pointing toward becoming more aware of how they deal with conflict and sharing with others their reactions and resolves.

PROGRAM EVALUATION

At the conclusion of the workshop, and 3 months later at the follow-up session, participants completed questionnaires regarding their overall reactions to the workshop and reactions to specific portions of the workshop. In addition, questions testing for knowledge of the content areas were asked. These were the same questions asked in the preworkshop questionnaire, making possible a precise assessment of the efficacy of the program vis-à-vis knowledge gained.

The responses of the participants were overwhelmingly positive, with about 95% of the participants indicating that their expectation of the workshop had been fulfilled or surpassed. Ratings by the participants of the major content portions, both didactic and experiential, were consistently high, ranging from good to excellent. Moreover, the participants unanimously indicated that the content of the workshop was relevant to their hospital roles. At the time of the follow-up session, a high percentage indicated that they were applying on their jobs the knowledge and skills learned in the workshop.

With respect to knowledge gained, comparisons of the data obtained prior to, at the completion of, and at the 3-month follow-up session indicated highly statistically significant gains in knowledge in all of the content areas, namely, patients' needs, patients' reaction to stress, problems of communication, and interstaff conflict. The gains were directly attributable to the learning experience of the workshop.

Opinions of the participants were also secured regarding the continuation of staff development sessions similar to the workshop. Again the opinions were enthusiastically supportive of ongoing programs, with about 95% indicating their favor for such a program.

Additional benefits cited by the participants were opportunities to meet personnel from other units of the hospital. Several of the participants indicated they had gained greater respect for and understanding of the problems of other administrative units—units with which they had experienced conflict in the past. Although there was a cross section of professional, business, secretarial, and technical staff, this mix did not affect the focus of the faculty or in any way deter the program sessions. It was notable that during the course of the workshop initial reserve and hesitation gradually yielded to a climate of openness and camaraderie, an unplanned but much-welcomed benefit.

CONCLUSIONS

Based on findings of this project, it was concluded that a carefully conceived program, such as the Human Relations Program, is an effective means of expanding participants' knowledge around major content areas.

If the program is planned and presented effectively, the participants will be receptive and enthusiastic and will make efforts to utilize the content in enhancing their job performance.

A program that incorporates an approach combining didactic and small-group experiential sessions is a powerful mechanism for teaching human relations. In addition, a well-designed program that encourages and plans for active involvement of the individual can achieve a high level of positive participant response. Hospital or medical center officials, in collaboration with other professional disciplines, can successfully activate a program to meet and accomplish specific institutional goals. Finally, social work should feel secure in assuming a leadership role in the design and presentation of such programs.

EPILOGUE

To this point, the highlights of our humanistic program as designed and presented at the University of Utah Medical Center have been described. The program was initially conducted as a pilot effort including detailed evaluation of both program content and presentation. As a result of the participants' positive responses to the Human Relations Program, exhibited in part by their expressions of appreciation and the findings of the pilot presentation, the program was continued. Three additional programs were conducted in January, February, and September 1974. Over 200 medical center personnel have completed the 2-day course, and plans are underway to extend the program to ongoing staff development or on an in-service basis.

The subsequent programs provided the opportunity to incorporate participant suggestions for strengthening the overall presentation. The major program revision resulted from participants' expressed interest in greater use of the small-group sessions. Participants felt that the group sessions were productive, and despite some reported discomfort during the initial sessions, they requested additional time in small groups. This suggestion resulted in reducing the early didactic sessions on the 1st day and adding two small-group sessions. Some material normally presented in the large didactic sessions was preserved, but presented in small groups, utilizing role playing and greater individual participation.

Finally it should be noted that the subsequent sessions were improved due to the incorporation of constructive participant suggestions, as mentioned above, but also due to the more relaxed atmosphere created by a tried and tested faculty. Although the same detailed evaluation was not used in subsequent programs, a modified evaluation procedure revealed even more positive response to the program content, presentation, and overall contribution.

REFERENCES

1. Switzer, Ellen. "Unless a Remedy Is Applied at Once." *Redbook,* October 1969, p. 65.

2. Upham, Frances. *A Dynamic Approach to Illness.* New York: Family Service Association of America, 1949.

3. Bernard, Jessie, and Jensen, Deborah. *Sociology.* Saint Louis: C. V. Mosley, 1962.

4. *Multidisciplinary Practice in Public Health.* Based on the Proceedings of the 1965 Annual Institute for Public Health Social Workers, edited by Joanna F. Gorman and Alice M. Varela. Berkeley: University of California, 1966.

5. Chin, Robert, and Benne, Kenneth D. "General Strategies for Effecting Changes in Human Systems." In *The Planning of Change,* edited by Warren G. Bennis, Kenneth D. Benne, and Robert Chin. New York: Holt, Rinehart & Winston, 1969.

6. Pfiffner, John M., and Fels, Marshall. *The Supervision of Personnel: Human Relations in the Management of Men.* Englewood Cliffs, N.J.: Prentice-Hall, 1965.

7. Hand, Herbert H., and Slocum, John W., Dr. "A Longitudinal Study of the Effects of a Human Relations Training Program on Managerial Effectiveness." *Journal of Applied Psychology* 56 (1972):412–17.

Chapter 18

Reflections
of a Social Work Administrator
on the Opportunities of Crisis

Martin Nacman, DSW

ABSTRACT. The climate of crisis in which hospital social work departments currently operate is contemplated by an undaunted administrator. Social workers as planners and innovaters are able to move ahead in such a climate. Constructive approaches that benefit the hospital and its consumers and enhance job gratification are discussed.

"READING" THE NATURE OF CRISIS

Yesterday the magic word was "audit." Today it is "containment." The government and consequently hospital administrators have become committed deeply to cost containment. It is a time of curtailment of some hospital programs, termination of others. Rising costs and limited reimbursements highlight the fiscal ineptitude of many hospital organizations. During a period of explosive growth, many hospital administrators paid little attention to the organization of work. As a result, waste, duplication of effort, and "organization obesity" were common. Some fiscal management was by medical specialists whose training in science had not prepared them for the rigors of organizational administration. Now government is trying to impose uniform and universal standards and a reduction in hospital beds and expenses. By 1990 we shall probably have fewer hospital beds but more diversified programs. The excess beds of the 1970's may look cost effective compared to the inflated construction costs of 1990. The astronomical rise in government controls adds to administrative frustrations and intensifies the climate of crisis that characterizes the hospital.

What does the crisis mean to social work? In some instances it has already resulted in the reduction of social work staff and the curtailment of programs. Not only social work, but other allied health professionals have been affected. Too often cutbacks have been instituted indiscriminately without regard to ultimate effect on patient care. In the search for fiscal solvency some hospital administrators have seized on decentralization as a means of achieving improved fiscal responsibility. Some medical administrators have attempted to break up peer control of allied health professionals in order to establish stronger administrative control over these personnel (Nacman, 1975-6). In some hospitals medical administration aided by meaningful data systems have lowered the expenditures for supporting services such as accounting, maintenance, laundry, and housekeeping as a means of balancing the hospital budget. Herzlinger (1977) identifies fiscal innovations such as self insurance to cover malpractice and liability claims, second reviews for surgery, peer review of utilization patterns, selected use of laboratory and radiological procedures, and preventive health care programming as holding promise toward controlling spiraling health costs without adversely affecting direct patient care.

CONFLICT IS INEVITABLE

In the agonizing arena of administrative ambiguity, conflict of interest can become severe because there are usually no objective measures of right or wrong courses of action. Action at the executive level is by no means always rational. There is no one best solution. Every administrator and many staff members become proselytizers trying to sell their alternatives, trying to influence others to reorient their choices or to collaboratively sponsor a compromise alternative.

There is no way of avoiding conflict or remaining aloof from struggles within an organization. The minute you are told that the scope of your program is to be reduced for the good of the hospital, you are involved in a serious conflict. Do you acquiesce for the sake of the common good or do you fight? To some social work administrators the word "fight" seems too harsh. However, the willingness to fight may serve the interests of the organization, by highlighting issues and stimulating thinking before final decisions are made (Kelly, 1970).

Living with conflict necessitates the innovative development of power alliances. In the changing environment of the hospital, the composition and nature of coalitions is a changing mosaic. One cannot rely on the same alliances all the time. Previous alliances may neither be available nor workable in the present; they may not be effective in relation to certain issues. New alliances offering different potentials need to be developed constantly.

CONFLICT, CHANGE, AND OPPORTUNITY

But neither the hospital nor its social work program can remain as they have been. Whatever exists in a hospital is aging. Sooner or later everything has to change. Hospital social work faces the same dilemmas as the hospital organization in general. Both must change. A hospital social work program must be capable of purposeful evolution in order to adapt to new conditions. It must be capable of purposeful innovation in order to change existing conditions. We must not only respond to opportunities but we must create our own opportunities.

—Opportunity exists when there is a disparity between needs and resources.
—Opportunity exists when conflict exists.

The problems confronting the hospital organization will produce further conflicts for social work administration but will also offer opportunities for growth and development. Social work can capitalize on existing conflict and stress by producing innovative ideas and programs capable of resolving some of the problems that confront hospital administration.

The realities of organizational life demonstrate that conflict of interests exist even among people who ultimately share common goals and work together. In the current situation in which resources are scarce, it is inevitable that conflict will arise and that the struggle for power over resources will intensify.

Drucker views conflict and dissent as the catalysts to decision-making. Conflict and dissent should not be feared. They should not be avoided. Drucker asserts that the effective decision-maker organizes dissent. In his opinion, dissent is needed (1) to safeguard the decision-maker against becoming the prisoner of the organization; (2) to provide alternatives in decision-making and (3) to stimulate the imagination of staff. It produces new and different ways of proceeding and understanding (Drucker, 1975).

It is said that managers make decisions and lovers make choices. But in fact, all of management involves making choices. Contemporary administrative mythology would have us believe that we obtain facts, become aware of all opinions and options and make the best decision. This is not true. Pascale, describing administration in Japan, says the Japanese define administration as choosing one option over the other. That philosophy acknowledges and appreciates more fully the inevitable sense of incompleteness that stems from having to choose. It also sensitizes administrators to the illusion of mastery. The Japanese delay decisions until after they can articulate the right questions. Formulating the questions is the serious work of management (Pascale, 1978).

It would be comforting to think there is one effective formula which would enable us to operate in an atmosphere of total cooperation, but that is not reality. Ambiguity and adversity are threatening and so, as generations before us have done, we too have sought a kind of "religious conversion" to resolve our problems. We approach administration with a blind faith in various rituals. There is a tendency for administrators to form elaborate structures, procedures, and other ceremonials which create the illusion of problem solving. We expend enormous energy carrying out these rituals with child-like expectations that our magical formulas will solve real problems. Some of our contemporary management "religions" are: the conservative religion called management by objectives; the reform movement called decentralization; the new form of orthodoxy called zero-based budgeting; and, lastly, a modification of Zen called sensitivity training. With the intensity of a fanatic we work towards our staff's conversion to one or all of these religions. We seduce them with promises of certainty. It is not that these approaches have no substance; they have their virtues if used in a limited context. Administrators should not transform these approaches into religions or make their organizations total institutions governed rigidly by these devices. For example, management by objectives is advantageous toward helping an organization to direct its energy and attention. At the same time an over zealous adherence to this approach may result in rigidities and discourage staff from looking toward new horizons (Levinson, 1970). We must guard against allowing achievement of stated goals to compromise ideals. Each of the stated techniques offers promise, none offers final solutions.

INNOVATION AND RISK

A major thesis is that a social work program must be constantly innovative. In a sense, social work administrators are investors. We try to determine what activity, what program offers the most for our investment. And as investors, we should realize that there are risks and that the outcomes cannot be totally determined.

As in business organizations, social work programs also need diversification. Diversification balances the vulnerabilities and weaknesses of an organization. Organizations that produce only one product or service are extremely vulnerable as external and internal needs require change. The specialties of today may become extinct tomorrow. Staff needs to engage in a variety of activities, if not, work may become a bore.

Risk is inevitable. Risk is inherent in the commitment of present resources for future expectations. To eliminate risks is to produce rigidity. There are no solutions with respect to the future. There are only choices between courses of action: each imperfect, each risky, each uncertain, each requiring diffferent efforts and involving different costs. There are no formulas. There is only understanding (Pascale, 1978).

As social work administrators we need to learn to tolerate ambiguity. Often we are driven to make quick decisions. We feel compelled to be right all of the time. Japanese potters create bowls with slight imperfections. These potters know that the perfection of mass produced bowls is less satisfying than ones not so perfect. Administrative decisions need not be perfect (Pascale, 1978).

THE OPPORTUNITIES OF CRISIS

This section addresses the connections between specific problems confronting hospital, medical, and social work administrators and opportunities for social work development.

Utilization Review and Professional Standards Review Organization

Hospital utilization review programs have become extremely complex as a result of federal, state, and local PSRO policies and procedures (PSRO Manual, 1974). The program now resembles the old cyclone ride in Coney Island. The ascent to the top of the ride is slow and tedious, the descent, rapid and designed to produce the fear that you may crash. Then, one repeats the same experience, going to the next elevation and the next and the next.

The one point that is clear in the PSRO amusement park of policies and procedures, changes and fluctuations is that early and accurate discharge planning is unavoidable. Otherwise the patient is in trouble and the hospital faces loss of revenue (PSRO Manual, 1974). While discharge planning is not solely the province of the social worker, the social worker can perform an important role by providing direct services to patients and their families, and by helping to create and coordinate sound discharge planning systems. Social workers, by becoming experts in utilization review policies and procedures, can use this knowledge in combination with their social work expertise to help hospital administration improve discharge programming and avoid unnecessary losses. In addition, the same knowledge can be used to guide patients through this complex system. Increased knowledge and sensitivity about PSRO policies and problems also offers greater opportunity to change the system.

The same knowledge base also offers the social worker additional opportunities for teaching medical and nursing staff. Although the initial entry into the teaching situation may be on the subject of discharge planning, these opportunities can be expanded and other topics introduced that may enhance the participants' understanding of social work in general.

The hospital administrator's concern about not being penalized as a result of improper planning affords social work the opportunity to build a more effective discharge program.

Preventive Risk Management

Recent hospital literature abounds with references to risk protection programs. Hospital and medical administration have become alarmed over the cost of malpractice and liability insurance and the skyrocketing awards that have been granted in malpractice and liability suits (Salman, 1979). The JCAH and State Departments of Health have both placed considerable emphasis on establishing safe, physical environments. It has not always been apparent to legal practitioners that one of the reasons for the increase in malpractice suits is the erosion of the doctor-patient relationship. Lawyers do suggest that malpractice suits may be reduced if hospitals can reduce consumer dissatisfaction (Ascobrook and Goldsmith, 1978). Recently, administrators, in response to patient dissatisfactions, have created ombudsman and patient representative programs. However, these programs usually represent only token investments toward improving patient-staff relations. In most instances, these programs are not preventive but are actuated only after problems are identified. Hospital and medical administration have failed to recognize that the patient's and family's reaction to the hospital and staff represent extremely complex and often times subtle psycho-social reaction patterns.

It is precisely because of the influence of psycho-social factors on the patient's perception of the hospital that social work staff can contribute to preventive risk management. The social worker's diagnostic acuity and therapeutic skills may help patients sort out and perhaps even resolve some of the conflicts and problems they perceive before these issues become distorted and increase dissatisfaction with the hospital system. In addition, as advocates, social workers provide patients with access to resources to which they are entitled, thus preventing the buildup of frustration that may result when patient and/or family feel that they have nowhere to turn and see no constructive way of altering their situation. Social work's role in preventive risk management can go beyond the treatment of individual situations. Social workers can provide hospital administration with consultation relevant to the improvement of the hospital environment. For example, the social worker's constant exposure to patients' reactions to the hospital's admission procedures may be used to offer constructive suggestions as to how delays and distorted communications can be avoided. The social worker's keen awareness of the needs and frustrations of patients and families offers valuable information to administration toward the improvement of preventive risk management programs.

Advocacy for the Handicapped

Another contemporary problem confronting hospital administration is the need to implement the Rehabilitation Act of 1973. Ever since the Department of Health, Education and Welfare published the regulations implementing Section 504 of that act, hospital administrators have struggled with the implementation of that program. By August, 1977, all hospitals that receive Medicare, Medicaid, Hill Burton, and other types of federal financial assistance were required to make their programs, services, and activities accessible to the handicapped. Where structural changes were necessary, implementation could be achieved by a later date. The regulations also require that interested persons, including the handicapped or organizations representing them, be consulted at each phase of the evaluation (Rehabilitation Act of 1973). Here again, social workers can help administration resolve an important problem and at the same time improve services to patients. Social work staff should take an active role in advising administration on the needs of the handicapped, the type of programs that can assure equal access to care, and help with the implementation of required programs. In addition, the social workers' knowledge of community resources can be extremely helpful to hospital administration in establishing contact with relevant community organizations as part of the hospital's planning process. Social workers can be useful also in educating staff about the special needs of the handicapped as well as the needs of patients from diverse cultural backgrounds. Social work staff can also train interpreters to work with deaf and non-English speaking patients. It is essential to recognize, however, that the inclusion of interpreters does not preclude the need for trained social work staff. The two are not interchangeable. Hospitals also need social workers with bilingual and sign language capabilities.

Abused People

Another problem that deserves the expertise of social work staff is the neglect or maltreatment of children and adults. Although initially the primary emphasis was on the abuse and neglect of children, the problems of the elderly as well as the battered wife syndrome are now apparent, and men are petitioning for a battered husbands' program. Regardless of age of the maltreated or neglected person, these acts represent a serious problem for both the offender and the recipient. Social workers need to recognize that hospital administration is confronted with both legal and therapeutic issues of serious proportion. Social work can be an institutional resource as therapist, as staff consultant, as planner.

At our hospital we have established a child protection committee as a subcommittee of the Hospital Executive Committee. This committee, chaired by a social worker, is responsible for the development and monitoring of programs relevant to child maltreatment. The appointment of a social worker as chairperson recognizes the relevant role of social work in working with these problems and affords us greater opportunities to further influence programming in this area. The hospital has established a "response program" in which a core group of specially trained social workers serve as consultants to other hospital staff and coordinate necessary activities. The social worker serving as consultant needs to be thoroughly versed in the legal aspects of child maltreatment and neglect in addition to possessing highly developed clinical skills.

These are only a few examples of the kinds of hospital problems that are amenable to social work intervention. There are others, and each social work administrator can identify unique problems particular to his hospital.

NURTURING INNOVATION

The social work organization that wants to create and maintain a spirit of achievement must stress opportunity. But too often we have a fear of flying. Staff hesitate to take risks because they fear failure. In part, they fear that their supervisors and administrators expect that each idea and each innovation will be successful. In many instances their perceptions are correct. Administrators must accept the reality that the mortality rate of innovation will and should be high. Positive incentives are needed to encourage innovation. Furthermore, innovation does not necessarily proceed along a linear progression. For long periods of time nothing may happen before progress is achieved. There is a Chinese adage that states, "success is going straight around the circle" (Pascale, 1978). The development of an innovation is uneven and some innovations may not be successful. While we must require goals in innovative projects it is important to recognize that innovation requires a separate measurement system as compared to ordinary production goals (Drucker, 1975).

Hospital social work departments are finally launching programs that will provide us with the capability of quantitative and qualitative analysis of our services. These are important programs, but at the same time, we must be cautious not to be consumed by an accounting orientation. We must not allow the cost and time commitment to these programs to distract from our patient service objectives. Dr. Bennett points out that while it is necessary to recognize the results of science to the fullest we should not deny that there is something more than science (Bennett, 1978). The importance of defining costs, of planning objectives, of producing data capable of yielding qualitative analysis of our programs is indisputable. But we also need to recognize that these approaches may have a stifling effect on staff and programs. To impose upon innovation the accounting conventions that fit the on-going business audit is misdirection and may cripple or kill creativity.

At every staff level there is a vital role to be played in the generation of ideas and innovations about programming policies and procedures. But a strong central administrative program is essential to the success of the program. When staff undercut central administration the program is in trouble.

An effective administrative system that will enhance the potential for innovative practice is one that enables staff at all levels to achieve personal goals by achieving organizational goals. This may be accomplished through implementation of the following steps: (1) allow staff broader authority to develop and carry out social work programs commensurate with the employee's skills within a specific assignment, and in concert with program goals; (2) give social workers a complete natural unit of work; (3) assign individuals specific or specialized tasks enabling them to become experts; (4) introduce new and more difficult tasks not handled previously, both for staff and administration; (5) create opportunities for increasing staff recommendations about social work priorities, policies, and procedures; (6) expand staff participation in hospital administration in a planned manner allowing for individual differences and potentials; and, (7) provide an assertive administration (Herzberg, 1966). These procedures, designed to enhance job enrichment, in turn provide opportunities for the future growth and development of the social work program. This is a developmental-administrative systems model that taps creative potentials.

It utilizes our ability to look at and plan in relation to events that have already happened but have not yet had their full psychosocial impact. For example, changes in patient populations, changes in law, and new community crises may suggest to social workers opportunities for programming and innovation. Social work can use this information to create new markets, to create new talents, and to improve the marketability of current programs. Social workers from our staff, in conjunction with two pediatricians, helped to develop a family counselor program in which housewives were trained to work with chronically ill patients and their families. Others helped to establish, under the auspices of the local chapter of the American Cancer Association, an interim housing facility for patients undergoing out-patient treatment of cancer. One staff member is working on a project involving the training of the police force. The Social Work Division has obtained grants from the federal government for the training of child protective workers and has developed a series of audio-visual programs to facilitate their training.

IN SUMMARY

The administration approach described focuses on what staff can do rather than what they cannot do. It is the primary task of administration to bring out whatever strength a social worker possesses and to use each staff member's strength to help other social workers to improve their performance and to grow. The text of administrative achievement is not conformance but performance. The focus of administration must be on opportunities. The organization must be inculcated from the top with the habit of achievement. Social work management must set high standards of performance for itself that are related to the accomplishment of organizational objectives and not the needs of administrators. The administrative track record will include mistakes and failures. The better social work manager will make more mistakes because more new things will be tried.

It is an administrative imperative to plan for crises, to make the unanticipated anticipated. The social work director, as architect, using a systems approach, can prepare for crisis and develop long-range plans for the social work program.

Dr. Bennett states it well:

> As scientists and as professional people we would all do well to examine our roles, our motives, our faults, our policies, our prides and our prejudices in the broad context of our evolving society. If we look searchingly, we may finally arrive at a new viewpoint which will enable us to be pragmatic without sacrificing ideals, and hopefully, more humble without sacrificing pride (Bennett, 1978).

REFERENCES

Ascobrook, H. B. & Goldsmith, L. S. *Medical malpractice*. Washington, D.C.: Federal Publications Inc, 1978, p. 564.

Bennett, I. L. Problems and alternatives. *Journal of Medical Education*, 1978, *53*, pp. 33–39.

Drucker, P., *Management*. New York: Harper and Row, 1975, pp. 465–480.

Herzberg, F. One more time: How do you motivate employees? *New insights for executive achievement*. Cambridge, Mass.: Harvard College, 1966, pp. 1–11.

Herzlinger, R. E. Fiscal management in health organizations. Presented at a workshop on "Management & Accountability—Theory and Application," sponsored by the Society for Hospital Social Work Directors, April, 1977.

Kelly, S. Make conflict work for you. *Harvard Business Review*, July-August, 1970, pp. 103–113.

Levinson, H. Management by whose objectives? *Harvard Business Review*, July-August, 1970, pp. 125–134.

Nacman, M. A systems approach to the provision of social work services in health settings: Part II. *Social Work in Health Care*, 1975, *1*(2), pp. 133–143.

Pascale, R. T. Zen and the art of management. *Harvard Business Review*, March-April, 1978, pp. 153–162.

P.S.R.O. program manual. U.S. Dept. of H.E.W., Office of Professional Standards Review, March 15, 1974.

Rehabilitation Act of 1973. Section 504, June, 1977.

Salman, S. L. A systems approach can ensure high-quality care and low costs. *Hospitals*, March 16, 1979, AHA.

Chapter 19

A Social Worker's Use
of a Patient Attitude Survey
in the Administration
of a Small Health Clinic

Philip Starr, ACSW
Gary L. Ellis
Seishi Oka, DDS, PhD

ABSTRACT. This paper describes the use of a patient attitude survey in the administration of a small health clinic. A survey conducted by social service staff on a randomly selected, stratified sample of 100 parents and/or adult patients identified strengths and weaknesses in the operation of the clinic. These findings were then used as the basis for taking corrective action. The study with the consequent action taken demonstrated the value of client feedback for agency operation.

INTRODUCTION

There has been increasing recognition of the value of client (consumer) feedback at the worker and agency level. Dailey and Ives (1978) reported on how evaluations by clients resulted in improvement of workers' interviewing practices. Rosenberg (1977) reported how veterans' perceptions of their hospital care identified the nature of interaction of some staff with some patients as needing improvement. Maluccio (1979) analyzed how "clients views can help to maintain accountability, identify service gaps or deficiencies, influence policy formulation and decision-making, and initiate changes within a specific agency or the broader service delivery system."

This present study is a report of a survey on 100 randomly selected parents of young patients or adult patients attending a small specialty clinic. It was undertaken to assess how our clients viewed the services, staff, and facilities of the clinic. We will describe the setting in which the

This study is, in part, based on experiences supported by NIDR, NIH, Research Grant DE 04779-02.

survey was undertaken, how the survey was conducted, and the results and their implications on the clinic's operation.

SETTING

The H. K. Cooper Clinic is the oldest, only fulltime, fully staffed clinic serving patients with a cleft lip and/or palate (CL/P). A CL/P can be described as a gap or slit resulting from a lack of fusion of components forming the lip and/or palate. It is the second most common birth defect in the U.S. and occurs once in every 750 live births (Oka, 1979).

The severity of the CL/P condition varies greatly. The more severe the cleft, the more extensive are the deformities in related oral-facial structures (Harkins *et al.*, 1962). For example, a child with a cleft lip and palate is more likely to have surgical, dental, speech, and hearing difficulties than will a child with only a cleft of the lip.

At the clinic, the child is evaluated every six months until six years of age and thereafter annually. Thus, each child's unique development is periodically monitored and the skills and talents of a number of health professionals are utilized as needed. As the child grows the services of many professionals may be needed at various times for a comprehensive and successful treatment program. These professionals include the plastic surgeon, dentist, speech pathologist, otolaryngologist, audiologist, pediatrician, geneticist, orthodontist, prosthodontist, social worker, radiologist, and growth development specialist (Peacock and Starr, 1980).

METHOD

During the summer of 1979, 100 randomly selected parents or adult patients were asked to participate in this survey through interviews by the social service staff concerning their visits to the clinic. This stratified sample of 100 represented one half of the population who visited the clinic on the days the interviews took place. All of the selected families agreed to participate, however, some expressed apprehension about the purpose of the study and its confidentiality. The purpose of the survey was explained to them with an assurance that the information will be held in strict confidence. Names did not appear on the forms; this resulted in 100% participation.

A personal interview rather than a questionnaire was selected as the methodology in order to assure complete understanding of each question and to provide the opportunity to pursue answers in depth.

The selected families were asked the following questions: Is parking a problem at the clinic? Do you feel the period of time you had to wait was a problem for you? Do you feel the reception personnel were friendly and understanding? Do you feel the assistants were friendly and showed concern for your problem? Did you understand the reason for your visit? Did you understand the self-care instructions given to you upon your departure from the clinic? Do you have any comments about the professional treatment you received at the clinic? Do you have any problems with the appointment-making arrangements of the clinic? Would you recommend the clinic to a friend or relative? Can you think of any changes we can make to improve our services to you?

These questions were selected because they focus on two important dimensions that have been identified as essential in assessing effectiveness of services (Maluccio, 1979). The first dimension relates to the interactional environment which characterizes how services are delivered (Lennard & Bernstein, 1969). The second dimension involves the relationship between the patient and/or their family to the practitioners (Truax and Mitchell, 1971).

The role of the social worker in this study and in the process of implementation of the results were four-fold. First, he was involved in the design of the interview schedule. Second, his efforts toward explaining the purpose of the survey, reassuring absolute confidentiality, assured 100% participation. Third, the social workers' interviewing skills facilitated a broader and deeper response from the clients (Hollis, 1972). Lastly, the social worker, working with his staff and the parents' group (see implications section), was able to suggest changes to correct for the weaknesses identified by the clients (Perlman, 1957).

RESULTS

Client parking was identified as a severe problem for 10% of the respondents. Moreover, 15 respondents did not know that the Clinic had off-street parking spaces.

Of the 100 respondents surveyed, only 13 indicated that they had to wait more than 15 minutes before being seen by a professional staff member. Nine respondents stated that with the recent establishment of a playroom with a television, waiting was no longer a problem for them.

The reception personnel and dental assistants were rated by the respondents as friendly and understanding of their needs in 98% of the situations. Ninety-four of the respondents indicated that they had no problem in making appointments and 92% of them had no problem with billing arrangements.

Ninety-two respondents indicated that they understood the reason for their visit. Most respondents understood the self-care instructions provided by staff. Some, however, had to ask specific questions in order to obtain particular instructions.

Most patients and/or their parents were pleased with the quality and humaneness of the services rendered by our staff. As one patient stated, "the clinic deals with each individual as a person, in a very caring way, not just as another patient."

The most frequent expressed constructive criticism made by the respondents was for more clear communication with the parents and patients about what is being done and why, and in lay language. The respondents clearly desire information in order to more fully understand specific procedures and the total treatment process.

Ninety-nine respondents indicated that they would recommend the clinic to a friend or relative. Seventy-nine respondents stated that they had no changes to make to improve the services of the clinic. Of the 21 respondents recommending change, 12 indicated that more and clearer communication was desired. Some of the families during their initial evaluations were unsure of what to ask. These people wanted to be better apprised of the purpose of their first visit and of the specific procedures that comprise the diagnostic process.

Another area of concern was the taking of x-rays and the risks associated with radiation. This follows the trend in the general public where there is more concern regarding the exposure to excess radiation.

IMPLICATIONS FOR CLINIC OPERATION

The results of the Patient Attitude Survey were analyzed by the social service staff. A written report of the results together with recommendations for corrective actions was prepared for the executive director and the director of program development. These administrators decided to have the report discussed at a meeting of departmental heads. The president of the Parents and Adult Patient (PAP) Group was invited to attend.

At this meeting, it was decided that special efforts were necessary to better orient new patients to our facility, to develop a more effective means for communication between professionals and parents and/or adult patients, and to inform our clients about available clinic parking spaces. It was further decided that the social service staff would work with the PAP group to implement these recommendations.

An orientation letter with some common questions to ask professionals has been prepared by a member of the PAP Steering Committee. This letter is now routinely sent to all new parents and/or patients prior to their first visit.

The president of PAP, in cooperation with a member of the social service staff, developed a plan for volunteers to be present at the clinic on plastic surgery days. The volunteers were trained by the social service staff. These volunteers meet with the parent and/or adult patient after all the professionals have seen the patient. The volunteer checks to make sure that the family understands what was accomplished during the initial visit, and if applicable, the self-care instructions. Finally, they determine whether all client questions were clearly answered. Plastic surgery days at the clinic were chosen for this project since most new patients are scheduled on these days.

This plan was approved at a meeting of the department heads. In the November newsletter of PAP, the feature article described this program. Training of the volunteers occurred in February and the plan was implemented within the month.

Preliminary experiences with these volunteers have identified unmet needs in two cases. The volunteers informed the social service staff of these situations and proper remedial action was taken. The ability of some of the parents and/or adult patients to discuss significant matters with other people like themselves, and not the professional staff, demonstrates the value of experiential knowledge (Borkman, 1976).

Finally, a map with a layout of the locations of the clinic parking spaces was prepared and placed in our waiting rooms.

SUMMARY

This paper has been a report of a patient attitude survey with 100 randomly selected parents and/or adult patients. It demonstrates that most consumers of our service were pleased with the humaneness and competence of the professional staff. It identified areas of weakness which needed improvement. Constructive action to correct these weaknesses has been initiated. Therefore, this process has demonstrated the value of client feedback for agency operation.

It is important to caution the reader that because of the vulnerability of the patients they learn to be accommodating even if unintentional agency practices embarrass and degrade them. The value of patient satisfaction as a measure of the humanism provided by an agency depends on the population being served—their expectations, fears, and hierarchy of concerns.

REFERENCES

Borkman, T. Experiential knowledge: a new concept for the analysis of self-help groups. *Social Service Review*, 1976, *67*, pp. 445–456.

Dailey, W. J. & Ives, K. Exploring client reaction to agency service. *Social Casework*, 1978, *59*, pp. 223–245.

Harkins, C. S., Berlin, A., Harding, R. L., Longacre, J. J. & Snodgrasse, R. M. A classification of cleft lip and cleft palate. *Plastic and reconstructive surgery*, 1962, *29*, pp. 31–39.

Hollis, F. *Casework—a psychosocial therapy*, second edition. New York: Random House, 1972.

Perlman, H. H. *Social casework—a problem-solving process*. Chicago: University of Chicago Press, 1957.

Lennard, H. L. and Bernstein, A. *Patterns in human interaction*. San Francisco: Jossey-Bass, 1969.

Maluccio, A. N. *Learning from clients: Interpersonal helping as viewed by clients and social workers*. New York: Free Press, 1979.

Oka, S. Epidemiology and genetics of clefting: with Implications for etiology, in H. K. Cooper, Sr., R. L. Harding, W. M. Krogman, M. Mazaheri & R. T. Millard (eds.), *Cleft palate and cleft lip: A team approach to clinical management and rehabilitation of the patient*. Philadelphia: W. B. Saunders Co., 1979, pp. 108–143.

Peacock, J. and Starr, P. An outreach program for the newborn with cleft lip and/or palate. *Children Today*, in press.

Rosenberg, J. Veterans' perceptions of their hospital care. *Social Work Research and Abstracts*, 1977, 13, pp. 30–34.

Truax, C. and Mitchell, K. M. Research on certain therapist interpersonal skills in relation to process and outcome, in W. E. Bergin and S. L. Garfield (eds.), *Handbook of psychotherapy and behavior change; An empirical analysis*. New York: Wiley, 1971, pp. 299–344.

PART VII

Managing the Community Linkage System

Social departments and health care agencies serve as links to community support systems. This is particularly significant today because of the emphasis on community and home care programs in health care and the process of deinstitutionalization. As such programs proliferate on the assumption that they are cost effective, social work has a new frontier to explore and develop. However, what is needed are techniques, knowledge, and skills which enable social workers in health care to assess needs in the community and to develop programs to meet these needs.

Funding sources for such programs are necessary because the usual sources are no longer readily available. Marketing social work services and health care has particular relevance. As the article by Rosenberg and Weissman indicates, it is important to develop an approach which will bring social work services to the attention of consumers and help to motivate them as well as other professionals to participate in developing community programs for patients in need of health care services, either to prevent institutionalization or to help them with problems that they may face after they leave the institution. The Rosenberg, Weissman article discusses marketing concepts and strategies which can be useful and which have been employed by other departments and helps to make the notion of making social work services important as well as attractive to consumers and to other groups in the community who can benefit from such services.

A further step in developing linkages is to help intra-agency relationships. The article by Flaherty and Martin describes seven parameters in a process which they believe to be effective in developing relationships between a new community agency and those which exist in a community. What emerges clearly is the importance of the quality of planning, and the recognition that the developing relationships among agencies can be conceptualized in terms of stages. This article provides information and techniques regarding the importance of the planning process in instituting and managing a community linkage system.

A third article in this chapter deals with the role of social workers in the coordination of health services. A good social work department in a health care agency should have a community organization function which enables the department to be attuned to the needs of the consumers in the community and the needs of institutionalized persons who may have specific needs. It helps to develop a methodology for working in the community to expand the human services role. The expanded social work role in the community under this framework is described in Wilson's article. They include such functions as an information broker, an opinion maker, and a definer of issues.

The final article in this section uses discharge planning in a medical center as an illustration of how this process can be used by a department of social work to establish an advocacy role. Aside from the advocacy function which, in the judgment of Lurie, facilitates discharge planning, there are three areas which this function can help in projecting the social work department into the community and to participate actively in the community linkage system. They include political advocacy for the development of needed governmental programs, resource development advocacy to meet unmet needs and case advocacy to insure that programs are accessible and appropriate for eligible patients and families.

Social work functions in health care agencies have been enlarged and are encompassing greater areas. Much of this is related to the current concepts of the medical center as a hub of health services which range from preventative work to tertiary care and to developing resources in the community to help patients avoid institutionalization. As social workers in health care agencies work in these areas it is logical and realistic for them to begin to become managers in a community linkage system for the reasons described and the specific skills needed to do this are defined in the article. It is well to remember that the social work profession began principally in the community and much of social work activity emerged from working in impoverished urban areas. Knowledge gained from learning about formal and informal systems that exist in such areas helped social workers develop various processes in which they became expert. Case finding, developing interviewing techniques, working with various groups in settlement houses and with various ethnic minorities, and participating in social action and social policy processes are all part of the historical tradition of social work. For some years, the profession has moved away from working in the community and toward a greater emphasis on working with individuals. The process seems to be reversing itself and a balance is beginning to emerge.

Abraham Lurie, PhD

Chapter 20

Marketing Social Services in Health Care Facilities

Gary Rosenberg, PhD
Andrew Weissman, DSW

ABSTRACT. Marketing is compatible with social work because of its emphasis on consumer needs and consumer satisfaction. This article discusses relevant marketing concepts and then presents examples of marketing strategies and programs developed by hospital social work departments.

A marketing frame of reference can be useful to social work departments in health care.[1] This article presents a working definition of the marketing approach and general definitional guidelines to its uses. It analyzes environmental pressures on health care and social work and differentiates between business marketing and health care marketing. Moreover, it examines the advantages of a marketing perspective and identifies the barriers that impede its use in hospital social work departments. Finally, it discusses relevant marketing concepts and presents examples of marketing strategies and programs developed by such departments.

DEFINITION OF MARKETING APPROACH

A marketing perspective is concerned with ways of helping an organization achieve its corporate purpose of attracting and holding customers. Marketing is thus a special view of the business process designed to attract and keep a customer. If a company does not attract customers or continue to meet the needs of its present customers, business will fail.

Selling is largely a one-way process: It involves the sending of products out from a company for the consumer to purchase. In contrast, market research is a two-way process: It gathers factual information regarding consumers' preferences for goods and services and sends this information

This chapter is reprinted with the permission of *Health & Social Work,* Vol. 6, No. 3, August, 1981, and the National Association of Social Workers, Inc.

back to the company so that the company may develop and supply the appropriate goods and services. A marketing perspective strengthens a company's ability to develop those products or services that clients need and want rather than those the company might wish to offer.[2] Thus, the goal of a marketing plan is to satisfy the needs of consumers.

Marketing was a major theme of the literature on health care management in 1979, but it has barely been mentioned in the social work literature.[3] Social work departments do engage in marketing, however; but they call their marketing strategies and actions by other names that seem more compatible with the values and beliefs held by social workers. A marketing perspective tends to be highly compatible with the social work point of view that envisions a health care system offering services developed out of meeting clients' needs and desires. Within the marketing definitional system, one of the major fits is that of consumer satisfaction, a main strategy in evaluative research on health care.[4] Cooper provides a more formal definition:

> [It is] a management orientation that accepts that the key task of the system is to determine the wants, needs and values of a target market and shape the system in such a manner to deliver the desired level of satisfaction.[5]

CURRENT CLIMATE IN HOSPITALS

Health care agencies are overwhelmed by regulations and are engaged in attempts to counteract the constraining effects of legislation. In many areas, hospitals have to deal with extended lengths of stays by patients who do not need medical care, but for whom other arrangements are unavailable. Under these conditions, the insurers often will not reimburse the hospitals. At the same time, the hospitals may have more beds available than the shrinking volume of demand requires. In addition, costs of labor and supplies are rising. As a result of these complications, a hospital's survival may be at stake. It is likely that these factors contribute markedly to the popularity of marketing strategies. Marketing openly acknowledges competition and is a helpful strategy for survival in a competitive and shrinking environment.[6] Hospital managements are hesitant about openly acknowledging the competitive stances of hospitals.

Health care has followed the history of other declining growth industries (for example, automobile manufacturing)—a self-deceiving cycle of expansion and undetected decay. Levitt suggests the following conditions that guarantee this cycle: (1) the belief that growth is assured by an expanding and more affluent population, (2) the belief that there is no competitive substitute for the industry's major product, (3) too much faith in mass production (for example, technological medicine), and (4) preoccupation with the idea that a product can lend itself to improvement and cost reduction by carefully controlled scientific experimentation.[7]

The health industry meets all four criteria. It is unfortunate that social work is expanding its functions into a larger number of health care settings at a time when the health care industry is in a cycle of regulation and decline. In the final section of this article, the authors will deal with segments of the health care environment that are in growth cycles and have potential for social work marketing.

BARRIERS TO MARKETING

There are three main barriers that impede the use of the marketing perspective in hospital social work departments. First, social work attaches a stigma to marketing because it is a technique of big business. It has an aversion to the whole concept of the hard sell.

The second barrier is the practical limitation on patients' choices in the health care system because the physician has a primary role as the agent for the patient. This role cannot be underestimated for it is the physician who chooses the health care services available to patients. Yet expert technical care does not always insure the satisfaction of consumers. Social workers remember that Richard C. Cabot, the physician who first marketed social work in medicine, earned the anger of his profession and almost lost his membership in the Massachusetts Medical Society for his efforts to make the physician more socially responsible.[8]

The third barrier is the impact of marketing efforts directed to consumer groups who are in the economic position to pay for services. Social work services are a scarce commodity, and there is some danger that such marketing strategies will divert social work services from those people who have traditionally used them to the newer market, which can also pay for them.

MARKETING MATRIX

One of the more interesting ideas in the marketing literature is the concept of the marketing matrix.[9] The idea is to locate a social work services department on a two-dimensional grid: one dimension is the department's commitment to the well-being of patients, and the other is the department's commitment to the welfare of the organization in which it is housed, such as a hospital, clinic, or nursing home.

The positioning on this grid has significance. For example, a social service department that combines a ''medium-client orientation'' and a "medium-organizational orientation" connotes a mid-point balance. That is, the department would operate with equal concern for both the patient's needs and the hospital's needs in providing, for instance, discharge-planning services. Although such a balance may be good, one implication is that the department would let other departments carry out the innovative work. At best, the department would be an imitator. The bulk of its efforts would be in small-scale, fire-fighting, survival mechanisms.

A social service department that values long-term survival should aim for both a "high-patient" and a "high-organizational" orientation; that is, it should make a strong programmatic commitment to meet both the patient's needs for services and the hospital's need for financial viability. When aiming toward this goal, it needs to work on six fronts:

—Studying patients' needs to see how the hospital's or department's services might be modified or augmented so they will serve the patients better.
—Extending the range of services and benefits to the patients, so that what cannot easily be changed can be augmented by developing tie-in arrangements with other service organizations to provide patients with a wider spectrum of benefits.
—Planning for the future by selecting adjustments to augment the present range of services, for example, helping plan beyond the immediate problem.
—Making all internal communication systems integrative and self-reinforcing so that social work's contribution is instantly and easily recognizable.
—Developing long-term plans based on predictions of external events and on an assessment of the department's own internal strengths and weaknesses.

This marketing matrix has certain advantages: First, it structures a way of thinking about the department's efforts that takes into account the needs of three equally important constituents: the patient, department, and hospital. Second, the ranges of this matrix provide a department with benchmarks for determining how far it has gone toward achieving its goals of serving the patient, conserving its resources to remain viable, meeting the institutional mission, and estimating what remains to be done. Third, the matrix provides avenues for using the different talents of staff in creative, innovative ways. Fourth, for each position in the department, the approach can be used to stimulate thinking about the appropriate mix of concern for the patient, department, and hospital. Finally, the marketing matrix compels the director of a department to develop a clear definition of the department's directions and services.

Many social work departments gear their services to the needs of their patients (high-patient orientation) without providing services to the institution, for example, services involving the use of social work knowledge and skill in employee relations programs. The patient's needs always take priority, with little thought given to the survival of the department or of the hospital as an organization.

In locating this type of social work department on a matrix grid, one would find it to be very high on the dimension relating to consumer orientation and very low on the organizational dimension. This is not necessarily bad or wrong. In a given hospital, it might be best for the social work department to be explicitly mandated to represent the patient's interest to the exclusion of the hospital's interest. Although that may be the stance the department is asked to take or finds itself taking, one should not forget that for institutional survival, other departments of the hospital must take different orientations. Having grasped the need to combine these two dimensions in a functional equilibrium, a marketing audit gives a social work department a way to proceed.

MARKETING AUDIT

A marketing audit is a longitudinal approach to assessing how the services a department has to offer "fit" with consumers' needs. The audit develops baselines of data from several perspectives, data from which marketing strategies can be developed.[10] It translates social work terminology—data-gathering, assessment, and planning—into business terminology. Business terms are helpful in developing a marketing stance for social work "products": services to people and organizations. The audit also outlines ways to evaluate the department's competitive position in the professional marketplace. It helps identify what social work services can be offered in that marketplace to a variety of potential consumers: clients, physicians, other health care professionals, and service organizations. The following components make up the marketing audit.

The Consumer Market and Its Segments

This component surveys the universe of potential consumers and sorts out their differing needs. It gets readings on how social workers are viewed by others and tests the viability of various markets. Some of the questions for study are these: What is the geographic area covered by the market, and how was this area determined? How is the consumer market grouped? What percentage of the market uses third-party payment? What are the effects of age, income, and occupation on this market? What proportion of potential consumers are familiar with the organization's services and programs? What image does the department project to the consumer, and what are the important components of that image?

Organizational Strengths and Constraints

This component taps the strengths and reveals the weaknesses in the administrative and functional structure of both the hospital and the social work department. It addresses the following questions: What is the basic policy of both the hospital and the social work department? What does the policy focus on—health care, profit? What has been the department's success with services that were promoted? How does the department compare with others in the country? Is the number of patient admissions and the hospital's revenue increasing or decreasing? Have there been fluctuations in case openings, number of direct services, or Medicaid billings? If so, why? What are the basic objectives and goals of the hospital? How can they be expressed beyond the provision of good health care? What are the social work department's present strengths and weaknesses in specified areas of program development, as, for example, in areas relating to prenatal or pediatric pulmonary care? What is the character of the labor-management environment of the hospital? Does the social work department participate in decisions and planning? Does an atmosphere of confrontation exist between the department and hospital? How is the department affected by the hospital environment and external controls?

Competition

This component is self-explanatory. It attempts to discover the uniqueness of the services offered and to assess competition. The questions addressed are the following: How many competitors are in the hospital? How are the competitors defined? Do the roles of psychiatrists and psychiatric nurses overlap? What are the choices offered patients in terms of choosing social workers over their competitors, in both services and payment? What is the social service department's position (size and strength) in the market relative to competitors?

Services

This component summarizes and lays out the scope of the services social workers can potentially offer to others. It represents the total potential universe of services social workers can provide, a universe from which to select those they will market.

This component requires the social work department to make a list of its services, both those present and those proposed. It raises the following questions: What are the general outstanding characteristics of each product or service? What areas in the department are superior to those in other departments? Does the superiority stem from the services provided or staff members' qualifications? What is the total cost per service in use? Is service over- or underused? What services are most heavily used? Why? What is the profile of patients, physicians, and others who use the service? Are there distinct groups of users?

Price

It is essential for a social work department to know the cost of services it renders. The price component focuses on these questions: Has the department developed its pricing strategy in terms of one or more of the following factors: cost of service, return on investments, stabilization, per diem, not-for-profit, no-cost-attached? How are prices for services determined? Are they set by the hospital, by both the social work department and the hospital, or by Medicare and Medicaid? What have been the price trends for the department's services in the past few years? How are the department's policies regarding pricing viewed by patients, physicians, third-party payers, competitors, and regulators?

Promotion

This component deals with how a social work department makes its services known and how it increases their visibility to an ever-expanding group. It raises the following questions: Does the department promote ongoing promotional activities such as a staff newsletter to increase the visibility of its services? What is the main purpose of these promotional activities? Has this purpose undergone any change in recent years? To whom has this promotional appeal been largely directed? What media have been used?

A marketing audit provides a way of assessing a department's competitive position. It examines where the department stands in relation to others providing similar services. It helps identify the strongest and "most salable" facets that can be marketed to a spectrum of consumers.

MARKETING STRATEGIES

The following sections of this article provide examples of marketing strategies and programs developed by hospital social work departments. The targets identified by the departments for a marketing effort were these: consumers, consumers and physicians, physicians, third-party payers, hospital administrators, and innovative health care services.

Consumers

Former patients of many hospital social work departments wish to use the departments' services and also refer their relatives or friends. Because of the need for services expressed by such patients, one hospital social work department has engaged in consumer marketing. It created a counseling unit so that individuals outside the medical center network could be referred for social work services. The issues regarding the development of this kind of program were these: (1) establishing a fee policy that was compatible with the general guidelines of the medical center, (2) obtaining the authority for the social work department to accept patients directly without their being required to register first in other parts of the hospital's system, and (3) generating publicity about the program to increase the potential patient population.

The actual value of such a service is that it provides social work with vendorship status in the medical center. By this, the department is seen functioning as an independent, self-directed division. In this example of consumer marketing, the important ingredients of the marketing perspective are the marketing skills that brought the program to consumers and the sensitivity to the needs of patients and to organizational dilemmas.

A second example of marketing social work services to patients or potential patients is the employee assistance program. Many employees recognize the need for personal social work services as well as services relating to alcoholism and drug addiction. Social work departments are in a key position to set up programs offering such services, and, indeed, some have begun to market them to their own hospitals, to industries, and to other hospitals. They act as consultants or program planners and enter into contracts on a fee-for-service basis to provide such services directly.

A problem encountered when marketing to consumers is the need to offset the cost of what is being marketed by the prices being paid by the consumer. Social work has always had difficulty with this notion, and direct consumer marketing does not frequently occur in social work practice, particularly since most third-party payers do not pay for such ventures. Other types of direct consumer marketing include programs of preretirement planning and of counseling to groups of people who are relocating their residences.

Consumers and Physicians

This example was drawn from the market of what many data collection systems label "courtesy services." These services are rendered to patients of attending physicians who are not part of the hospital system, to patients' families, to physicians' families, to the physicians themselves, and to other staff members. Usually, no charge is made for such services.

In analyzing courtesy services, one hospital decided to develop a program for one segment of this population, namely, the elderly and the children of the elderly who are faced with planning for current and future needs. An essential ingredient in providing such a program is the availability of staff members who have acquired knowledge concerning the needs of the elderly, who can plan for the continued stay of the elderly in their natural environments, who can organize appropriate support services, and who can, in working with both the family and patient, arrive at the best institutional plan.

One such successful marketing program for consumers and physicians was developed by making the availability of courtesy services known to physicians treating the elderly in their offices and the community. Many have used these services for their hospital patients and want to help the elderly stay in the community rather than prematurely enter an institution.

Physicians

Often, physicians express the wish that some of their private patients could benefit from social services. An effective marketing strategy in this case is to assign social workers to the private office of the physician, to the outpatient hospital clinics in which the physician works, or to the hospital of the attending physician. This kind of marketing strategy works best with physicians who specialize in specific disease entities with highly visible social sequelae. The authors have been successful in "marketing" social workers to physicians for patients who suffer from myasthenia gravis, amyotrophic lateral sclerosis, and lupus erythematosis. In each case, the physician pays a significant portion of the social worker's salary to the department, the department pays a small amount, and the social worker collects fees from some patients. The social worker has a practice that focuses on specific patients, and he or she sees all patients with the specific disease in any of three places: the hospital, the clinic, and private office of the attending physician.

Another example of marketing efforts directed to physicians concerns a psychiatrist who had hired a social worker for his private practice. While practicing in the psychiatrist's office, the social worker remarked that she felt isolated from her professional colleagues in the hospital social work department. Because the psychiatrist wanted to retain her services, he had a discussion with the director of the department concerning the options open to the social worker in obtaining professional stimulation from the department. The director suggested to the physician that the social worker's salary be paid directly to the department rather than to the social worker. This made the social worker a member of the department. She practiced exclusively in the physician's office but received many additional benefits, including access to the psychiatrist's hospitalized patients and inclusion in the hospital team meetings. The department's peer review system reviewed the quality of her work.

Third-Party Payers

Although the social work profession as a whole needs to convince third-party payers that social workers are primary vendors and should be paid directly for their services, an excellent marketing strategy was developed by a hospital that marketed and negotiated a package of services for coverage by the third-party, per diem, hospital reimbursement rate. Any additional services were charged to the third-party payers of the clients. This is an innovative way of approaching basic support for the departments of social work services and for increasing the financial support for additional services offered to patients.

Hospital Administrators

The attitudes hospital administrators express toward social work departments range from support within the limits of the fiscal constraints the institution is experiencing to a lack of understanding and appreciation for social work functions. In-house marketing of social work to the hospital administration is an imperative. Because of their multifaceted activities, social work departments are in a good position to market key functions within health care organizations. Their good relationships with community networks put them in a key position to market additional, nondirect social work functions such as forming and staffing community boards to streamline community input into health care planning and submissions to health regulatory agencies.

Because of its discharge-planning functions and its wide network of liaison with other agencies, a hospital's social work department is also in a key position to market a program to other hospitals. For instance, a department of social work noticed a decline in the number of psychiatric beds occupied in its facility. It proposed that overcrowded hospital departments of psychiatry transfer their patients to its underused facility. The social workers became the natural marketing agents because of their knowledge of the status of other hospitals' bed census, their planning and programmatic perspective, and their administrative know-how. They coordinated the negotiations with other facilities for the transfers, which were based on criteria set by the departments of psychiatry and finance. Patients benefited and several institutions profited, showing that a high commitment to patients and a high commitment to the hospital are compatible and beneficial to both.

Innovations in Health Care Services

Although the health care industry is in a general state of decline, some segments of it are in a growth cycle. Health maintenance organizations, primary care centers, perinatal services, and group practices are examples of health delivery systems experiencing growth. Marketing social work services to these innovative programs is a key task of the profession. Data suggest that social work services are cost-effective for these programs. For example, the provision of such services results in a decrease in the rate of inappropriate use of physicians' services, in the actual time spent by physicians with patients and families, and in patients' use of health services for social reasons.[11] Social work skills are useful in marketing such programs, in recruiting patients to them, in promoting consumer satisfaction, and in improving the quality and comprehensiveness of services offered.[12]

Marketing concepts can be useful to social work departments in health care. They are compatible with social work because of their emphasis on consumer needs and consumer satisfaction. One note of caution is needed, however. In her article Levy reminds the reader that "anticipated events never live up to expectations."[13]

REFERENCES

1. *See* Philip Kotler, *Marketing for Non-Profit Organization* (Englewood Cliffs, N.J.: Prentice-Hall, 1975); Kotler, "Strategies for Introducing Marketing into Non-Profit Organizations," *Journal of Marketing*, 43 (January 1979), pp. 37–44; and Mara Melum, "Hospitals Must Change, Control Is the Issue," *Hospitals* (March 1, 1980), pp. 67–72.

2. *See* Raymond C. Ford, "Business Is Not As Usual in Hospitals," *Hospitals* (April 1, 1980).

3. Ibid.

4. *See* Barbara Berkman and Helen Rehr, "Social Work Undertakes Its Own Audit," *Social Work in Health Care*, 3 (March 1978), pp. 273–286; and Rehr and Berkman, "Patient Care Evaluations (Audits): Social Work Prerequisites and Current Approaches," in Rehr, ed., *Professional Accountability for Social Work Practice: A Search for Concepts and Guidelines* (New York: Prodist, 1979), pp. 92–110.

5. Philip D. Cooper. "What Is Health Care Marketing?" in Cooper, ed., *Health Care Marketing* (Germantown, Md.: Aspen Publications, 1979), p. 7.

6. Ibid., pp. 3–10.

7. Theodore Levitt, *The Marketing Mode* (New York: McGraw-Hill Book Co., 1969).

8. Harris Chaiklin, "Role and Utilization of the Social Worker in Clinical Practice," in George Balis, ed., *The Psychiatric Foundations of Medicine*, Vol. 5 (Boston: Butterworth Publishers, 1978), p. 476.

9. *See* Levitt, op. cit.

10. *See* Eric N. Berkowitz and William A. Flexner, "The Marketing Audit: A Tool for Health Service Organizations," in Cooper, ed., *Health Care Marketing*.

11. *See* Cooper, "What Is Health Care Marketing?"

12. For examples of such results, *see* John Wax, "Power Theory and Institutional Change," *Social Service Review*, 45 (September 1971), pp. 274–88; Martin Nacman, "A Systems Approach to the Provision of Social Work Services in Health Settings: Part 1," *Social Work in Health Care*, 1 (Fall 1975), pp. 47–53; and Nacman, "A Systems Approach to the Provision of Social Work Services in Health Settings: Part 2," *Social Work in Health Care*, 1 (Winter 1975–76), pp. 133–143.

13. Marion Levy, "Levy's Nine Laws of the Disillusionment of the True Liberal," *Midway*, 10 (Winter), unfolioed.

Chapter 21

The Process of Development
of Interagency Relationships

Eugenie Walsh Flaherty, PhD
Frances G. Martin, BS

ABSTRACT. Seven parameters of an interagency relationship were examined for their importance to the process and perceived effectiveness of the relationships between a new community agency and seven established agencies. Perceptions of performance of the new agency on these seven parameters changed over time, primarily in a positive direction. In the first 6 months of a relationship, the quality of planning for projects was correlated with perceived effectiveness. When a relationship was 12 to 18 months old, clarity of goals and of activities, presentation of the agency's mission, the agency's resources, and the agency's communications were related to perceived effectiveness. Implications for the development of interagency relations are discussed.

Although in the past 15 years there has been a proliferation of work on the characteristics of interorganizational coordination, relatively few studies are reported on the development of such relationships. The development of a coordinating relationship between two agencies is a sensitive and extended process for two major reasons: (a) the concern each agency has for preserving its own domain, and (b) the lack of an overall authority structure (Litwak & Hylton, 1962). We are all aware of instances in which mistakes by one or both agencies permanently terminated the development of their relationship. If we are to accept the assumption that each development of an interagency relationship is not a unique process but rather that there are some generic parameters in this process, then we must seek out these parameters in order to avoid such costly mistakes in the future.

The literature suggests that developing interagency relationships may have much in common, if only because warnings against the same mistakes are often found. For example, Freeman and Parry (1972) and Halpert and Silverman (1967) warn that a functional coordinating relationship cannot develop if it is based solely on "getting-acquainted" meetings and abstract discussions of services and goals. Freeman and

Parry add that even highly structured information-sharing does not seem to be sufficient support for a coordinating relationship. Although many feel that information-sharing meetings are a necessary first step in developing a relationship between two agencies, in order to understand each other's services, goals, and domains (Benson & Kunce, 1974; Levine & White, 1961; Levine, White, & Paul, 1963), they are apparently not sufficient for the establishment of a coordinating relationship.

If information-sharing meetings are a necessary but not sufficient first step, what steps follow in the development process? Litwak and Hylton (1962) suggest the mechanism of the coordinating agency, whose "major purpose is to order. behavior between two or more other . . . organizations" (p. 399). However, too often a coordinating agency of this kind does not exist, or if it does, it has limited power to "order behavior." Even when two agencies are trying to develop a coordinating relationship under the umbrella of a third agency, they are still in the position of asking what steps follow the information-sharing meetings.

Halpert and Silverman (1967) review a series of interagency coordination efforts and conclude that the most practical models involve "planned activities." Freeman and Parry (1972) describe the lengthy development of a community mental health network and report that genuine working relationships evolved only after the staff worked together on active projects in the community.

Important steps in the development of coordinating relationships thus seem to be information-sharing meetings, including discussion of each other's domains, followed by joint participation in an active project. It is, however, unlikely that these two exhaust the list of parameters important to the development of relationships. In the study reported here, seven additional parameters were selected for examination in the development of several interagency relationships. These were: the clarity of the agency's goals, the ability of the staff to present the agency's mission, the agency's resources, the clarity of the agency's activities, the communication by the agency, the agency's project planning, and the skills of the agency staff. It is important to note that in the relationship studied here, information-sharing and joint participation in a project had taken place. Therefore, the findings concerning the contribution of the seven parameters are limited to relationships that include these steps.

These parameters differ from the two steps discussed above, information-sharing and joint participation in a project, in the role they may potentially play in the development of a relationship. The two steps make a positive contribution to the relationship, even though they are apparently not sufficient to cement it. The seven parameters, on the other hand, may make a positive or negative contribution, depending upon both their quality and the way in which they are perceived. Therefore, in this study we sought to ask both how these parameters were perceived and what the contribution of each parameter was to the coordinating relationships. Unfortunately, we were not able to obtain an objective assessment of the quality of the seven parameters.

The parameters were examined in the relationships between a new community agency, the Early Childhood Program (ECP), and seven established community agencies. Staff of the established agencies who were involved in the relationship rated the performance of the ECP on each parameter; this was the measure of their perception of the quality of each parameter. The staff also provided a rating of the relationship's impact on their own work; this rating was considered a reflection of the effectiveness of the coordinating relationship, although admittedly a subjective one.

Because the development of a relationship is undoubtedly a dynamic process, the importance of individual parameters might be expected to change with time. To examine this issue, the staff of the seven established agencies provided *two* ratings of the ECP's performance on the parameters: one for the first 6 months of the relationship and one for the subsequent time, varying between 6 and 12 months for individual agencies. All ratings were provided at the same time, in the summer months of 1976.

The study was thus designed to answer two questions. First, is there indeed a process of development? Do the ratings on these parameters improve or decrease over time? Second, is there a link between any of these parameters and the perceived effectiveness of the relationships, and does this change with time? In other words, which, if any, of these parameters seem to enhance the probability that a relationship will be perceived as effective, in the first 6 months, and thereafter?

METHODOLOGY

Agencies Participating in the Study

The agency initiating these relationships, the ECP, is a special unit for the prevention of mental health problems in young children. It works with young children, their parents, and other caretakers. A long-term goal of this unit was to create a network of coordinating agencies to work in the area of prevention; the intermediate goal was to establish coordinating relationships with individual agencies, by means of collaboration on active projects. The projects included parent education, child development classes and assessments, development of a preschool day-care program, and staff training in a variety of intervention strategies.

The seven established community agencies participating in the study had had contact with the ECP for at least a year. All seven agencies had collaborated with the ECP on two or three projects during that time. Two of the agencies were family service agencies concerned with foster placement, adoption, and follow-up services. A third agency provided special services to school-aged parents. Two of the agencies were city hospitals; the ECP worked with staff of the obstetrics-gynecological, maternity, and pediatric departments. The sixth agency was a local health center, and the seventh a methadone drug rehabilitation program, many of whose clients were parents of young children.

One hundred and thirty-eight staff members from these agencies worked with the ECP, of whom 79 (or 57%) responded to the questionnaire (described below). Much of the loss seemed to be due to staff turnover and extended summer vacations. Unfortunately, only 48 staff members (35% of the total) provided data for both time periods, as many were not involved in the first 6 months of the relationship.

Procedure

Questionnaires were intended for distribution to all staff of the seven community agencies who had been involved in the relationship with the ECP. Distribution was through their supervisors, after careful explanation of the study, and completed questionnaires were collected by the supervisors. Because we felt that staff might bias their responses in anticipation of the supervisors reviewing them, all questionnaires were completed anonymously.

Respondents rated the ECP's performance on each of the seven parameters on a 6-point scale, with 1 indicating the most positive response. Instructions were to note "the ECP's performance as you perceived it." Each parameter was first noted for the first 6 months of the relationship and then for the subsequent time period. The agency staff's perception of the effectiveness of the coordinating relationship, at the time of questionnaire completion, was also obtained on a 6-point rating scale, with 1 for the strongest effect. The staff were asked for the rating "which best describes the effect on your work regarding early prevention."

FINDINGS

The Process of Development of the Relationship

The mean ratings for each parameter for both time periods are presented in Table 1. When all parameters are combined, there is a trend toward a more positive perception of the ECP's performance over time. Five of the seven parameters received higher ratings in the second time period (two significantly so), one received a lower rating, and only one

TABLE 1

Change in Interorganizational Relationships [a]

Parameters of Relationship	Perceived Effectiveness		
	First 6 Months	6--12 Months	Significance of change
Clarity of agency's goals	2.7	2.3	significant[***]
Ability of staff to present agency's mission	2.3	2.4	not significant
Agency's resources	2.6	2.4	not significant
Clarity of agency's activtites	2.6	2.5	not significant
Communication by agency	2.7	2.6	not significant
Project planning	2.9	2.7	not significant[**]
Agency staff skills	2.3	2.3	not significant
All cagegories combined	2.6	2.4	Trend toward significance[*]

[a] Only those respondents who completed the ratings for both time periods (n = 48) are included in the analyses.

[b] On the scale used, 1 is the most positive rating and 6 the least positive rating

[*] $p < .10$.
[**] $p < .05$.
[***] $p < .02$.

parameter's rating did not change. The two parameters that changed significantly in a positive direction were the clarity of the ECP's goals and its project planning.

The unavailability of objective assessments of the quality of these parameters leaves the results open to at least two interpretations. First, the ECP performance may have remained stable, and the agency staff then changed their ratings as their knowledge about the ECP increased. If this interpretation is correct, we would expect the ratings to be somewhat similar in the first time period, and to be more differentiated in the second time period, as agency staff became more knowledgeable about the parameters. In fact, the effect is in the opposite direction: The range decreases from .6 in the first time period to .4 in the second time period.

The second interpretation suggests that the ECP's performance in reality changed with time, and that the agency staff's perception accordingly also changed. This interpretation provides a better explanation of the differential degrees and direction of rating changes.

Although these findings should be interpreted with caution, they do suggest that the process of development is a dynamic one. Whether the cause was an actual change in performance or a change in the perception of that performance, the agency staff perceived a change over time in the other agency's performance on seven parameters. Furthermore, the change in perceptions of at least two parameters was significantly different for the two time periods. The implication is that an agency initiating a relationship cannot expect to establish a stable relationship in 6 months, even when there is collaboration on projects. The significant changes in perceived clarity of the ECP's goals and project planning suggest that these two areas should receive special attention in the beginning stages of a relationship.

The Relationship Between the Parameters and Perceived Effectiveness

In order to examine the possibility of links between the seven parameters of interagency relationships and the perceived effectiveness of the relationships, the ratings of effectiveness were correlated with the parameter ratings for both time periods (Table 2). There is a striking difference between the two time periods. For the first 6 months, there was only one parameter related (at a very low level of significance, $p < .10$) to perceived effectiveness: the ECP's project planning.

In the second time period, five parameters of the relationship were related to perceived effectiveness: the clarity of the ECP's goals; the ability of the staff to present the ECP's mission; the ECP's resources; the clarity of its activities; and the ECP's communication. Project planning was not related to perceived effectiveness in the second time period.

The results must be accepted with caution, both because of the inherent ambiguities in a correlational relationship and because of the retrospective nature of the study. On the one hand, the findings very tentatively suggest that performance of an agency on certain parameters affects the perception of effectiveness of that agency by a second agency, especially after the first 6 months. On the other hand, the correlational approach used leaves open the possibility that the perception of effectiveness influenced the perception of the parameters. The sole cause for support of the first interpretation is the differential nature of the various parameter/effectiveness relationships. If perceived effectiveness influenced the perception of parameter quality, then we would expect all the correlations to be similar. They are not: One of the seven in the first 6 months (at a low level) and five of the seven in the subsequent time period are significant.

DISCUSSION

If we can tentatively accept these results, if only as stimuli for a subsequent study with stronger design, then we must begin to think in terms of the differential importance of certain parameters during the course of an

TABLE 2

Correlations between Parameters and Perceived Effectiveness [a]

Parameters of Relationship	First 6 months		6 -- 12 Months	
	Correlation	Significance	Correlation	Significance
Clarity of agency's goals	-.145	Not significant	.291	Significant***
Ability of staff to present agency's mission	-.002	Not significant	.326	Significant***
Agency's resources	.191	Not significant	.292	Significant***
Clarity of agency's activities	-.03	Not significant	.274	Significant**
Communication by agency	.160	Not significant	.346	Significant****
Project Planning	.249	Trend toward significance	.236	Not significant
Agency staff skills	.233	Not significant	.226	Not significant

aOnly those respondents who completed the ratings for both time periods ($\underline{n}$ = 48) are included in the analyses.

* $\underline{p} \geqslant .10.$
** $\underline{p} \leqslant .05.$
*** $\underline{p} \leqslant .025.$
**** $\underline{p} \leqslant .01.$

277

interagency relationship. The quality of planning seems to play an important role in the early stages, and to be less important as the relationship progresses, possibly because planning is usually more prominent in the early stages. As the relationship develops, parameters concerned with the agency's resources, the clarity of its services, and the staff's ability to communicate those services become important.

In a study of Model Cities programs, during the planning period and part of the 1st program year, Gilbert and Specht (1977) also found differences in characteristics of program directors with outcome as a function of the time period. A process orientation by the director was associated positively with both process and task objectives during the planning year. In the subsequent program year, directors with task orientations were associated with programs receiving high ratings on both sets of objectives. The authors suggest that "the phasing of role orientations—that is, the shifting from process to task orientations—may be the most appropriate response in programs where process and task objectives are emphasized simultaneously."

The findings of the present study cannot be compared to those of Gilbert and Specht because the time periods used are different and because categorization of our parameters as "process" and "task" oriented would be ad hoc. Both studies, however, share an important finding: In the study of program development and the associated parameters, one must conceptualize the development in terms of stages, in which the role of the parameters varies with the particular stage.

CONCLUSIONS

In the beginning of this article it was suggested that only two factors emerge from the literature as important to the development of an interagency relationship: early information-sharing meetings and collaboration on a project. The results of this study suggest that there are additional parameters that play an integral role in the growth of a relationship. Furthermore, the results suggest that one must conceptualize a relationship in terms of stages, in which the importance of the parameters varies with the particular stage.

REFERENCES

Benson, J. K., & Kunce, J. T. Co-ordinating human services: A case study of an interagency network. *Social and Rehabilitation Record,* 1974, *1*(7), 28–33.

Freeman, S. J. J., & Parry, R. Modes of co-ordinating a community mental health network. *Canadian Psychiatric Association Journal,* September 1972, *17*, 15–24.

Gilbert, N., & Specht, H. Process versus task in social planning. *Social Work*, May 1977, *22*(3), 178–183.

Halpert, H., & Silverman, C. Approaches to interagency cooperation. *Hospital and Community Psychiatry*, 1967, *18*, 84–87.

Levine, S., & White, P. E. Exchange as a conceptual framework for the study of interorganizational relationships. *Administrative Science Quarterly*, March 1961, *5*, 583–597.

Levine, S., White, P., & Paul, B. D. Community interorganizational problems in providing medical care and social services. *American Journal of Public Health*, August 1963, *53*, 1183–1195.

Litwak, E., & Hylton, L. F. Interorganizational analysis: A hypothesis on co-ordinating agencies. *Administrative Science Quarterly*, 1962, *6*, 395–420.

Chapter 22

Expanding the Role of Social Workers in Coordination of Health Services

Paul A. Wilson, PhD

ABSTRACT. The lack of connection between the two approaches to coordination—the structural approach and the case coordination approach—has hampered efforts to coordinate health care services. This article discusses the bases for integrating the two approaches and presents guidelines for expanding the role of social workers in coordination.

The health care system is plagued by escalating costs; economic, social, and geographic barriers to care; and the maldistribution of facilities and personnel. As long as these conditions exist, there will be efforts to coordinate various aspects of the health care system. Coordination, however ill defined and elusive, will continue to be a goal of service delivery.

Two distinct, unrelated approaches to coordination exist. One is case coordination; the other is structural and deals with organizational arrangements and broad planning efforts. This article argues that the lack of connection between these two approaches militates against greater coordination of health services. It explicates the bases on which the two can be brought together and suggests guidelines for expanding the role of social workers in coordination.

TWO APPROACHES

In case coordination, individual professionals lead individual patients in need of the multiple services of numerous organizations through the health care system. This function is critical, especially for patients with many problems who often see the system as a bewildering array of professions, organizations, and specialty services, each demanding different information, schedules, and regimens. The fragmented, bureaucratized, and often impersonal nature of the system led Mechanic to suggest that the medical ombudsman should be trained.

This chapter is reprinted with the permission of *Health & Social Work* and the National Association of Social Workers, Inc.

. . . to be sensitive to the social and behavioral aspects of care; the coordination of services, and the need for and availability of services in general. Such a person might serve to improve coordination among the various persons involved in providing health care . . . and serve as the point of unification of all medical, rehabilitation, and social services provided the patient within the context.[1]

Social workers in various health settings perceive case coordination as their legitimate role. And, although health care organizations need this function to provide continuous comprehensive care, the specification of an individualized professional role is not enough because of the main limitation of case coordination in complex organizational and interorganizational context—its inefficiency. In case coordination, the worker must determine, case by case, which of a variety of organizations provides the specific elements of service needed by a particular client. Then the specific types of service to be offered to each client must be negotiated with each of the organizations involved with the client. Often, additional organizational resources have to be located for any unusual problems.

The structural approach to coordination is meant to overcome the limitations of case coordination by establishing a particular set of relationships among organizations characterized by cooperation, joint programs, mutual referrals, and joint planning and policymaking. The most pervasive example of this approach to coordination is the health planning efforts of health systems agencies (HSAs). The intent of such efforts is to develop a multi-organizational system on the local and regional levels that will enhance service and be cost effective. Established by the National Health Planning and Resources Development Act of 1974 (P.L. 93-641), HSAs were mandated to provide accessible services to residents of a health service area for the purpose of improving the residents' health. These agencies attempt to increase the acceptability, continuity, and quality of health services while keeping down the costs of providing services. One way to contain costs is to eliminate the unnecessary duplication of functions and capabilities. The priorities of HSAs are specifications of what is commonly referred to as a coordinated system of care.

SOME PROBLEMS

The preeminence of the structural approach to coordination and its separation from case coordination present problems. The establishment of a coordinated system of cooperative relationships among health care organizations does not necessarily resolve the problems of practitioners even though it satisfies structural or administrative requirements. As Hasenfeld noted in reference to Management Information Systems (MIS), a specific type of coordination mechanism:

> First the system fails to articulate with and respond to the needs of the staff [and second] . . . MIS makes a series of assumptions about the service and delivery process that are aimed at satisfying the technical needs of the system rather than reflect[ing] the true modes of operation in the agency.[2]

The structural approach focuses exclusively on variables of the system that relate to aggregates of people and organizations. The emphasis is on data such as morbidity rates, service areas, and "at-risk" populations. This focus is appropriate for planning and research and is necessary for administration. However, practitioners have little control over or influence on the suggestions for practice or administrative programs that are derived from these data. Levine, White, and Paul suggested that it is difficult to solve some coordination problems at the practitioner level of the system.[3] As Benson et al. asserted in their study of the relationships among social welfare agencies in Missouri:

> . . . degrees of work coordination at the level of service delivery must be understood in a political-economic context. The agencies are enmeshed in a complex system of relations in which they pursue a supply of resources. Thus, to explain fully the variation in equilibrium components at the level of service delivery, the analyst must move to higher systemic levels and invoke a different set of concepts. By the same token, the practitioner must appreciate the strategic significance of the levels' distinction. It is our judgment that substantial changes in the effectiveness and coordination of interorganizational networks require alterations of the political economy in which the agencies are entangled.[4]

The belief that problems occurring at lower levels of a system can be addressed and resolved only at higher levels carries with it the assumption that different personnel at different levels in a system carry different responsibilities for coordination. For example, resource providers channel financial and other resources to organizations best suited to provide a full array of unduplicated services. Administrators establish contractual and other interorganizational arrangements that foster continuity of care. Direct-service professionals steer clients through the system. The questionable implication of such an approach is that if everyone meets his or her respective responsibilities at his or her respective level in the system, then everything will be coordinated.

Such a division of labor is explicit in the work of Aiken et al., who

studied the coordination of service programs in the area of mental retardation.[5] To these writers, the problem of coordination is exhibited at the
resource-provision, organizational, and direct-service levels. For overall
coordination to exist, each level must be comprehensive; it must
cooperate with the other levels and be compatible with them.

The approach of Aiken et al. raises the following serious conceptual
questions: What types of problems are resolvable at which level in the
system? How does one know that the appropriate "higher" level has
been reached in addressing a given difficulty in coordination? The basic
logical problem is that there is no way of knowing when to stop in one's
search for "higher" levels. Also, having reached a higher level, are any
of the components of that level controllable by anyone?

On a more political and practical note, however, the structural approach is evident in the debate over reform of the health care system.
Alford identified two types of reformers who take the opposite extreme
positions on the issue of levels: the "market reformers" and the "bureaucratic reformers."[6] The market reformers insist that only the choices and
activities of individuals can insure the proper functioning of the health
care system—not the policies, programs, and regulations of the government. The bureaucratic reformers are convinced that higher levels of the
political, economic, and regulatory systems must be brought into play to
achieve a more rational organization and integration of health care and
that reliance on the individual approach has created the need for reform.

The structural approach to coordination assumes that some fixed form
of organization can assure "good" care and is capable of delivering comprehensive, integrated, continuous health care services. Market and bureaucratic reformers, as well as researchers of interorganizational relationships, are convinced that some form of organization represents a
greater degree of coordination. The controversies over the particular form
of organization to be attempted, however, are carried on with subjective
and ideological trappings that have little to do with effective
coordination. An expanded role for social workers is possible only if the
preoccupation with and unfounded faith in the efficacy of structural
arrangements is challenged and qualified.

BASIS FOR INTEGRATION

The government's development of policies and programs for health
services and the attempts by providers of resources to offer incentives for
organizational and professional behaviors are still important for the
coordination of services. However, the structural emphasis has led to the
neglect of other promising alternatives. In this regard, Warren's warning
is appropriate:

. . . the failure to take informal networks and processes into consideration often makes the actual behavior of organizations toward each other unexplainable. It leads to a false picture of the extent to which integration or coordination among organizations is actually taking place in the community, and it tends to confine change objectives to setting up new structures of new formal relationships and to neglect the possibility that more may be accomplished through changing network relationships, often on an informal, ad hoc basis.[7]

Although a well-coordinated delivery system can be achieved partly through manipulation of the political economies of health care organizations (the macro level), more can be done at the informal level of the individual practitioner (the micro level). However, before coordination can occur at the micro level and the direct-service role can be expanded, the meaning of coordination must be reexamined. Coordination must be seen as a political process by which health care professionals and organizations mobilize and form linkages in response to health problems and issues—what the author terms the "mobilization view" of coordination.[8]

The mobilization view has several advantages. First, it eliminates the attempt to reach an ideal state of affairs. Thus, there is no need for normative judgments about the best way of delivering services or for determining beforehand what better service is. Second, it assumes that coordination can be initiated at any level in the system and thus allows for a greater degree of correspondence between direct-practice and other activities in the system. Third, it avoids the categorical approach to coordination—the view that coordination is either present or absent—and emphasizes different degrees of coordination relative to various issues.

The service needs of a patient hospitalized for a condition that is complicated by alcoholism provide an illustration of the mobilization approach. Social service staff of the hospital provide support services during the patient's stay in the hospital. But the broad spectrum of services that may be required after discharge could involve a combination of child welfare agencies, a council on alcoholism, Alcoholics Anonymous, a detoxification center, counseling agencies, and public welfare, social security, and Supplemental Security Income offices. The degree to which the community agencies can mobilize to establish appropriate linkages indicates the degree of coordination in the system. Such linkage could range from telephone contacts between direct-service workers to a highly developed joint program between two or more agencies to a comprehensive community-wide program for alcoholics and their families.

Another requirement for expanding the social work role is that the point of contact between practitioners and policymakers and planners must be articulated so practice problems and perspectives may have an impact on policymaking and planning. Practitioners and those who function at the organizational and community levels (such as board members, administrators, and planners) need to be in greater agreement if they are to unify their efforts for coordination of the health care delivery system.

Social workers, as in the alcoholism illustration just given, are in an advantageous position to suggest that the extensive contacts between professionals in two or more agencies may indicate that more formal arrangements are possible and desirable. Or their experience with such clients and the service network may prompt them to suggest that specific services should be incorporated into the HSA plan for their area. Social workers can contribute to such concerted efforts by knowing and making use of factors associated with interorganizational mobilization.

RELATED FACTORS

No theory of interorganizational relationships has received general acceptance, nor have the results of research in this field been consistent or cumulative. Nevertheless, common themes and general parameters can serve as the basis for a beginning practice model.

Exchange theory is the most prevalent conceptual base for research on interorganizational relationships. Organizations need each other to acquire and control the resources necessary for their continued survival and growth. In turn, the resources needed by organizations depend on the various functions they perform. Their respective functions determine the amount of financial resources required, the quantity and types of personnel to be recruited, and the kind of equipment needed.[9]

In an ideal world these general requirements for cooperative, coordinated action among health care organizations would be simple and straightforward. The various functions to be performed and an explicit division of labor would be agreed on. Which organizations would perform which function would be clarified so there would be no confusion about the interrelationships among functions. Consequently, there would be no competition for scarce and overlapping resources; thus all the health agencies in a community could make their individual and unique contribution to the delivery of health care. Moreover, this idyllic state of affairs would receive the active support of community groups and political, social, and fraternal organizations.

Such a scenario is a far cry from reality, but it illustrates several key ingredients of coordination: mandates from the community for specific functions to be performed by various agencies, a consensus on the domain or division of labor among organizations, and appropriate and adequate resources within and outside a community.

Other aspects of the health care system, however, make coordination both more necessary and more difficult. First, the delivery of health care cannot be neatly divided into mutually exclusive functions. Consequently, some degree of competition and conflict is inevitable concerning which organizations should perform a particular function and thereby receive the necessary resources for doing so. As HSAs proceed with project review and, in the interest of cost containment, insist on a limitation of the number and kinds of functions to be performed by health agencies, this aspect of the health system may be minimized but cannot be eliminated. Because of the inevitable overlap in functions, organizations and individual practitioners are needed who, on the basis of broad, general values, can initiate and support joint action to resolve such issues.[10]

Second, the array of services offered by health care organizations in a community and the distribution of responsibilities for delivering those services are constantly changing. The delicate balance of alliances, supports, agreements, and joint programs that make it possible for an organization to be secure today may not be maintained.[11] However, some semblance of stability is maintained through an elaborate network of interorganizational and interpersonal ties in a community.[12]

COMMUNITY NETWORKS

The following four characteristics of community networks are the bases of coordination and provide further indications of what may be built into the social worker's role.

Common Views

Organizational ties are maintained in part by the common philosophical and ideological positions held by members of the participating organizations regarding how the health care "game" is to be played and the rules by which it is to be played.[13] Casual observation of community health organizations makes clear that there is an organizational "pecking order." This pecking order is often reflected in the common classification of health agencies into (1) official and public, (2) voluntary nonprofit, (3) hospitals and nursing homes, and (4) health related.[14] Such a classification provides a preliminary means of assessing the relative position of each organization in a community. Those with similar status and ideological commitments are most likely to engage in joint efforts.

Mutual Regard

Mutual respect for and appreciation of the professional competence and work performance of the respective members of each organization are conditioned by the type of training received by the respective staff members, the professional schools they attended, and their general orientation toward the health system. Similarities of background are likely to result in respect for each other's work and foster cooperative joint action.[15]

Similarity of Technology

Organizations that are similar in technological approaches and capabilities are most likely to undertake cooperative ventures.[16] For instance, a medical center specializing in the latest advances in scientific medicine is likely to refer clients to similarly oriented institutions, not to faith healers or others who are regarded as medically marginal. Furthermore, neighborhood health centers, which often incorporate broad goals of social, economic, and political change into their mandate and hence define their tasks as more than the delivery of scientific medicine, may find it difficult to attain full membership in a community network.[17]

Troublesome Clients

An organization is more likely to engage in coordination when faced with a client group whose needs do not correspond too closely to the organization's definition of its function. This factor should help bring neighborhood health centers and other organizations into a community network, since traditional medicine cannot readily deal with the complex and multiple problems of some client groups. Thus coordination is enhanced when cause-and-effect relationships are not clear and what is required for particular clients is uncertain.[18]

In summary, coordination requires both diversity and integration. On the one hand, there is a need for broad diversity in client groups, types of agencies to perform different functions, and resources. Out of this diversity, needs are more likely to be identified and actions initiated to meet them.[19] On the other hand, diversity creates conflict and competition, which must be managed, usually through the use of other community organizations and professionals as mediators to foster integration of programs. The balance between diversity and integration is accomplished through the interorganizational and interpersonal networks that capitalize on the four bases of coordination just mentioned.

EXPANDED SOCIAL WORK ROLE

The four bases of coordination just described offer some initial guides for an expanded social work role. The transmission of information has long been recognized as a necessary condition for coordination.[20] Therefore, the first function in an expanded social work role would be that of *information broker*. The transmission of information as a form of power requires discipline in its use. The function of broker involves translating the problems of clients as presented or observed into terms that clearly indicate which organizational actions are possible or represent challenges to the policies and practices of organizations. The transmission of information among staff members of various organizations and the ways it shapes their respect for each other are salient aspects of the function of information broker, especially for those social workers who act as links between health organizations and social welfare agencies in the community.

The second function of the expanded social work role is that of *opinion maker*. This function involves interpreting the philosophies, perspectives, and technologies of agencies to each other. It can be performed through setting up meetings of significant participants in the network or through one's own interpretation of the ways in which agencies perceive their roles, their place in the community, their clientele and their technologies. The direct approach of formalized discussions among various participants in the system may enhance the network's resources and, consequently, increase coordination. Increasing agencies' knowledge and appreciation of each others' activities, whether directly or indirectly, raises the probability of concerted action.

The third function is that of *definer of issues*. This function involves the ability to redefine the problems of a system and the possible approaches to them. It is essential because it allows for the analysis and definition of situations to optimize the potential for coordination in response to identified problems. Preparation of detailed analyses of the service needs of particular client groups is a significant part of this function. Coordination is more likely if such analyses emphasize multi-institutional requirements for meeting the needs of clients.

The following example of the experiences of the director and staff of a social service department in a medium-sized municipal hospital illustrates the major features of the coordinator's role. The specific concern of the department was for low-income unmarried pregnant teenagers whose babies were to be delivered at the hospital. Childbirth often was these girls' first contact with the health care system and with a social worker. Problems of housing, employment, education, child care, finances, and general coping became evident at the very time when these girls were least able to deal effectively with them.

The staff members of the hospital's social service department identified the public health department, family planning agency, a neighborhood health center, the two city high schools, and two private physicians who accepted Medicaid patients as the relevant providers of service. They discovered, however, that the two physicians saw few patients for ongoing prenatal care. The family planning agency assumed that the public health department provided adequate prenatal care and thus referred clients who came for pregnancy tests to that department. The public health department informed the social service staff that although it provided some prenatal care, its primary emphasis was a well-baby clinic.

The counselors at the two high schools were keenly aware of the problem of teenage pregnancy and had referred pregnant students to the public health department and the family planning agency. Their attempt to institute a program whereby pregnant students could continue going to school had met with resistance from the school administrators. The neighborhood health center provided prenatal care to the pregnant girls who came for its services; however, staff members of the center were aware that the clients they saw represented a small proportion of those in need, even in the center's service area.

The hospital's social workers included the key providers of service in several staff meetings. In these meetings, the social workers concentrated on the way each participant perceived the problem and defined it. They also determined which agencies had the most contact with each other for other purposes and which had little contact with the others.

From these conversations, several alternatives were suggested. Proposals included sex education programs and a wider distribution of family planning materials, outreach programs, prenatal care, and financial resources for abortion services. The social workers noted, however, that the most critical need was for prenatal care.

Moreover, the need for prenatal care turned out to be the basis on which action could be mobilized. A staff member of the local HSA identified a source of federal funds for community groups seeking to establish prenatal and related services. She also indicated that the goal of reducing the infant mortality rate for the area was being incorporated into the HSA's health systems plan.

The prospect of increased financial resources, along with the public interest generated in the issue of teenage pregnancy, stimulated the public health department to consider expanding its prenatal services. The neighborhood health center was also prepared to concentrate on this area of service. All agreed that special support services, especially child-care training and counseling, should accompany medical services.

The successful expansion of the program, which received considerable attention from the community, was accompanied by renewed efforts to establish the school program for pregnant teenagers. The increased interaction between the social service department and the HSA staff member also resulted in a new goal, incorporated into the HSA's annual implementation plan, to provide ongoing prenatal care to 70 percent of the low-income women needing such care.

The foregoing example illustrates how social workers can manipulate community networks to mobilize for greater coordination of services. In this case, not only was a program instituted for a particular client group, but clearer lines of communication and referral were established among the relevant agencies. Other parts of the community network were also activated, which opened up the possibility of undertaking additional efforts.

FURTHER QUESTIONS

Several preliminary questions emerge from the foregoing discussion. For example, of all the possible issues that could emerge in a community, how do particular problems and concerns come to the forefront? Are there special organizational or community positions that social workers must occupy if they are to be effective in a coordinating role? How can pivotal people and organizations in the network be identified? Must personnel in certain positions be involved in coordination regardless of the issue involved? Or do the relevant participants change, depending on which issue is addressed? Are there particular domains of interest and resources that must be selectively represented for coordination to occur? As these and other questions begin to be addressed and social workers begin to assess their experience in such a role, a more fully developed practice model for coordination should emerge.

REFERENCES

1. David Mechanic, "Human Problems and the Organization of Health Care," *Annals of the American Academy of Political and Social Science*, 399 (January 1972), p. 11.

2. Yeheskel Hasenfeld, "Teaching Management Information Systems to Social Work Administrators." Paper presented at the Annual Program Meeting, Council on Social Work Education, New Orleans, La., February 26, 1978.

3. Sol Levine, Paul E. White, and Benjamin D. Paul, "Community Interorganizational Problems in Providing Medical Care and Social Service," *American Journal of Public Health*, 53 (August 1963), pp. 1183–1195.

4. J. Kenneth Benson et al., *Coordinating Human Services: A Sociological Study of an Interorganizational Network*, Research Series No. 6 (Columbia: Regional Rehabilitation Research Institute, University of Missouri, June 1973), pp. 121–122.

5. Michael Aiken et al., *Coordinating Human Services* (San Francisco: Jossey-Bass, 1975).

6. Robert Alford, *Health Care Politics: Ideological and Interest Group Barriers to Reform* (Chicago: University of Chicago Press, 1975).

7. Roland L. Warren, *Social Change and Human Purpose: Toward Understanding and Action* (Chicago: Rand McNally & Co., 1977), p. 16.

8. A similar definition of coordination is elaborated by Herman Turk, *Interorganizational Activation in Urban Communities: Deduction from the Concept of System*, Rose Monograph Series (Washington, D.C.: American Sociological Association, 1973), pp. 1–4.

9. Karen S. Cook, "Exchange and Power in Networks of Interorganizational Relations," *Sociological Quarterly*, 18 (Winter 1977), pp. 62–82, Sol Levine and Paul White, "Exchange as a Conceptual Framework for the Study of Interorganizational Relationship," *Administrative Science Quarterly*, 5 (March 1961), pp. 583–601; and Ray Elling and Ollie Lee, "Formal Connections of

Community Leadership to the Health System," *Milbank Memorial Fund Quarterly*, 44 (July 1966), Part I.

10. Turk, op. cit.

11. For an elaboration of the turbulence in modern organizational environments, *see* S. E. Emery and E. L. Trist, "The Causal Texture of Organizational Environments," *Human Relations*, 18 (February 1965), pp. 21–31.

12. The relevance of organizational ties is demonstrated by Turk, op. cit. Personal network ties and their impact on the community are discussed in Edward O. Laumann and Franz Pappe, *Networks of Collective Action* (New York: Academic Press, 1977).

13. Richard Hall et al., "Patterns of Interorganizational Relationships," *Administrative Science Quarterly*, 22 (September 1977), pp. 457–474.

14. Sol Levine and Paul E. White, "The Community of Health Organizations," in Howard Freeman, Levine, and Leo G. Reeder, eds. *Handbook of Medical Sociology* (2d ed.; Englewood Cliffs, N.J.: Prentice-Hall, 1972), pp. 359–385.

15. Benson et al., op. cit.

16. Hall et al., op. cit.

17. *See* Daniel Zwick, "Some Accomplishments and Findings of Neighborhood Health Centers," *Milbank Memorial Fund Quarterly*, 50 (October 1972), Part 1, pp. 387–420; and Sol Levine, "Summary and Implications for Further Research," in Edgar Borgatta and Robert Evans, eds., *Smoking, Health, and Behavior* (Chicago: Aldine Publishing Co., 1968), pp. 274–281.

18. *See* Basil Mott, *Anatomy of a Coordinating Council: Implications for Planning* (Pittsburgh, Pa.: University of Pittsburgh Press, 1968); Rita Barito, Steve Paulson, and Gerald Klonglon, "Domain Consensus: A Key Variable in Interorganizational Analysis," in Merlin B. Brinkerhoff and Phillip Kuna, eds., *Complex Organizations and their Environments* (Dubuque, Iowa: William C. Brown Co., 1972), pp. 176–192.

19. Michael Aiken, "The Distribution of Community Power: Structural Bases and Social Consequences," in Aiken and Paul Mott, eds., *The Structure of Community Power* (New York: Random House, 1970), pp. 487–525.

20. *See,* for example, William Reid, "Interagency Coordination in Delinquency Prevention and Control," *Social Service Review*, 38 (December 1964), pp. 418–429; and Levine, White, and Paul, op. cit.

Chapter 23

The Social Work Advocacy Role in Discharge Planning

Abraham Lurie, PhD

ABSTRACT. The social work role in discharge planning must include an advocacy function. This is important to facilitate discharge planning and can be carried out in three related areas: (1) political advocacy—to improve governmental programs, (2) resource development advocacy—to meet unmet needs, and (3) case advocacy—to ensure that programs are accessible and appropriate for eligible patients and families. This role is particularly suited for social workers because of their training and experience and should be included as part of their contribution to comprehensive health care.

INTRODUCTION

For some time, hospital discharge planning has been the focus of much discussion, planning, and scrutiny. Rising health care costs have enhanced our opportunity to contribute to adequate discharge planning. Health care professionals and planners have become more interested in developing alternate levels of care programs to meet the growing demands for effective discharge planning procedures.

The creation of seminars, planning groups, and educational programs devoted to discharge planning is evidence of the importance social workers and others attribute to this area of their practice; a function recognized by the hospital hierarchy as a social work activity and which in recent times has become more complicated and frustrating to perform.

The impetus for effective discharge procedures dovetails with the view that prolonged hospital stays can have a negative impact on patients and their convalescence and result in hospital overutilization (Greater New York Hospital Association, 1980; Sirkis, 1981). Alternative levels of care, which refers to providing the level of care needed by the patient as the patient passes through the acute phase of illness, requires improving other kinds of facilities and services such as nursing homes, rehabilitation centers and home care programs (Rogatz, 1980). The discharge planning process is inextricably tied up with developing these resources. The social work role of helping families cope effectively with patient illness is also tied into appropriate discharge planning, as family members can become more active in the recuperation process once the patient leaves the acute care facility.

In assessing cost factors, the cost of hospitalization compared to alternate level of care programs may or may not be proven to be significantly more expensive in terms of general tax payer dollars, but the financial burden to hospitals in maintaining long-term patients, such as the aging patient past the acute phase of illness, is extremely serious and is one of the major factors in driving up the cost of health care (Hitt and Harristhal, 1980).

However, what must be looked at is the potential improvement in the quality of care when medical services are appropriately matched to the patient's continuously changing medical needs. A pattern of experience of ill people has been identified by sociologists as the concept of "career of illness" which may be used as a framework to understand the processes related to the effects of illness. It has been suggested that this framework would be helpful to social workers in matching appropriate resources to the different courses of illness and preventative endeavors (Dinerman, Schlesinger and Wood, 1980). Costs for alternative care placements may be less than long-term hospitalization but this is secondary to the improved state of the patient's condition when treatment and services offered more accurately parallel needs.

What are some of the current obstacles to good discharge planning? Foremost are the lack of adequate resources to meet the needs of patients ready for discharge from hospitals. One of the serious obstacles to effective discharge planning has been that much of the planning is based on the availability of governmental programs and financial resources. Because federal/state/county bureaucracies move slowly, by the time programs are established the rationale for the consideration of these programs has changed and what was thought to be necessary is either currently not as needed, or as is more usually the case, needs have changed and different kinds of programs are required. An example is the goal of reducing length of hospital stays, an excellent priority. But with an increasingly aged population and more chronic patients, more extensive as well as more intensive ambulatory and home care programs are essential. The attempt to reduce hospital stays by financially penalizing the hospitals may be effective in the short run, but will ultimately fail due to increased readmissions of patients who cannot get appropriate care in the community. These are the isolated or powerless people whose ability to cope is diminished because of physical illness or disorganizing emotional reactions (Dinerman, Schlesinger and Wood, 1980, p. 14).

For a significant number of people ready to leave the hospital, two areas of major concern are appropriate facilities in which to live, such as in a nursing home or other group living arrangement to avoid being alone, and financial assistance to pay for ongoing medical and/or psychological support services.

While there exist federal and state programs such as Social Security, Community Support Programs, and Home Care to address the continuing needs of the discharged patient, many patients and their families have difficulty in obtaining such resources because they are either unaware of the programs or do not have the necessary mobility, strengths or knowledge to search them out. To go through the process of requesting such services can also be very difficult for many who oftentimes have been intimidated by public agencies. The lack of experience about how to present their case effectively limits success in obtaining services that legally are available. To match the needs of those who are leaving hospitals with the appropriate governmental support programs is, therefore, not always an easy undertaking and the function of discharge planning often places the social workers in the role of patient advocate.

This advocacy function, to facilitate discharge planning, can be carried out in three related areas: (1) political advocacy—to improve governmental programs, (2) resource development advocacy—to meet unmet needs, and (3) case advocacy—to insure that programs are accessible and appropriate for eligible patients and families.

ADVOCATING FOR IMPROVED GOVERNMENTAL PROGRAMS

The history of the social work profession has in large measure been based on the premise of client advocacy. Social work roots in this country is the history of those whose total commitment was to advocacy: Adam Smith, John Howard, Dorothea Dix, Jacob Riis, Jane Addams (Thursz, 1977). Although putting this rhetoric into practice techniques has been underutilized in the past, the skills and knowledge amassed by the profession can be used to turn the social work role into a political instrument to gain assistance for those who are in need.

Community organization is a method through which social workers learn political strategies. Skills for influencing governmental programs are taught as a two pronged technique: mobilizing a community through developing community coalitions and developing liaisons with legislators on local, state and national levels.

Building coalitions of citizen groups and/or local agencies is an area of expertise used as a political tool by social workers to gain influence in directing the course of governmental services. There are many illustrations of successful coalitions, particularly in relation to the creation of local programs. One example of the positive effects of building a coalition of local drug agencies and community groups helped this medical center obtain additional local funding for substance abuse programs.

This was accomplished in about a year's time by uniting administrators of community-based drug treatment programs and staff of the Medical Center. They organized a data gathering effort which was presented as a report to the local county government and agency responsible for these services to show that a necessary service was not being provided to the target population. Pooling information enabled the coalition to have a strength that could not have been developed by one or two agencies acting alone, even though each agency had data which was valid.

A coalition of local providers of a service can have an impact on local government when it is recognized that the mandate to that local government from state and federal funding sources is to provide their community with the needed services for which they are receiving their grants. In this case, the need for additional outreach workers was demonstrated to be essential to the mandate of providing drug treatment services in the community. Political clout can be developed when a group, in this example, a local agencies' coalition, can validate its needs in terms of the funding source's mandate.

As changes in agency programs take place, in this case through funding for additional workers, these new workers and the work created by these new positions must be presented back to the local government as the agencies' increased abilities to provide services to the target population. This is the necessary feedback to the funding source which can help to institutionalize the changes in program sought by the agencies. This validation of the use of the increased funding will help to institutionalize worker time spent on new programs and will enhance the chances of the new staff being viewed as part of the whole operation.

Another illustration of coalition building involved uniting a group of hospitals, a variety of social agencies and day programs in one area to pressure local government agencies to take advantage of urban transportation regulations to have buses available for the transportation of patients. These vehicles are now used not only to transport patients to local agencies and socialization programs, but also to bring them to outpatient treatment clinics at the hospitals.

The second technique in developing a political influence system is to create liaison committees with legislators. This requires considerable staff time but is well worth it. By understanding that legislators need information about their constituents, social workers can plan to provide the information at the same time presenting possible solutions to problems that also impact directly or indirectly on the social work profession within its particular setting. Several liaison committees have been established by Long Island Jewish-Hillside Medical Center staff with local state legislators. For example, a committee of social workers is presently working with a member of the New York State Assembly's Health Committee and his chief council to recommend improvements for implementing a discharge planning law.

In order to establish this committee there had to be an issue that could be dealt with on a legislative level. While there are always problems, the scope of the issue selected must match the level at which it will be addressed. At Long Island Jewish-Hillside Medical Center, as at many other area acute care hospitals, the problem of delayed discharge of patients has become quite serious—both for the patient and the institution. Incomplete financial arrangements or inadequate facilities at a lower level of care kept patients in the acute care hospitals longer than they required acute care. The complications inherent in this problem could not be addressed at just an agency to agency level because of the political nature of the potential solutions, which might include increasing nursing home beds and/or financial supports. Therefore, a more encompassing level at which to address the situation was needed, i.e., changing a law.

Information on the scope of the problem was assembled to present to the assemblyman's chief council. Meetings were held to discuss the extent of the problem and to validate to the assemblyman how his interests in developing a discharge planning bill could be enhanced with social work professional support. The chief council saw the role of Long Island Jewish-Hillside Medical Center social workers as arranging a large metropolitan constituency of social workers to provide information on all aspects of the problems for patients and institutions. The hospital social workers, in conjunction with the clerical support from the assemblyman's office, arranged a state-wide conference on the problem of discharge planning, at which both the assemblyman and the president of the Medical Center were the keynote speakers. Professionals from all areas of the state were invited to prioritize their recommendations for a discharge planning bill. The outcome of the workshop sessions were sent to all participants to again prioritize their recommendations. From this final list a discharge planning bill was written and presented to the legislature the following year. The major change sought was to enact legislation providing for presumptive Medicaid eligibility for patients in the hospital so they could be processed for lower levels of care without waiting in the hospital, sometimes for months, until the State Social Service Department validated their eligibility for outpatient or nursing home services.

Through providing legislators with feedback on the types of problems encountered by their constituents in finding adequate post acute medical care, legislators become acquainted with the significant problems of the hospitals that keep patients beyond their medically appropriate discharge time as well. In return for supplying legislators with realistic information on the effects of existing laws, social workers learn more about the workings of the legislature and can bring to bear, even in a small way, some influence on political decisions. The skills taught in social work schools develop negotiating skills that professionals use to address both client and agency needs. These skills are specifically used by social workers engaged in C.O. to develop influence in directing the legislative process concerned with health care legislation.

A third way to advocate for improved governmental programs is for the health disciplines in the health care field to develop interdisciplinary committees. These committees, which may serve as task forces, can develop expertise in programming ideas for the unmet needs of their patients. By preparing position papers for conferences and seminars, inviting government agency officials to agencies and preparing statements for hearings, momentum for legislative changes in existing programs can be created. There are numerous illustrations of social workers' activities in these areas.

Through these methods and acquired skills social workers can play a very major role in helping to influence governmental programs.

DEVELOPING RESOURCES TO MEET UNMET NEEDS

As in other areas, innovative approaches are needed to develop programmatic ideas based on the assessment of patient need and availability of resources. The implementation of innovative ideas is often difficult because of bureaucratic obstacles, which are not the making of any single group, but often are inherent in the manner in which program accountability is developed. Nevertheless, there is generally an interest on the part of governmental agencies, as well as others, to make changes in programs and to be cooperative. The governmental bureaucracy is not always the adversary and by developing innovative programs which may be successful, one finds that the governmental agencies can be extremely helpful. It has been our experience that when innovative plans have been introduced, justifiable critiques are instructive in shaping programs. In some instances in which we have developed alternate living arrangement programs for discharged patients, governmental support was vital. Specifically, a congregate living apartment program was developed with the cooperation of the state and local agencies involved. As a result, a pilot project which began with approximately eight patients has now been expanded to sixteen, with the plan to increase the number further. Obviously, this will not meet the needs of patients discharged from other medical centers, but it can be a prototype program which can be used by hospitals in other areas. The advantage of the program is that it uses existing resources, such as apartments in urban areas, for congregate living arrangements for frail and elderly patients as well as in some instances for psychiatric patients. The use of these apartments is one illustration of how resources can be modified or made available to meet unmet needs for different levels of care for different types of problems. It is interesting to note that although the hospital initiated the programs, after they were implemented governmental agencies took the initiative and encouraged the hospital to expand them.

Social workers, by virtue of their knowledge of the needs of the most disadvantaged groups in our society, have a special role to play in program development. Since much of this work has to do with having programs available for patients discharged from institutions (general, acute care hospitals and psychiatric hospitals), the knowledge gained in working with patients and their families provides the basic information necessary for making a significant contribution in this area. Social workers help also to mobilize family support for the patients who require alternate levels of care placement and are in an excellent position to know the obstacles that prevent transfers to appropriate resources as well as the resources that are needed.

ENSURING ACCESSIBILITY OF APPROPRIATE SOCIAL AND HEALTH INSURANCE PROGRAMS TO PATIENTS AND FAMILIES

There are many reasons why patients and their families have difficulty obtaining governmental benefit programs (Lurie, Rizzo and Talbot, 1981). Often there is a lack of information or misinformation which can result in failure to take advantage of programs for which these patients and their families qualify. Sometimes there are psychological reasons which stand in the way of having patients apply for programs. This is particularly true of elderly people who may have minimal resources, but who feel a particular insecurity in having to dip into these resources to qualify for benefit programs. Very often the children and families of potential recipients are reluctant to apply for public services because they feel that governmental scrutiny will invade their privacy or stigmatize them. Because of their training and knowledge of such programs, social workers can provide information and support to patients and families to help them overcome some of these obstacles. Through their personal contacts with their counterparts in governmental agencies, social workers can develop linkages through which patients and their families can gain access to services such as those provided by Social Security, local Departments of Health and Human Resources, and home care services.

One of the most important ways to help patients cope with adjustment difficulties is to make knowledge of appropriate programs available. Social workers, because of their constant use of these programs, should be able to develop resource manuals and directories which can be used to transmit information. Another technique to employ when necessary is the fair hearing procedures which will enable patients and their families, when they feel helpless to challenge governmental decisions, obtain legal support for their legitimate requests. A report of a committee composed of community volunteers, social workers and lawyers which monitored fair hearings experiences in New York City indicates the potential of these hearings to insure appropriate reviews of Medicaid applications (Salomon, Bletter, Prosnitz and Sohmer, 1980).

Social workers can move into positions as consultants to admitting offices or accounting departments to develop expertise about third party payors and how to help families meet the established criteria. In some instances these criteria can be very difficult and it may be that social workers, through developing coalitions and using legislation, can modify some of these difficult restrictions to more properly reflect the intention of public programs to meet the needs of patients and their families. Often there is not a negative reaction to suggested changes, but rather it is a lack of knowledge and information which makes these governmental programs so difficult to implement. An illustration is the Home Care Program which was developed as "nursing homes without walls." The intention of the program was admirable and is successful today. But, prior to its becoming successful, knowledge about the program was lacking and several modifications were necessary before the program became viable. With the help of social workers and others who participated in making referrals of patients and their families to the program, the obstacles such as the rigid financial requirements and some criteria for availability of home care personnel were pointed out to interested legislators. Gradually these limitations were modified so that the program is functioning well.

What are the social work skills that contribute to taking an activist role in working with the voluntary, private and public sectors to high quality discharge planning?

IMPLEMENTATION

The first is to develop methods and techniques that will effectively address the problem to yield the desired outcome. This requires an accurate identification of the problem, mobilization of resources, management of methodology and skills and constant monitoring of new information entering the system which can change that system (Shulman, Rosenberg, Rock and Jefferson, 1976). A series of actions have to be taken to begin the development of this process. The first is a sequence of moves that establishes a beginning power base. In community action this can mean the bringing together of provider groups with hospitals, social agencies, advisory boards and local associations to link provider and consumer groups in a given geographic locality.

Another step is to select a key issue which needs to be emphasized. This requires considerable skill because the issue has to be realistically addressed to meet a definite need or the task cannot be accomplished successfully. Further, the issue has to be acceptable to the constituency of the coalition and achievable within a reasonable time frame. Often the issues which are less controversial and threatening are preferable and if medical centers are involved, the issue should be one in which the hospital can stand to benefit.

Once the issue is selected an attempt to broaden the coalition membership should be made. The broader the membership, the greater the amount of community pressure which can be brought to bear on the issue. These coalitions should include consumer and professional groups and legislators whose interests coincide with that of the resolution of the issue.

Today there would not be much controversy on developing issues which pertain to helping the frail elderly patient. The task then is not to develop this issue, but the implementation skills in the form of an action plan to achieve the goal.

Social workers can make a significant contribution in politicizing issues because they have had experience in creating liaisons at the interfaces between various groups in the community. The strategy consists of developing (1) long range goals (2) short range goals, (3) techniques for identifying and weighting the strengths and weaknesses of issue and (4) developing a series of actions (Shulman, Rosenberg, Rock and Jefferson, 1976, p. 103).

Social workers can apply these steps to develop a discharge planning process. It is important for social workers and others who are interested in discharge planning to develop identifiable action strategies both from within and without the medical center. This requires a multidisciplinary group, preferably under social work leadership, including nurses, physicians, accountants and others involved in the discharge process. A second step is to develop an advocacy committee within the institution. The advocacy committee should consist of volunteers, professionals from different disciplines, and if possible community agency liaison persons who have access to governmental agencies. An important addition is legal consultative help. This is not for the purpose of developing an adversarial position to governmental agencies but to develop strong liaison contacts. Quite often agencies are more than pleased to work together with such advocacy committees, benefiting from the results of efficient application procedures.

At present discharge planning is a complicated process involving several professional disciplines, community groups and local agencies. For the patient leaving the hospital, discharge plans to return to the community are often complicated by local resistance to having physically or emotionally disadvantaged people living in residential neighborhoods. Misinformation and lack of skillful professional involvement to help communities understand the needs and limitations of these patients often intensifies this resistance.

To deal with this problem, as well as with the various forces represented by political, professional, and health and welfare agencies, requires a wide range of skills. From a social work point of view, it requires the understanding of political processes such as compromise, mediation, arbitration and negotiation. It also requires an understanding of the psychological factors that sometimes underlie resistance. Strategies to overcome community fears might include an educational program to bring needed information to the communities which will be more acceptable to them; community meetings explaining programs and having the patients themselves participating; recruiting community volunteers to work on housing proposals; developing liaison committees with local legislators and developing a political environment in which it may be possible to develop innovative programs that will offer incentives to communities to accept a housing program.

Relatives of patients are another resource for a health pressure group who often live in local communities. They are able to form and direct coalitions and community activities to promote health activities such as educational programs and supportive efforts for discharged patients. They can be aided by social workers who can offer community organization skills in these endeavors.

Most important, it is necessary for social workers and those who are interested in discharge planning to understand the political implications of all phases of the discharge planning process and how it can effect social agencies, communities, patients and their families (Shulman and Tuzman, 1980).

A major strategy for change, therefore, is forging relationships amongst different groups to enhance understanding for the need to work together to develop mutually advantageous programs.

The result of effective planning will be ability to justify programs to monitoring agencies whose duty and responsibility it is to insure that funds for health care, particularly in the area of discharge planning, is appropriately spent. From a human services perspective, the most important need is to improve the quality of care of patients as they leave the hospital and to insure that there is a continuity of care which will maintain the gains that patients have made while they were in the hospital. This can only be done with proper discharge planning.

REFERENCES

Dinerman, M., Schlesinger, E. G., and Wood, K. M., "Social Work Roles in Health Care: An Educational Framework," *Health and Social Work,* 1980, 5, 13–20.

Greater New York Hospital Association, "Hospital Discharge Planning—Report of Discharge Planning Task Force," New York, New York, 1980, page 3.

Hitt, D. H. and Harristhal, M. P., "Financing Health Care in the 1980's," *Hospitals,* 1980, 54, 71–74.

Lurie, A., Rizzo, A., and Talbot, L., "Medicare Beneficiary Aide Plan Relieves Reimbursement Woes." *Hospitals* , 1981, 55, 66–68.

Rogatz, P., "Directions of Health System for New Decade," *Hospitals,* 1980, 54, 67–70.

Salomon, P. R., Bletter, G., Prosnitz, P., and Sohmer, H., "Report on D.S.S. Fair Hearings: Regulations and Case Experiences." Sub-committee on Fair Hearings, Community Council of Greater New York. New York, New York, November 1980. Mimeo.

Shulman, L., Rosenberg, G., Rock, B., and Jefferson, E., "Political Skill in Social Work Practice." In A. Lurie and G. Rosenberg (Eds.) *Social Work in Mental Health.* New Hyde Park, New York: Long Island Jewish-Hillside Medical Center, 1976, 97–110.

Shulman, L. and Tuzman, L., "Discharge Planning—A Social Work Perspective." *Quality Review Bulletin,* 1980, 10, 3.

Sirkis, C. J. (Ed.), "Discharge Planning." Health Care Financing Administration, U.S. Department of Health and Human Services. Kensington, Maryland, January 1981.

Thursz, D., "Social Action." In J. Turner (Ed.) *Encyclopedia of Social Work,* 17th Edition, Volume II. Washington, D.C.: National Association of Social Workers, 1977, 1274–1280.

Conclusion

The social work administrator in health care has become one of the major administrative functionaries in a very large bureaucratic structure. In a number of institutions the social work administrator sits on the highest level of the management of the health care agency and since some of these health care institutions resemble large industrial plants, it is imperative that the social work administrator not only becomes knowledgeable about administration from the specific point of view representing a social work discipline per se, but also as a manager in a generic sense. Social work processes can make a contribution to generic management, but specifically the social worker must first be capable to translate social work concepts, knowledge, and skills into social work administrative practice. A social work department in a hospital may be one of the largest or smallest departments in the institution. Regardless, the social work administrator must be grounded in social work principles, ethics, and concepts, and must also be aware of the health care agency as a system unto itself.

The articles in this book have illustrated principles which social work administrators have used in a variety of health care settings. They have reflected a variety of functions to underscore the importance of social work administration which helps to motivate, train and hold accountable a social work staff so that it can provide the fullest measure of its competence and knowledge for the purpose of helping patients and families who come to the institution for health care.

We anticipate that the future of social work in health care is, despite temporary budgetary constraints, very bright. It is so because there is increasing recognition that the psychosocial aspects of illness must be dealt with in a variety of ways, from prevention through the various levels of care that are increasingly available. There has to be continuity of the caring process for the patient and the family from the community, to the institution, and returned into the community. It is increasingly recognized that the caring element social work brings to the patient and the family can have a great deal to do with maintaining people in the community, which can be cost effective provided the necessary support systems are there. Social workers can play an increasingly significant role in helping to see that these support systems are in place. This will enable home care programs to flourish, prevention to take place, linkages to many agencies to be developed and exploited for the benefit of patient care and in the short and long run to aid the hospital team to provide its care in the best possible way.

Abraham Lurie, PhD
Gary Rosenberg, PhD

Index